Ten Women *of* The Bible

ONE BY ONE THEY CHANGED THE WORLD

....

STUDY GUIDE

....

BY JENNA LUCADO BISHOP

FROM THE WRITINGS OF

MAX LUCADO

HarperChristian Resources

CONTENTS

INTRODUCTION

THE CAST

The ten women of the Bible we're going to focus on in this study came from a range of different backgrounds. Some we know only by clues as to their nationality left in the Scripture. Some we know only by the place they are believed to have lived. Some were queens and women of power and influence in their world. Others were relegated to the fringes of society.

Some of their stories are inspiring. In a society in which the contributions of women were often overlooked, their actions stood out for one reason or another to the writers of Scripture. Others, marked by scandal and intrigue, provide a cautionary tale for us. Yes, all of their stories are different. And yet all of them provide lessons for us today . . .

Sarah, the woman whom God promised would give birth to a nation, but who would also at times try to rush God's plans.

Rahab, a prostitute in the Canaanite city of Jericho, who would save herself and her family through her faith in the one true God of the Israelites.

Abigail, a woman whose wisdom and well-placed words quieted the wrath of King David and prevented the deaths of many people.

Esther, a young queen whom God placed in the Persian court for "such a time as this" to prevent the genocide of the Jewish people.

Mary, the young virgin pledged to Joseph, whom God would choose to give birth to Jesus, the promised Messiah who would save the world.

The Samaritan Woman, who would meet this Messiah at a well one day. His words would forever after change her life.

The Canaanite Woman, who made God smile with her wit and faith, and who received from Jesus an answer to her prayer.

Mary of Bethany, a friend of Jesus who witnessed the resurrection of her brother, Lazarus, and then anointed Christ in anticipation of his death and resurrection.

Mary Magdalene, who traveled with Jesus as one of his followers and was given a unique front-row seat to his victory over death.

Sapphira, a woman in the early church who, along with her husband, made the unfortunate (and deadly) decision to lie to the Holy Spirit.

The lives of these women are very different from our own. And yet, in many ways, we often find ourselves facing the same issues they faced. The promises of God that don't seem to come to pass. The barbaric behavior of others in our world that forces us to play peacemaker. The overwhelming nature of the tasks the Lord has set before us. The injustice of a world that judges us for our past, finds us guilty, and says we will always be considered a failure.

Even more, these stories show us there is a God who sees us where we are and loves us for who we are. He is the one who hovers over all the pages of the Bible, shaping lives, rescuing hearts, healing sicknesses, raising what was dead to life, and passing out high callings to those who choose to follow him and have faith in him.

So, if you ever feel like a second-class citizen in this world and wonder how God could possibly use you to change lives, just look at the stories of these women in the Bible. As you do, you will come to the conclusion—as the disciple Peter did—that God "does not show favoritism but accepts from every nation the one who fears him and does what is right" (Acts 10:34–35). And as you study their lives, you will uncover important truths God wants you to grasp.

Let's get started!

HOW TO USE THIS STUDY

This study guide is designed to help you delve into God's Word and learn more about these ten fascinating women in the Bible. Each session contains the following elements:

OPENING INSIGHTS: To help you get to know more about these ten women, each session opens with an insight and a retelling of the character's story as drawn from Max's books. Two reflection questions will then get you thinking about how each person's story relates to your own.

DAILY BIBLE STUDY: Each session contains five days of Bible study with insights drawn from Max's books and leading questions to help you navigate the stories of these women in Scripture.

POINTS TO REMEMBER: Each day's session concludes with a summary of the main points in the study. These serve as reminders to the key points of Max's teaching and a review at the close of your study time.

PRAYER FOR THE DAY: Each day's session includes a prayer to help you focus your thoughts on God and move into your quiet time with him.

WEEKLY MEMORY VERSES: Our lives are changed when we encounter Jesus, and our hearts are changed by what is kept there. The weekly memory verse will relate to the main theme of the session and help you hide God's Word in your heart.

SCRIPTURE QUOTATIONS: Many Scripture quotes have been provided in the margins to help you follow the retelling of the story in your Bible.

During the daily Bible study portions, in addition to answering the questions that have been provided, you will also want to make notes of what comes to mind as you read the selected passage of Scripture. Be sure to have pen and paper for writing. Commit this time to the Lord and ask him to reveal himself to you as you work through each of the sessions.

FOR LEADERS

If you would like to lead a group through the material in this study guide, please see the section at the end of the guide for a basic design of how to set up your group time, navigate problems and opportunities that may come up during your discussion time, and get the most out of the study as a group.

SARAH

LIFE IN THE KINGDOM OF THE ABSURD

THE KINGDOM OF HEAVEN. Its citizens are drunk on wonder. Consider the case of Sarai. She is in her golden years, but God promises her a son. He says to her husband, Abram, "I will make you into a great nation, and I will bless you" (Genesis 12:2).

So Sarai gets excited. She visits the maternity shop and buys a few dresses. She plans her shower and remodels her tent . . . but no son. She eats a few birthday cakes and blows out a lot of candles . . . still no son. She goes through a decade of wall calendars . . . still no son.

So Sarai decides to take matters into her own hands. (*Maybe God needs me to take care of this one.*) She convinces Abram that time is running out. (*Face it, Abe, you ain't getting any younger, either.*) Sarai then commands her maid, Hagar, to go into Abram's tent and see if he needs anything. (*And I mean "anything"!*)

Hagar goes in a maid. She comes out a mom. And the problems begin.

Hagar is haughty. Sarai is jealous. Abram is dizzy from the dilemma. And God calls the baby boy a "wild donkey." It's an appropriate name for one born out of stubbornness and destined to kick his way into history. This isn't the cozy family Sarai expected. And it isn't a topic Abram and Sarai bring up very often at dinner.

Finally, fourteen years later, when Abram is pushing a century of years and Sarai ninety . . . when Abram has stopped listening to Sarai's advice, and Sarai has stopped giving it . . . when the wallpaper in the nursery is faded and the baby furniture is several seasons out of date . . . when the topic of the promised child brings sighs and tears and long looks into a silent sky . . . God pays them a visit and tells them they had better select a name for their new son. Abram and Sarai have the same response: laughter.

The LORD had said to Abram, "Go from your country, your people and your father's household to the land I will show you. I will make you into a great nation, and I will bless you; I will make your name great" (Genesis 12:1–2).

Now Sarai, Abram's wife, had borne him no children. But she had an Egyptian slave named Hagar . . . (16:1).

Abraham fell facedown; he laughed and said to himself, "Will a son be born to a man a hundred years old? Will Sarah bear a child at the age of ninety?" (17:17).

Be joyful in hope, patient in affliction, faithful in prayer (Romans 12:12).

They laugh partly because it is too good to happen and partly because it might. They laugh because they have given up hope, and hope born anew is always funny before it is real. They laugh at the lunacy of it all.

1. Put yourself in Sarai's shoes. It had been fourteen years since God's original promise of a son. Now, she is *ninety*. *Ninety*! God must have forgotten his promise, right? Wrong. God does the unthinkable—a son. No wonder she laughed! Have you ever let out a "Sarai laugh" because of God interrupting your familiar life with the unexpected? Describe what happened.

   _____

   _____

   _____

   _____

   _____

2. What blurs your kingdom vision? What is it that gets in the way of your seeing the world with spiritual eyes—with believing God can do the impossible?

   _____

   _____

   _____

   _____

   _____

He called a little child to him. . . . And he said: "Truly I tell you . . . whoever takes the lowly position of this child is the greatest in the kingdom of heaven. And whoever welcomes one such child in my name welcomes me" (Matthew 18:2–5).

As citizens of the kingdom of heaven, we are often surprised when God does the "absurd," works miracles, and moves in unimaginable ways. All too often we grow comfortable in a life that we see, touch, and manage on our smartphones. But Jesus said, "Unless you . . . become like little children, you will never enter the kingdom of heaven" (Matthew 18:3). A child lives in constant wonder and faith in the unimaginable. Yet Sarah's childless life would test her childlike faith. As you read her story, it is possible that you will relate to her journey. And it's probable that God will grow your childlike faith along the way.

❧ PRAYER FOR THE WEEK ☙

Jesus, nothing is impossible for you. Forgive us for the times we get so wrapped up in the kingdom of earth that we forget about the kingdom of heaven. We want to live expecting the unexpected, trusting in a God whose thoughts are higher than our thoughts and whose ways are higher than our ways (see Isaiah 55:9). In your mighty name, amen.

Day One: Promise Given

INTEGRITY FOR SECURITY

When we first meet Sarai, she is living in the land of Ur of the Chaldeans, located in modern-day Iraq. In addition to being told she is Abram's wife, we also read she is childless because she was not able to conceive (see Genesis 11:30). When Sarai's father-in-law, Terah, takes the family on the move, she and Abram end up in the city of Haran. It is there the Lord appears to Abram, tells him to go to Canaan, and promises to make him into a great nation.

Abram's wife was Sarai . . . [she] was childless because she was not able to conceive. . . . and together they set out from Ur of the Chaldeans to go to Canaan (Genesis 11:29–30).

The writer of Hebrews tells us, "It was by faith Abraham obeyed God's call to go to another place God promised to give him. He left his own country, not knowing where he was to go" (11:8 NCV). Yet in spite of this faithfulness, we wouldn't exactly expect to see either his or Sarai's names listed in "Who's Who in Purity and Sainthood."

By faith he made his home in the promised land like a stranger in a foreign country (Hebrews 11:9).

Why? Well, for Abram's part, he has a fibbing tongue that won't stop!

Shortly after the first visit from God, a famine in the land of Canaan sends the couple and their family down to Egypt. It is here we read an interesting detail about Sarai: she was exceptionally beautiful. So beautiful, in fact, that Abram fears the Egyptians will kill him to get to her. So, in order to save his neck, he lets the word get out that Sarah isn't his wife but his sister . . . which is only half true.

"Say you are my sister, so that I will be treated well for your sake" (Genesis 12:13).

And then, not long after, he does it again! "Abraham moved south to the Negev and lived for a while between Kadesh and Shur, and then he moved on to Gerar. While living there as a foreigner, Abraham introduced his wife, Sarah, by saying, 'She is my sister.' So King Abimelech of Gerar sent for Sarah and had her brought to him at his palace" (20:1–2 NLT).

Abimelech called Abraham in and said . . . "You have done things to me that should never be done" (20:9).

Twice Abram and Sarai trade integrity for security. Is that what you call confidence in God's promises? Can you build a nation on that kind of faith? As it turns out, God can. God took what was good, forgave what was bad, and used Abram and Sarai to change history.

1. Read Genesis 12:1–9. Sarai was sixty-five, and Abram seventy-five, when God asked them to journey approximately 400 miles from their home to a strange land called Canaan. Not exactly an easy move to the suburbs. How do they respond to the call? When was a time God called you into the unfamiliar? How did you respond?

He took his wife Sarai . . . and they set out for the land of Canaan (12:5).

_____

_____

_____

_____

By faith even Sarah, who was past childbearing age, was enabled to bear children because she considered him faithful who had made the promise (Hebrews 11:11).

2. Check out Hebrews 11:8–12. How did Sarai and Abram demonstrate their faith (see verse 8)? What is the spiritual implication of dwelling in tents (see verse 10)? How can we be modern-day "tent dwellers" in the way we trust and follow God?

_____

_____

_____

_____

Now there was a famine in the land, and Abram went down to Egypt to live there (Genesis 12:10).

3. The story of Sarai and Abram is one of phenomenal faith, but this doesn't mean they didn't stumble at times. Read Genesis 12:10–20. What takes Abram from a place of faith in God's promise to forgetting God's promise? What circumstances cause your own heart to forget God's promises?

_____

_____

_____

_____

4. The idea of "God's promises" is tossed around a lot in Christian circles, but what does it mean? What are God's promises? What do these verses say about the promises of God?

Numbers 23:19: "God is not a man, that He should lie, nor a son of man, that He should repent. Has He said, and will He not do? Or has He spoken, and will He not make it good?" (NKJV).

_____

_____

_____

1 Kings 8:56: "Blessed be the LORD, who has given rest to His people Israel, according to all that He promised; not one word has failed of all His good promise, which He promised through Moses His servant" (NASB).

_____

_____

_____

2 Corinthians 1:20: "For no matter how many promises God has made, they are 'Yes' in Christ. And so through him the 'Amen' is spoken by us to the glory of God."

_____

_____

_____

2 Timothy 3:16: "All Scripture is inspired by God and is useful for teaching, for showing people what is wrong in their lives, for correcting faults, and for teaching how to live right" (NCV).

_____

_____

_____

_____

TOUGH TO SWALLOW

By the time the Lord again appears to Abram, he and Sarai are finding God's promises about as easy to swallow as a chicken bone. "Master," he says, "what use are your gifts as long as I'm childless . . . ? You've given me no children, and now a mere house servant is going to get it all" (Genesis 15:2–3 MSG).

God's response? "No problem."

Abram must have looked over at Sarai at that point as she shuffled by in her gown and slippers with the aid of a walker. The chicken bone stuck for a few minutes but eventually slid down his throat. Just as he was turning away to invite Sarah to a candlelight dinner, he heard promise number two.

"Abram."

"Yes, Lord?"

"All this land will be yours."

Imagine God telling you that your children will someday own Fifth Avenue, and you will understand Abram's hesitation.

"On that one, Father, I need a little help." And a little help was given.

God told Abram to take three animals, cut them in half, and arrange the halves facing each other. To us, the command is mysterious. To Abram and Sarai, it wouldn't have been at all. They'd seen the ceremony before. Abram had participated in it. He'd sealed many covenants by walking between the divided carcasses and stating, "May what has happened to these animals happen also to me if I fail to uphold my word" (see Jeremiah 34:18).

Abram's heart must have skipped a beat when he saw the lights in the darkness passing between the carcasses. The soft golden glow from the coals in the firepot and the courageous flames from the torch. What did they mean? The invisible God had drawn near to make his immovable promise. "To your descendants I have given this land" (Genesis 15:18 NKJV).

And though God's people would often forget their God, he didn't forget them. He kept his word. The land became Abram and Sarai's.

> The word of the LORD came to him: *"This man will not be your heir, but a son who is your own flesh and blood will be your heir"* (Genesis 15:4).

> So the LORD said to him, *"Bring me a heifer, a goat and a ram, each three years old, along with a dove and a young pigeon."* Abram brought all these to him, cut them in two and arranged the halves opposite each other (verses 9–10).

> When the sun had set and darkness had fallen, a smoking firepot with a blazing torch appeared and passed between the pieces. On that day the LORD made a covenant with Abram (verses 17–18).

5. Take a look at the conversation between God and Abram in Genesis 15. The Hebrew name that Abram calls God in verse 2 is *Adonai*, which means "Lord, Master."[1] What does this tell you about how

Abram viewed God? How do you view God when the waiting is long and his promises seem bleak?

_____

_____

_____

_____

He took him outside and said, "Look up at the sky and count the stars—if indeed you can count them" (Genesis 15:5).

6. Abram assumes God's promise will be fulfilled through Eliezer, the head of his household. But then God instructs Abram to "look up at the sky" (verse 5). God not only tells Abram that his lineage will be as numerous as the stars, but also, in this, he draws Abram's gaze upward. What do you think gazing at the stars did for Abram's perspective? How can you "look up at the sky" in your daily life?

_____

_____

_____

_____

The words "it was credited to him" were written not for him alone, but also for us, to whom God will credit righteousness—for us who believe in him who raised Jesus our Lord from the dead. He was delivered over to death for our sins and was raised to life for our justification (Romans 4:23–25).

7. Reread Genesis 15:6 and compare it to Romans 4:18–25. What is God's promise to us as Abram and Sarai's descendants?

_____

_____

_____

8. God commanded Abram to cut in half a heifer, ram, and goat—a pretty graphic mental picture! Yet it was common in Abram's day for two parties to walk between animal halves while making a treaty. It was as if to say, "May I become like these animals if I don't keep my part of the deal."[2] But in this vision, who passes between the animals—one party or two? What does this gesture say about God's promises?

_____

_____

_____

For the LORD God is a sun and shield; the LORD bestows favor and honor; no good thing does he withhold from those whose walk is blameless (Psalm 84:11).

At the beginning of Genesis 15, God says, "Do not be afraid, Abram. I am your shield, your exceedingly great reward" (verse 1 NKJV). This is where we start. We start with "I am." We start with remembering our "shield" and our "great reward." Before looking at the promises, we look at the Promise Maker. If we focus on trusting in his promises before trusting in him, or receiving his promises more than receiving him, then we have missed it. Missed what? That the same God who spoke with, met with, and walked with Abraham wants to speak with, meet with, and walk with us. This is the ultimate promise—the greatest gift. And as we grow in relationship with God, we grow in our trust of his promises burgeoning in our lives.

❧ POINTS TO REMEMBER ❧

❖ Our imperfect, doubting faith cannot prevent God from keeping his promises.
❖ God may call us to move outside of our comfort zone, but being "tent dwellers" will prepare us to be ready when God calls.
❖ God *never* forgets his promises, and our confidence in those promises is rooted in our relationship with him.

Immediately Jesus reached out his hand and caught [Peter]. "You of little faith," he said, "why did you doubt?" (Matthew 14:31).

❧ PRAYER FOR THE DAY ❧

Lord, thank you for grafting us into your promise of salvation. Thank you for the example of Sarai and Abram. Give us the confidence they had to call you "Adonai," Master, Lord, no matter the circumstances. And help us to remember that above all, the ultimate promise is fulfilled in relationship with you. In Jesus's name, amen.

𝒟ay Two: "Helping" God

RACKING UP CHARGES

Wouldn't it be nice if someone credited your charge card account? All month long you *rrack-rrack* up the bills, dreading the day the statement comes in the mail. When it comes, you leave it on your desk for a few days, not wanting to see how much you owe. Finally, you force yourself to open the envelope. With one eye closed and the other open, you peek at the number. What you read causes the other eye to pop open. "A zero balance!"

There must be a mistake, so you call the bank that issued the card.

"Yes," the manager explains, "your account is paid in full. A Mr. Max Lucado sent us a check to cover your debt."

You can't believe your ears. "How do you know his check is good?"

"Oh, there is no doubt. Mr. Lucado has been paying off people's debts for years."

By the way, I'd love to do that for you, but don't get your hopes up. I have a few bills of my own. But Jesus would love to, and he can! He has no personal debt at all. And, what's more, he has been doing it for years. For proof, Paul reaches into the two-thousand-year-old file marked "Abram of Ur" and pulls out a statement.

"He himself bore our sins" in his body on the cross, so that we might die to sins and live for righteousness (1 Peter 2:24).

What then shall we say that Abraham, our forefather according to the flesh, discovered in this matter? (Romans 4:1).

If, in fact, Abraham was justified by works, he had something to boast about—but not before God (Romans 4:2).

Abram and Sarai certainly had their share of charges on this statement. They were far from perfect. As we have seen, there were times when Abram trusted the Egyptians before he trusted God. He even lied, telling Pharaoh that Sarai was his sister. But Sarai had her failings as well. One of the most memorable occurred just after God made his covenant with Abram—when Sarai decided to take matters into her own hands.

"Sarai said to Abram, 'See now, the Lord has restrained me from bearing children. Please, go in to my maid; perhaps I shall obtain children by her.' And Abram heeded the voice of Sarai" (Genesis 16:2–3 NKJV). The result? Disaster.

1. Read Genesis 16 and write down the "charges" Abram and Sarai rack up. Why do you think Sarai decides to "help" God's plan in this passage? Based on Abram's response, what desires did he have to "help" God's plan as well?

2. Think about a time when you took control of a situation instead of entrusting it to God. What were some of the results of that decision? Sarai believed taking over would fix the problem (see Genesis 16:2), and this gave her a false comfort. What false "comforts" tag along with control?

Then Sarai said to Abram, "You are responsible for the wrong I am suffering. I put my slave in your arms, and now that she knows she is pregnant, she despises me. May the LORD judge between you and me" (verse 5).

3. It had been ten years since Abram and Sarai had picked up and left all they knew to follow this promise of God. Sarai's hope and patience were wearing thin, and she was beginning to cast blame. Who do you see her blame in Genesis 16? Who do you tend to blame when your dreams or plans don't unfold as you had hoped?

You will keep in perfect peace those whose minds are steadfast, because they trust in you (Isaiah 26:3).

4. Read Proverbs 3:5–7 and James 1:6–8. Which passage best describes Sarai in Genesis 16, and why? In Isaiah 26:3, how does the prophet encourage us to avoid doubt and control and have a heart of peace and trust?

In Need of a Little Grace

"So after Abram had been living in Canaan ten years, Sarai his wife took her Egyptian slave Hagar and gave her to her husband to be his wife. He slept with Hagar, and she conceived" (Genesis 16:3–4). Abram and Sarai now have an heir, but it isn't the heir God intended. They have gone outside of God's plan, and soon things begin to unravel.

Hagar starts to despise Sarai. Sarai starts to despise Hagar. Abram is caught in the middle. The situation gets so bad that Abram finally gives up trying to work it out. "Indeed your maid is in your hand," he says to his wife. "Do to her as you please" (verse 6 NKJV).

When she knew she was pregnant, she began to despise her mistress (Genesis 16:5).

In many ways, strange as it may seem, Sarai's humanness is refreshing. Should you ever need a reminder of God's tolerance, you'd find it in her story. If you ever wonder how in the world God could use you to change the world, just look at this couple. They made a lot of bad decisions. But Abram also made one for his family that changed everything: "He trusted God to set him right instead of trying to be right on his own" (Romans 4:3 MSG). Because of this, God offered grace to both Sarai and Abram in spite of their faults and missteps. He credited their charge account and covered their debts.

Abram believed the LORD, and he credited it to him as righteousness (15:6).

My father had a simple rule about charge cards: own as few as possible and pay them off as soon as possible. So you can imagine my surprise when he put one in my hand the day I left for college. I looked at the name on the plastic. It wasn't mine; it was his. His only instructions to me were, "Be careful how you use it."

I went several months without needing that card. But when I needed it, I *really* needed it. On an impulse, I skipped class one Friday morning and headed out to visit a girl in another city, six hours away. Everything went fine until I rear-ended a car on the return trip. I can still envision the phone where I stood in the autumn chill to call my father. My story wasn't much to boast about. I'd made a trip without his knowledge, without any money, and wrecked his car.

"Well," he said after a long pause, "these things happen. That's why I gave you the card. I hope you learned a lesson." Did I learn a lesson? I certainly did. I learned that my father's forgiveness predated my mistake. He had given me the card before my wreck in the event that I would have one. He had provided for my blunder before I blundered.

Need I tell you that God has done the same? God knew that Abram and Sarai would falter. He knew they would someday need grace. And he knew that someday we, too, would need his grace.

We all stumble in many ways (James 3:2).

5. What are the negative results of Sarai's decision to step outside of God's plan, both relationally and emotionally?

_____

_____

_____

6. How does Abram react to Sarai's decision? How do you think he should have responded? How can you help a friend or relative who is trying to take control or manipulate God's plans?

_____

_____

_____

_____

7. How did God's promise to Abraham in Genesis 15:6 provide for his "blunder before his blunder"?

_____

_____

_____

_____

8. God gives us forgiveness, knowing we will step outside of his desired plan, just as Sarai and Abram did. But he also gives us grace to grow in our faith along the way. Based on the following verses, how does our faith and trust in God grow?

Matthew 26:41: "Stay awake and pray for strength against temptation. The spirit wants to do what is right, but the body is weak" (NCV).

_____

_____

_____

_____

Mark 9:23–24: "Jesus said . . . 'All things are possible for one who believes.' Immediately the father of the child cried out and said, 'I believe; help my unbelief!'" (ESV).

_____

_____

_____

_____

Romans 10:17: "So then faith comes by hearing, and hearing by the word of God" (NKJV).

_____

_____

_____

_____

Philippians 4:6–7: "Be anxious for nothing, but in everything by prayer and supplication with thanksgiving let your requests be made known to God. And the peace of God, which surpasses all comprehension, will guard your hearts and your minds in Christ Jesus" (NASB).

_____

_____

_____

Philippians 4:12–13: "I know how to live when I am poor, and I know how to live when I have plenty. I have learned the secret of being happy at any time in everything that happens . . . when I have more than I need and when I do not have enough. I can do all things through Christ, because he gives me strength" (NCV).

_____

_____

_____

This story gives us a glimpse of what happens when we seek to go our own way instead of God's way. Sarai is left contempt and bitter. Abram is weary and consenting. Hagar is abused. Ishmael is left to die. We all have "Sarai moments"—times when we want life to go our way instead of God's way. We all have moments when we ask God to scoot over so we can sit in the driver's seat. This should make us love God even more—for we know that during such times he protected us from our own selves. He knew all the mistakes we would make—the "charges to the credit card"—yet he still chose us before the foundation of the world. No matter how much we foul up, God's plan of salvation is never thwarted, and his grace is never threatened.

We all, like sheep, have gone astray, each of us has turned to our own way; and the LORD has laid on him the iniquity of us all (Isaiah 53:6).

─❧ POINTS TO REMEMBER ❧─

❖ "Fixing" a situation by using our own means to move God's plan forward may give us a sense of comfort and control, but the results lead to disaster.
❖ God's forgiveness predates our mistakes, and his grace when we fail gives us the faith to grow in contentment with his plans.
❖ God often has to protect us from ourselves!

─❧ PRAYER FOR THE DAY ❧─

*Lord, we need help trusting you with all of our heart (see Proverbs 3:5–7). It's so easy to lean on our own understanding, and we don't want to **be wise** in our own eyes. Humble us and give us a heart that fears you. Thank **you** for your grace and love that predates all of our mistakes. Amen.*

Day Three: Staying Hopeful

DREADFULLY ROUTINE

When Abram was ninety-nine years old, the LORD appeared to him (Genesis 17:1).

By the time God makes his next appearance in Genesis 17, twenty-five years have passed since he first promised to make Abram and Sarai into a great nation. Abram is now ninety-nine, and Sarai is not much younger. She knits, and he plays solitaire. He has lost his hair. She has lost her teeth. And neither spends a lot of time anymore lusting for the other.

Twenty-five years. A lot has happened during that time. The couple has overcome scandal in Egypt. Their nephew Lot has been captured and rescued. Then there was that whole Hagar-and-Ishmael ordeal. But still, no son has been born, no promised heir.

For Abram, whose name meant "exalted father," the conversations must have become dreadfully routine.

"Say, what is your name?"

"Abram."

"Oh, 'exalted father'! Wow, what a great title. Tell me, how many sons do you have?"

Abram would sigh. "None."

Occasionally, I'm sure he'd think of God's promise and give Sarai a wink. She'd give him a smile and think, *Well, God did promise us a child, didn't he?* And they'd both chuckle at the thought of bouncing a boy on their bony knees.

"As for me, this is my covenant with you: You will be the father of many nations" (verse 4).

God was chuckling too. With the smile still on his face, he began getting busy doing what he does best—the unbelievable. But first he had to change a few things, beginning with their names. "I am changing your name from Abram to Abraham," he said, "because I am making you a father of many nations. . . . I will change the name of Sarai, your wife, to Sarah. I will bless her and give her a son, and you will be the father" (Genesis 17:5, 15–16 NCV).

Abram, the father of one, would now be Abraham, the "father of a multitude." Sarai, the barren one, would now be Sarah, the "mother of nations." It was another assurance from God that the promise would be fulfilled. Somehow, the couple chose to believe it and never give in to doubt.

1. Spend some time reading Genesis 17. This is the fourth time, during a twenty-five-year span, that the Lord visits Abram, and he opens this visit with the command, "Walk before me faithfully and be blameless" (verse 1). What does this mean?

_____

_____

_____

2. If you were in Sarai's place, how would you have reacted to this command to walk before God after twenty-five-years of waiting? How does Abram react? What can we learn from his obedience (see verses 23–27)?

_____

_____

_____

_____

On that very day Abraham took his son Ishmael and all those born in his household or bought with his money, every male in his household, and circumcised them, as God told him. . . . And every male in Abraham's household, including those born in his household or bought from a foreigner, was circumcised with him (Genesis 17:23, 27).

3. In Isaiah 40:31 the prophet writes, "Those who wait on the LORD shall renew their strength" (NKJV). What is the promise of waiting/hoping in the Lord? What lessons have you learned during your seasons of waiting?

_____

_____

_____

_____

_____

4. According to 2 Peter 3:8–9, "With God, one day is as good as a thousand years, a thousand years as a day. God isn't late with his promise as some measure lateness" (MSG). What does this verse say about God's timeline versus our own? How should we view God's timing?

_____

_____

_____

_____

_____

THE UNWANTED AND OBNOXIOUS GUEST

Ah, *doubt*. He's a nosy neighbor. He's an unwanted visitor. He's an obnoxious guest. Just when you are all prepared for a weekend of relaxation . . . just when you pull off your work clothes and climb into your Bermuda shorts . . . just when you unfold the lawn chair and sit down with a magazine and a glass of iced tea . . . his voice interrupts your thoughts.

"Hey, Rebecca. Got a few minutes? I've got a few questions. I don't mean to be obnoxious, Bec, but how can you believe that a big God could ever give a hoot about you? Don't you think you are being presumptuous in thinking God wants you in heaven?

"You may assume you are on pretty good terms with the man upstairs, but haven't you forgotten that trip in Atlanta? You think he won't call your cards on that one?

"How do you know God gives a flip about you, anyway?"

When you ask, you must believe and not doubt, because the one who doubts is like a wave of the sea, blown and tossed by the wind (James 1:6).

Got a neighbor like this? He'll pester you. He'll irritate you. He'll criticize your judgment. He'll kick the stool out from under you and refuse to help you up. He'll tell you not to believe in the invisible yet offer no answer for the inadequacy of the visible.

He's a mealymouthed, two-faced liar who deals from the bottom of the deck. His aim is not to convince you but to confuse you. He doesn't offer solutions; he only raises questions. Don't let him fool you. Though he may speak the current jargon, he is no newcomer. His first seeds of doubt were sown in the Garden of Eden in the heart of Eve. He undoubtedly worked hard to sow those same seeds in the hearts of Sarah and Abraham.

But Sarah and Abraham never gave up trusting God. Although their get-up-and-go had got up and gone, and all they had was a Social Security check and a promise from heaven, they decided to trust that promise rather than focus on the problems. As a result, the Medicare couple were the first to bring a crib into the nursing home.

You, dear children, are from God (1 John 4:4).

He predestined us for adoption to sonship (Ephesians 1:5).

We are heirs—heirs of God and co-heirs with Christ (Romans 8:17).

5. We have an enemy who loves to steal away our hope. When we listen to his voice, we call ourselves names like *forgotten*, *unlovable*, *unimportant*. More than likely, Abraham and Sarah felt this way during their twenty-five years of waiting. But then they listened to God's names for them—*Abraham* meaning "father of many," and *Sarah* meaning "princess." Read 1 John 4:4, Ephesians 1:4–5, and Romans 8:17. What does God call you? How does this breathe new hope into you?

_____

_____

_____

_____

_____

Yet he did not waver through unbelief regarding the promise of God, but was strengthened in his faith and gave glory to God, being fully persuaded that God had power to do what he had promised (Romans 8:20–21).

6. God's plan is so outlandish that Abraham asks, "How could I become a father at the age of 100 . . . and how can Sarah have a baby when she is ninety years old?" (Genesis 17:17 NLT). Yet in spite of how crazy the plan sounds, he and Sarah never give up trusting God. Read Romans 4:18–21. What do these verses say about their faith?

_____

_____

_____

_____

7. Abraham is clearly in disbelief that Sarah will give birth to a son at such an old age. So he asks God to bless Ishmael, thinking that he *must* be the rightful heir after all. How does God respond (see

Genesis 17:19–20)? What does this say about God's generosity and grace even when we misunderstand or doubt his plan?

_____

_____

_____

_____

_____

8. What doubts are you hearing these days? Write them down, and then beside them write out these promises: 2 Peter 3:8–9, Deuteronomy 7:9, 2 Thessalonians 3:3.

_____

_____

_____

_____

_____

Then God said, "Yes, but your wife Sarah will bear you a son, and you will call him Isaac" (Genesis 17:19).

He is patient with you, not wanting anyone to perish (2 Peter 3:9).

The LORD your God is God; he is the faithful God (Deuteronomy 7:9).

The Lord is faithful, and he will strengthen you (2 Thessalonians 3:3).

In Hebrews 11:13, the author writes that the greatest biblical heroes "died in faith, not having received the promises" (NKJV). Sometimes we won't see God's promises unfold during our lifetime. Other times, it may take only a matter of minutes. Regardless, in seasons of doubt we must remember that God doesn't need an alarm clock. He hasn't dozed off or forgotten his plan for our lives. He is faithful, and his timing is perfect. May we, like Abraham and Sarah and all the heroes of faith, trust in God regardless of promises seen or unseen.

❧ POINTS TO REMEMBER ❧

❖ God's timeline is not our own, and we cannot measure his faithfulness by our clock or calendar.
❖ It is the enemy's goal to confuse us, raise questions in our minds about God's plans, and lead us into doubt.
❖ Our trust needs to be in God and God alone, or we will lose sight of him and sink into hopelessness when we grow impatient waiting on his plan.

❧ PRAYER FOR THE DAY ❧

Thank you, Lord, that your timing is perfect. You are never late to fulfill your promises. Help us to focus on you, on your faithfulness, and to keep our eyes fixed on your love and grace. May we grow in faith as we wait expectantly for what you are going to do in our lives. In Jesus' name, amen.

*D*ay Four: Promise Fulfilled

UNEXPECTED VISITORS

With God all things are possible (Matthew 19:26).

Sarah's name isn't the only thing God changes in her life. He soon changes her mind. He changes her faith. He changes the number of her tax deductions. He changes the way she defines the word *impossible*. But most of all, he changes her attitude about what it means to trust in him. It begins one day when three visitors arrive at her tent.

Abraham looked up and saw three men standing nearby (Genesis 18:2).

Abraham sees them first. He runs to greet them and then goes to find Sarah. "Quick," he says, "get some flour and bake some bread." Sarah does so, but as she kneads the dough in the tent, she does some eavesdropping as well. "I will surely return to you about this time next year," she hears one visitor say, "and Sarah your wife shall have a son" (Genesis 18:10 ESV).

Sarah laughed to herself as she thought, "After I am worn out and my lord is old, will I now have this pleasure?" (verse 12).

When Sarah hears the news, a cackle escapes before she can contain it. Her shoulders shake, and she buries her wrinkled face in her bony hands. She knows she shouldn't laugh. It's not kosher to laugh at what God says, for this visitor indeed is the Lord speaking to her. But just as she catches her breath and wipes away the tears, she thinks about it again—and a fresh wave of hilarity doubles her over.

1. Spend some time in Genesis 18:1–15. Why do you think Sarah laughed? What emotions were behind her laughter (doubt, joy, shock)? Use the context and history you know to support your thoughts.

   _____

   _____

   _____

2. Why do you think the Lord asks Abraham, "Why did Sarah laugh?" in verse 13? Usually when God asks a question, he is communicating a lesson. What lesson is he teaching Sarah?

   _____

   _____

   _____

So she lied and said, "I did not laugh" (verse 15).

3. Why does Sarah lie about laughing? How do you see her attitude toward God change from verse 12 to verse 15? Why does it change?

   _____

   _____

   _____

4. God changes the way Sarah defines the word *impossible* and changes her attitude about what it means to trust in him. When was a time God did this to you? How did he change the way you trusted him? How has he opened your eyes to the impossible?

_____

_____

_____

_____

Lord GOD . . . there is nothing too hard for You (Jeremiah 32:17 NKJV).

THE LORD PROVIDES

Later on, after the visitors have left, Abraham looks over at Sarah—toothless and snoring in her rocker, head back and mouth wide open, as fruitful as a pitted prune and just as wrinkled. And he cracks up. He tries to contain it, but he can't. He has always been a sucker for a good joke.

But one year later, it's God who has the last laugh. "The LORD visited Sarah as he had said, and the Lord did to Sarah as he had promised. And Sarah conceived and bore Abraham a son in his old age at the time of which God had spoken to him" (Genesis 21:1–2 ESV).

Sarah and Abraham's name for God was *Jehovah-jireh*, which means "the Lord who provides." It's a bit ironic, perhaps, that they would call God *provider*, given the fact the couple had been well provided for already before their trek to Canaan. They had lived in a split-level tent with a four-camel garage. Life was good in Ur.

To this day it is said, "On the mountain of the LORD it will be provided" (Genesis 22:14).

"But life will be better in Canaan," Abraham had told Sarah and the rest of the family. So off they had gone. When she had asked, "Where will we live?" Abraham had answered, "God will provide." And God did.

When they later got caught in an Egyptian scandal, the family wondered, "How will we get out?" Abraham assured them, "God will provide." And he did.

When they split up the land and nephew Lot took the grassland and left Uncle Abraham with the rocks, the family wondered, "How will we survive?" Abraham knew the answer: "God will provide." And he did.

And when Abraham and Sarah stood next to the empty crib, and she wondered how she'd be the mother of nations, he'd put his arm around her, whispering, "The Lord will provide." And God did.

Were Sarah to hear Jesus' statement in Matthew 5:3 about being poor in spirit, she could give a testimony. "He's right," she would say. "I do things my way, I get a headache. I let God take over, I get a son. You try to figure that out. All I know is I am the first lady in town to pay her pediatrician with a Social Security check."

Blessed are the poor in spirit, for theirs is the kingdom of heaven (Matthew 5:3).

Abraham and Sarah had truly learned that God provides. But what God would ask them to do next must surely have tested their trust in him once again.

God has brought me laughter, and everyone who hears about this will laugh with me (Genesis 21:6).

5. Read Genesis 21:3–7. The name *Isaac* means "he laughs." How would you describe Sarah's laughter in this chapter (see verse 6) as compared to her laughter in Genesis 18?

6. Sarah learned a lesson on how to be "poor in spirit" (Matthew 5:3). What does being poor in spirit mean? Why does it bring blessing? In what ways are you poor in spirit?

7. "The poor in spirit are those who recognize they need God's help."[3] How does seeing our need for God affect the way we live out our daily lives as compared to not seeing our need for God?

My God will meet all your needs according to the riches of his glory in Christ Jesus (Philippians 4:19).

8. *Jehova-jireh* means "the Lord will provide." God provided for Abraham and Sarah every step of the way. All they had to do was trust in him. In the space below, write down a time in your past when God provided an answer to a worry or need. Now write down a worry of today, and next to it write down God's name, *Jehova-jireh*. Take a minute to remind yourself that God was faithful in your past and will be faithful in your present.

Everything is possible for one who believes (Mark 9:23).

God had once asked Abraham, "Is anything too hard for the LORD?" (Genesis 18:14 NKJV). In the question we find the answer—absolutely not. Approximately 2,000 years later, we find the same truth proclaimed about another promised child yet to be born. "For with God nothing will be impossible," the angel said to Mary as he announced the birth of the Savior (Luke 1:37 NKJV). Are you gripped by worry? Plagued with doubt? If so, just remember that if God could do the "impossible" by giving a ninety-one-year-old woman a child and a teenage virgin a child, he can do the impossible in your life. And just as Sarah joyously laughed the day she held that impossible miracle in her weathered arms, may you joyously laugh today as you hold on to the incredible promise that *nothing is impossible with God*. Nothing.

❧ POINTS TO REMEMBER ❧

❖ When God provides the impossible, our understanding of his character and our trust in his faithfulness grow.
❖ Remembering how God has provided for us in the past will help us to trust him to be faithful in the present.
❖ God can do the impossible in our lives.

❧ PRAYER FOR THE DAY ❧

We praise you, Lord, for your faithfulness in the past—for those promises you have fulfilled and those impossible needs that you have already met. Your love and care are beyond measure! Thank you that our needs for today are safely in your hands. Amen.

Day Five: A Test of Faith

THE MOST DIFFICULT COMMAND

She added, "Who would have said to Abraham that Sarah would nurse children? Yet I have borne him a son in his old age" (Genesis 21:7).

It's hard to say which is more amazing: that Sarah became pregnant at ninety, or that she and Abraham at that age were still trying to conceive. Of all the gifts God gave them, Isaac was the greatest. But of all the commands God would give them, this one would be the hardest: "Take your dear son Isaac whom you love and go to the land of Moriah. Sacrifice him there as a burnt offering on one of the mountains that I'll point out to you" (Genesis 22:2 MSG).

Some time later God tested Abraham. He said to him, "Abraham!" "Here I am," he replied (22:1).

The Bible doesn't tell us what was running through Abraham's mind when he heard this command. It doesn't tell us Sarah's reaction as she said goodbye to her son. All we know is that Abraham saddled the donkey, took Isaac and two servants, and traveled to the place of sacrifice. When he saw the mountain in the distance, he instructed the servants to stay and wait. And he made a statement that is worthy of special note: "Stay here with the donkey. My son and I will go over there and worship, and then we will come back to you" (verse 5 NCV).

Early the next morning Abraham got up and loaded his donkey. He took with him two of his servants and his son Isaac (verse 3).

Look at Abraham's confident "we will come back." As the writer of Hebrews would later note, "Abraham reasoned that if Isaac died, God was able to bring him back to life again. And in a sense, Abraham did receive his son back from the dead" (Hebrews 11:19 NLT).

1. Turn to Genesis 22. In verse 1, we read that "God *tested* Abraham" (NKJV, emphasis added). What does it mean to "test" one's faith? Note that God never *tempts* our faith, only tests it (see James 1:13). What is the difference between testing and tempting?

   _____

   _____

   _____

   _____

2. Read 1 Peter 1:7. Describe a time when you think the Lord was testing your faith. How was your faith "refined by fire" during that test?

   _____

   _____

   _____

3. In Sarah and Abraham's story, just when the waiting and trials are over—just when life is feeling good again with their promised son, Isaac—God sends the hardest test yet. Why did God test Abraham's faith? Hadn't Abraham proved faithful enough?

   _____

   _____

   _____

4. Read Hebrews 11:17–19. How does the author say Abraham reacted toward God during this trial of faith? What can we learn from his example?

   _____

   _____

   _____

GIVING EVERYTHING BACK TO GOD

Up the mountain the father and son go. "Where is the lamb we will burn as a sacrifice?" Isaac asks at one point (Genesis 22:7 NCV). One wonders how the answer made it past the lump in Abraham's throat. "God will give us the lamb for the sacrifice, my son" (verse 8 NCV). Jehovah-jireh, the Lord will provide.

Abraham ties up his son. He places him on the altar. He raises the knife . . . and then an angel stays his hand. God has interrupted the sacrifice and spared Isaac's life. Abraham hears a rustling in the thicket and sees a ram caught by his horns in a bush. He offers it as a sacrifice and gives the mountain a name: Jehovah-jireh, the Lord provides.

In the New Testament, we find Jesus reaching out to parents of stricken children. The Canaanite mother. The father of an epileptic boy. Jairus. They held one end of their rope in one hand and reached toward Christ with the other. In each case, Jesus responded. His consistent kindness issues a welcome announcement: God heeds the concern in a parent's heart.

After all, our kids were his kids first. "Don't you see that children are God's best gift? the fruit of the womb his generous legacy?" (Psalm 127:3 MSG). Before our children were ours, they were his. Even as they are ours, they are still his. We tend to forget this and regard our children as "our" children, as though we have the final say in their health and welfare. We don't. All people are God's people, including the small people who sit at our tables.

Wise are they who regularly give what they have received from God back to him. This is exactly what we see in Sarah and Abraham's lives. They were willing to withhold nothing from God and entrust him with the very life of the one they had waited so many years to receive. Their example shows us that God rewards us when we do the same.

Jairus, a synagogue leader, came and fell at Jesus' feet, pleading with him to come to his house because his only daughter . . . was dying (Luke 8:41–42).

5. Think of a gift that God has given to you that you cherish deeply. If God asked you to return this gift to him tomorrow, how would you respond?

_____

_____

_____

Now I know that you fear God, because you have not withheld from me your son (Genesis 22:12).

6. In Matthew 6:21 Jesus says, "Where your treasure is, there your heart will be also." If we aren't careful, we can allow our gifts to outweigh the Gift-giver. Do you have any earthly gifts that you treasure too much? If so, how can you reach a place where you view God as the ultimate treasure and not the gifts he gives to you?

_____

_____

_____

Do not store up for yourselves treasures on earth . . . but store up for yourselves treasures in heaven (Matthew 6:19–20).

7. A thousand years after Abraham, the temple in Jerusalem would be built on Mount Moriah. Although the Bible doesn't specify, many scholars believe the temple and the place where Abraham offered the sacrifice of Isaac were the same location. If that is the case, what would be the significance of the shared location (see Genesis 22:14)?

_____

_____

_____

8. Abraham's sacrifice of Isaac was an act of worship—an offering to God of his absolute best, and his giving back to God what was rightfully the Lord's in the first place. How can we likewise sacrifice our most prized possessions to God in a physical and spiritual sense?

_____

_____

_____

_____

_____

God responded to Abraham's faithfulness with these words: "Because you have done this and have not withheld your son, your only son, I will surely bless you and make your descendants as numerous as the stars in the sky and as the sand on the seashore. Your descendants will take possession of the cities of their enemies, and through your offspring all nations on earth will be blessed, because you have obeyed me" (Genesis 22:16–18).

In the end, the Lord blessed Sarah and Abraham for their trust in him. Yes, Satan had used an empty crib to stir up tension and dissension and doubt in their household. Sarah could have easily served as the enemy's *prima facie* evidence as to why a person could never trust God. But instead, as we have seen, she modeled just the opposite. Her story has ever since instructed millions that God saves the best for last.

Other examples stand out in the pages of the Bible. When Daniel and Jerusalem's best young men were led into captivity, it appeared to be a victory for Satan. Hell's strategy was to isolate the godly young men. But again the plan boomeranged. Daniel was soon asked to serve in the king's court. The very man Satan sought to silence spent most of his life praying to the God of Israel and advising the kings of Babylon.

Peter is another example. Satan sought to discredit Jesus by provoking Peter to deny him. But the plan backfired. Rather than be an example of how far a fellow can fall, Peter became an example of how far God's grace extends.

Or consider Paul. Satan hoped the prison would silence his pulpit. It did, but it also unleashed his pen. The letters to the Galatians, Ephesians, Philippians, and Colossians were all written from a jail cell. Can't you just see Satan kicking the dirt and snarling his lips every time a person reads those epistles? He helped write them!

Every time Satan scores a basket, the other team gets the points.

Sarah's story tells us that God always keeps his promises. It shows us that God gives grace to those in need of it. It reveals that God stays with us and works in our lives even when we try to move against his will. And it shows us that he will care for us when we entrust to him the gifts that he has given to us.

❧ POINTS TO REMEMBER ☙

- ❖ Times of testing refine our faith, making it genuine, and allow us to give God glory, honor, and praise.
- ❖ Our willingness to give God what we value the most is an act of worship that God will bless.
- ❖ We know our hearts are right toward God when he is more valuable to us than any treasure he gives us.

❧ PRAYER FOR THE DAY ☙

Everything we have is yours, Lord. We love and care for your treasures, but we recognize that they pale in comparison to you. Help us to worship you by having hearts that are willing to give you our all each and every day of our lives. Amen.

❧ WEEKLY MEMORY VERSE ☙

Understand, therefore, that the LORD your God is indeed God. He is the faithful God who keeps his covenant for a thousand generations and lavishes his unfailing love on those who love him and obey his commands.

DEUTERONOMY 7:9 (NLT)

For Further Reading

Selections throughout this lesson were taken from *No Wonder They Call Him Savior* (Nashville: Thomas Nelson, 1986); *The Applause of Heaven* (Nashville: Thomas Nelson, 1990); *In the Grip of Grace* (Nashville: Thomas Nelson, 1996); *Great House of God* (Nashville: Thomas Nelson, 1997); *Six Hours One Friday* (Nashville: Thomas Nelson, 2004); and *Fearless* (Nashville: Thomas Nelson, 2009).

Notes
1. Earl Radmacher, Ronald B. Allen, H. Wayne House, eds., *Nelson's New Illustrated Bible Commentary* (Nashville: Thomas Nelson, 1999), p. 30.
2. Ibid., p. 32
3. *The ESV Global Study Bible* (Wheaton, Ill.: Crossway, 2012), note on Matthew 5:3.

LESSON 2

RAHAB

WHEN A CHECKERED PAST MEETS GOD'S GRACE

SOME KIDS IN CATEURA, on the outskirts of Asunción, Paraguay, are making music with their trash. They're turning washtubs into kettledrums and drainpipes into trumpets. Other orchestras fine-tune their maple cellos or brass tubas. Not this band. They play Beethoven sonatas with plastic buckets.

On their side of Asunción, garbage is the only crop to harvest. Garbage pickers sort and sell refuse for pennies a pound. Many of them have met the same fate as the trash. They've been tossed out and discarded.

But now, thanks to two men, they are making music.

Favio Chavez is an environmental technician who envisioned a music school as a welcome reprieve for the kids. Don Cola Gomez is a trash worker and carpenter. He had never seen, heard, or held a violin in his life. Yet when someone described the instrument, this untutored craftsman took a paint can and an oven tray into his tiny workshop and made a violin. His next instrument was a cello. He fashioned the body out of an oil barrel and made tuning knobs from a hairbrush, the heel of a shoe, and a wooden spoon.

Thanks to this Stradivarius, the junk gets a mulligan, and so do the kids who live among it. Since the day their story hit the news, they've been tutored by maestros, featured on national television programs, and put on a world tour. They've been called the Landfill Harmonic and also the Recycled Orchestra of Cateura.

We could also call them a picture of God's grace.

God makes music out of riffraff. Heaven's orchestra is composed of the unlikeliest of musicians. Peter, first-chair trumpeter, cursed the name of the Christ who saved him. Paul plays the violin. But there was a day when he played the religious thug. And the guy on the harp? That's David. King David. Womanizing David. Conniving David. Bloodthirsty David. Repentant David.

Be strong in the grace that is in Christ Jesus (2 Timothy 2:1).

The king of Jericho was told, "Look, some of the Israelites have come here tonight to spy out the land" (Joshua 2:2).

Take special note of the woman with the clarinet. Her name is Rahab. Her story occupies the second chapter of Joshua. "Now Joshua the son of Nun sent out two men from Acacia Grove to spy secretly, saying, 'Go, view the land, especially Jericho.' So they went, and came to the house of a harlot named Rahab, and lodged there" (verse 1 NKJV).

1. If you are honest, how do you see yourself today? As a piece of garbage, unusable and forgotten? Or as God's instrument, redeemed and valuable? Or maybe a mixture of both? Explain your thoughts.

_____

_____

_____

_____

_____

_____

2. How has God taken the garbage in your life—maybe bad decisions you've made in your past or a current struggle you are facing—and mercifully turned it into music?

_____

_____

_____

_____

_____

_____

_____

Worship the LORD with gladness; come before him with joyful songs (Psalm 100:2).

A pan made into a violin. A cello made out of a barrel. Who would have thought music could come out of something so messed up, so discarded, so rotten? Yet God does this every day. He tunes our off-pitch hearts to match his song. Our only job is to let him do his work. If we think he can't use us, we're wrong. So today, let's ask God to help us see ourselves as landfill instruments—once dirty, now clean; once silent, now singing his music.

⤳ PRAYER FOR THE WEEK ⤳

Lord, you tell us that "anyone united with the Messiah gets a fresh start, is created new. The old life is gone; a new life burgeons!" (2 Corinthians 5:17 MSG). Thank you for transforming our trash into your song. Today, we ask that you would continue to make our life song sound more and more like you. Amen.

𝒟ay One: Trial in the Wilderness

CANAANITE-SIZED FEARS

The Promised Land was actually the third stop on the Hebrews' iconic itinerary. Their pilgrimage had begun in Egypt, where they had been enslaved to Pharaoh. After God raised up Moses to be the leader of the people, the Israelites stepped on dry ground through the Red Sea and entered the wilderness. There, in the desert, they were liberated from Egyptian bondage. But you wouldn't have known it by listening to them.

Just three days into their freedom, "the people grumbled to Moses and asked, 'What shall we drink?'"(Exodus 15:24 NCV). A few more days passed, and "the whole Israelite community grumbled to Moses and Aaron in the desert. . . . 'It would have been better if the Lord had killed us in the land of Egypt. . . . You have brought us into this desert to starve us to death'" (16:2–3 NCV). The people "quarreled with Moses" (17:2 NCV), and they "grumbled against Moses" (verse 3 NCV). They inhaled anxiety like oxygen. They bellyached to the point that Moses prayed, "What can I do with these people? They are almost ready to stone me" (verse 4 NCV).

Finally, when God called the people to cross over into Canaan, Moses sent twelve spies into the land. When they returned, all but two of them said the mission was impossible. The giants were just too big for them. "We were like grasshoppers," they said (Numbers 13:33 NKJV). *We were tiny, tiny bugs. They will squash us.*

So God gave them time to think it over. He put the entire nation in time-out for nearly forty years. They walked in circles. They ate the same food every day. Life was an endless routine of the same rocks, lizards, and snakes. Victories were scarce. Progress was slow. They were saved but not strong. Redeemed but not released. Saved from Pharaoh but stuck in the desert. Redeemed but locked in a routine. Four decades of tedium.

But the day came when God appeared to Joshua, Moses' successor, and said, "Arise, go over this Jordan, you and all this people, to the land which I am giving to them" (Joshua 1:2 NKJV). The time had come for a second chance, and Jericho was the first test.

How would the people respond this time?

1. Before we step inside the Jericho walls, let's look back at the Israelites' journey to get there. Read Exodus 3:7–10. What did God promise to Moses and the people in these verses? What can you gather about God's affection toward Israel?

_____

_____

[Moses] led them out of Egypt and performed wonders and signs in Egypt, at the Red Sea and for forty years in the wilderness (Acts 7:36).

But our ancestors refused to obey him. Instead, they rejected him and in their hearts turned back to Egypt (verse 39).

I have come down to rescue them from the hand of the Egyptians (Exodus 3:8).

Sing to the LORD, for he is highly exalted. Both horse and driver he has hurled into the sea (Exodus 15:21).

2. Turn to Exodus 15:20–21. God freed the Israelites after 430 years in captivity through an epic series of plagues and the parting of the Red Sea. Once they are out of Egypt, they begin to worship the Lord. What do Miriam and the women proclaim about God in their song? What is their attitude and demeanor?

_____

_____

_____

In the desert the whole community grumbled against Moses and Aaron (16:2).

3. Now skip down a few verses and read Exodus 16:1–3. The people were just worshiping God, but now they are grumbling. What do you think led to the change? Describe a time when you, like the Israelites, were guilty of praising God one moment only to turn around and doubt him the next.

_____

_____

_____

Not one of them will ever see the land I promised on oath to their ancestors (Numbers 14:23).

4. Look up Numbers 13:28–29. The Israelites' doubt in God's plan didn't stop. After Moses sent spies into the Promised Land, they returned with bad news. What did the spies say they feared? What Canaanite-sized fears do you have right now?

_____

_____

_____

_____

A FORTY-YEAR LESSON IN TRUST

To understand how the Israelites would respond to God's command in Joshua 1:2 to enter the Promised Land, we need to look at what they had learned during their forty years of wandering in the wilderness. As we saw, the people had taken anxiety to a new art form. You'd think they would have given seminars on faith based on everything they had witnessed. They had beheld one miracle after another, but still they worried.

Just a month into freedom, the same Hebrews who had cried out to God for deliverance were speaking as if Egypt were a paid vacation. They had forgotten the miracles they saw and the misery they knew, and forgetfulness sires fretfulness. So God had to teach them how trust in him and depend on him. And they needed to depend on him *one day at a time*.

If only we had died by the LORD's hand in Egypt! There we sat around pots of meat and ate all the food we wanted (Exodus 16:3).

In the evenings, God sent quail to cover the compound. In mornings, manna glistened like frost. Meat for dinner. Bread for breakfast. The food fell every day. Not annually, monthly, or hourly, but daily. The people learned that God had resources they knew nothing about, solutions outside their reality, provisions outside their possibility. They saw the scorched earth; God saw heaven's breadbasket. They saw dry land; God saw a covey of quail behind every bush. They saw problems; God saw provision.

In Romans 8:28 Paul writes, "We know that in everything God works for the good of those who love him" (NCV). I think it's one of the most helpful, comforting verses of the entire Bible, announcing God's sovereignty in any painful, tragic situation we face. Why? Because it tells us not only that *God works*—that he is active in our situation—but also that he *works for our good*. God uses our struggles to build character.

James makes the same point in his letter. "My brethren, count it all joy when you fall into various trials, knowing that the testing of your faith produces patience. But let patience have its perfect work, that you may be perfect and complete, lacking nothing" (James 1:2–4 NKJV). Today's trial leads to tomorrow's maturity.

Hasn't the oyster taught us this principle? The grain of sand invades the comfort of the shell, and how does the oyster respond? How does he cope with the irritation? Does he go to the oyster bar for a few drinks? Does he get depressed and clam up? Does he go on a shopping binge and shell out a bunch of money to get over the pain? No. He emits the substance that not only overcomes the irritation but also transforms the irritation into a pearl. Every pearl is simply a victory over irritations.

So what do we do in the meantime? We do what the people of Israel did: we learn to trust completely, day by day, for all of our needs. And we remember that "God is working . . . God is working for the good . . . God is using all things."

You will know that it was the LORD when he gives you meat to eat in the evening and all the bread you want in the morning, because he has heard your grumbling against him (Exodus 16:8).

5. Read Numbers 14:1–10. How did the people react when they heard from the ten spies about the size and strength of the Canaanites? What did Joshua and Caleb do to try to convince them to trust God?

_____

_____

_____

_____

All the Israelites grumbled against Moses and Aaron, and the whole assembly said to them, "If only we had died in Egypt!" (Numbers 14:2).

6. Turn to Mark 11:22–25. What does Jesus say in this passage about the power of having faith in God? What does he say about doubting in God's promises?

_____

_____

_____

Whatever you ask for in prayer, believe that you have received it, and it will be yours (Mark 11:24).

7. When in your life did doubt and/or fear prevent you from stepping into a place of "milk and honey"—a place of more freedom and joy?

Why are you troubled, and why do doubts rise in your minds?
(Luke 24:38).

What steps did you take to overcome that doubt? How did you see God leading you?

_____

_____

_____

_____

8. No one enjoys trials, but Scripture is clear they serve a purpose. Read the passages below and write down some of the ways God uses difficult times to shape our character.

Romans 5:3–4: "We also exult in our tribulations, knowing that tribulation brings about perseverance; and perseverance, proven character; and proven character, hope" (NASB).

_____

_____

_____

2 Corinthians 1:3–4: "The Father of mercies . . . comforts us in all our affliction, so that we may be able to comfort those who are in any affliction, with the comfort with which we ourselves are comforted by God" (ESV).

_____

_____

_____

2 Corinthians 4:17: "For our present troubles are small and won't last very long. Yet they produce for us a glory that vastly outweighs them and will last forever!" (NLT).

_____

_____

_____

1 Peter 4:12–13: "Do not be surprised at the terrible trouble which now comes to test you. . . . But be happy that you are sharing in Christ's sufferings so that you will be happy and full of joy when Christ comes again in glory" (NCV).

_____

_____

_____

In Egypt, generations of God's people had sat around the dinner table, telling their children, "One day the Lord will deliver us. He promised!" But when that day actually came, the people forgot the promise and focused on the fear. We do the same when we allow the words of the enemy or our own insecurities to overshadow God's truth. So today, let's shift our eyes off of our Canaanite-sized fears and onto the promise of God—the same promise He made to the Israelites: "I am the LORD . . . I will free you from being slaves . . . I will redeem you with an outstretched arm . . . I will take you as my own people, and I will be your God" (Exodus 6:6–7).

Then the LORD said to him, "Know for certain that for four hundred years your descendants will be strangers in a country not their own and that they will be enslaved and mistreated there" (Genesis 15:13).

⤷ POINTS TO REMEMBER ⤶

❖ Trusting God and depending on him one day at a time builds our confidence in him and in his plans.
❖ God has resources and solutions outside of our reality and beyond our concept of what is possible.
❖ Trials serve a purpose . . . they build character, allow us to empathize with the pain of others, bring God glory, and help us be more like Christ.

⤷ PRAYER FOR THE DAY ⤶

Lord, forgive us when we forget your promises. When fear creeps in, flood our hearts with your promise that you have freed us, redeemed us, taken us in as your children, and given us the privilege to call you our God. Use the trials in our lives to shape us into the kind of people that you want us to be—people more like your Son, Jesus. Amen.

Day Two: The First Step of Faith

GOD LEADS THE WAY

The Israelites' first exercise in faith would come in the form of the Jordan River. During most months of the year, this river was thirty or forty yards wide, and maybe six feet deep.[2] But Joshua received his orders during the season of the harvest. At that time, the Jordan swelled to a mile in width, turbulent with the melted snows of Mount Hermon.

You will cross the Jordan here to go in and take possession of the land the LORD your God is giving you (Joshua 1:11).

Early in the morning Joshua and all the Israelites . . . went to the Jordan, where they camped before crossing over (Joshua 3:1).

The priests who carried the ark reached the Jordan and their feet touched the water's edge (verse 15).

Get ready to cross the Jordan River into the land I am about to give to them—to the Israelites (1:2).

They answered Joshua, "Whatever you have commanded us we will do" (verse 16).

Especially with millions of people! God wanted every man, woman, child, and infant across the river. Not just the hearty and healthy, but the old and feeble, sick and disabled. No one would be left behind. Joshua might well have gulped at this command. Two million people crossing a mile-wide river? Yet he set the process in motion.

For three days the people camped on the eastern edge of the river, watching the copper-colored waters and yeasty waves carry debris and trunks of trees. Three days. Plenty of time to ask how in the world they would get across. But on the third day the answer came: "When you see the ark of the covenant . . . you shall set out from your place" (Joshua 3:3 NKJV).

When God said, "Follow the ark," he was saying, "Follow me." God led the way. Not soldiers. Not Joshua. Not engineers and their plans or Special Forces and their equipment. When it came time to pass through the impassable waters, God's plan was simple: trust me.

The people did, though the Bible does not try to veil their fear. The priests "dipped" their feet into the edge of the water. They did not run, plunge, or dive into the river. They placed ever so carefully the tips of their big toes in the river. It was the smallest of steps, but with God the smallest step of faith can activate the mightiest of miracles. And as they touched the water, the flow stopped as if someone had shut off the water main.

The first obstacle had been overcome. But there was a bigger challenge waiting for them on the horizon: the conquest of the mighty city of Jericho. And, as we shall see, Rahab would play a key role in the Israelites' plans to take it.

1. Check out Joshua 1:1–6. After forty years, the doubting generation of Israelites dies in the wilderness, and God appoints Joshua to lead the next generation into the Promised Land. What did God tell Joshua to do? What promises did he give?

2. Look at Joshua 1:10–18. Joshua immediately orders the Israelites to prepare for battle. How do the Israelites respond to the order this time? How does this generation of Israelites differ from the one that came before?

3. Read Joshua 3:8–13. Try to put yourself in the Israelites' shoes (or should I say sandals) as they approached the first test of faith: crossing the Jordan River. What was unusual about God's instructions for how they would cross? How did this require faith?

The ark of the covenant of the LORD of all the earth will go into the Jordan ahead of you (Joshua 3:11).

_____

_____

_____

_____

4. Read the rest of the story in verses 14–17. God had led the people out of Egypt by making a way for them to cross on dry land through the Red Sea. Now he was leading the people into Canaan by making a way for them to cross on dry land through the Jordan River. What "rivers" is God leading you through in your life? What steps of faith is he asking you to take to reach the other side?

All Israel passed by until the whole nation had completed the crossing on dry ground (verse 17).

_____

_____

_____

_____

A GNARLED FAMILY TREE

Jericho was a formidable town that sat just north of the Dead Sea. The Canaanites indwelled the city. To call the people barbaric is to describe the North Pole as nippy. These people turned temple worship into orgies. They buried babies alive. The people of Jericho had no regard for human life or any respect for God.

Destroy them . . . otherwise, they will teach you to follow all the detestable things they do in worshiping their gods (Deuteronomy 20:17–18).

It was into this city that Joshua sent two men to spy out the enemy's defenses. It was in this city that the spies met Rahab, the harlot.

Much could be said of her without mentioning her profession. She was a Canaanite. She provided cover for the spies of Joshua. She came to believe in the God of Abraham before she ever met the children of Abraham. She was spared in the destruction of her city. She was grafted into the Hebrew culture. She married a contemporary of Joshua's, bore a son named Boaz, had a great-grandson named Jesse, a great-great-grandson named David, and a descendant named Jesus. Yes, Rahab's name appears on the family tree of the Son of God.

They went and entered the house of a prostitute named Rahab (Joshua 2:1).

Her résumé needn't mention her profession. Yet in five of the eight appearances of her name in Scripture, she is presented as a "harlot." Five! Wouldn't one suffice? Couldn't that one reference be nuanced in a euphemism such as "Rahab, the best hostess in Jericho," or, "Rahab, who made everyone feel welcome"? It's bad enough that the name Rahab sounds like "rehab." Disguise her career choice. Veil it. Mask it. Put a little concealer on this biblical blemish. Drop the reference to the brothel, please.

But the Bible doesn't. Just the opposite. It points a neon sign at it. It's even attached to her name in the book of Hebrews Hall of Fame. The list includes Abel, Noah, Abraham, Isaac, Jacob, Joseph, Moses . . . and then, all of a sudden, "the harlot Rahab" (11:31 NKJV). No asterisk, no footnote, no apology. Her history of harlotry is part of her testimony.

The prostitute Rahab, because she welcomed the spies, was not killed with those who were disobedient (Hebrews 11:30).

5. Turn to Hebrews 11:30–31. What does the author say about Rahab in this passage?

_____

_____

_____

_____

Was not even Rahab the prostitute considered righteous for what she did? (James 2:25).

6. Look at James 2:25–26. Who does James mention in this passage? What does she embody according to these verses?

_____

_____

_____

_____

Salmon the father of Boaz, whose mother was Rahab (Matthew 1:5).

7. Now take a look at Matthew 1:1–16. Did you find Rahab in that list? What is the significance of her being in this lineage, given her reputation?

_____

_____

_____

_____

8. The Israelites had a tainted past, and so did Rahab. Yet God used them both, even making Rahab a model of exemplary faith all throughout the Bible! What does this teach us not only about our past but also about our future?

_____

_____

_____

_____

The LORD is compassionate and gracious, slow to anger, abounding in love (Psalm 103:8).

Perhaps you come from a lineage of faithlessness. Or maybe your lineage is more of the faithless variety. Regardless, aren't you glad we have a God who works according to his goodness and not ours? Because he is faithful, we still have a future. Because he is good, we still have a hope. We can praise him because he "does not treat us as our sins deserve or repay us according to our iniquities" (Psalm 103:10). Instead, he forgives us and sees us as clean. As a result we, like Rahab, can find ourselves in the lineage of Christ.

∽ POINTS TO REMEMBER ∾

❖ The smallest step of faith can activate a mighty miracle.
❖ Our history can become part of our testimony of God's goodness.
❖ Our future—which is secured by God's grace alone—can give us hope and a place in God's family.

If you have faith as small as a mustard seed, you can say to this mountain, "Move from here to there" (Matthew 17:20).

∽ PRAYER FOR THE DAY ∾

Lord, thank you for promising us a future regardless of what we have done in our past. Thank you for using us in your great kingdom plan, just like you used Rahab. Give us eyes to see ourselves the way you see us— as forgiven, clean, and yours. Amen.

Day Three: Provision Through a Prostitute

AN UNLIKELY SANCTUARY

Rahab's story begins like this: "The king of Jericho was told, 'Look, some of the Israelites have come here tonight to spy out the land'" (Joshua 2:2). The king could see the multitude of Hebrews camped on Jordan's eastern banks. As Rahab would later disclose, the people of Jericho were scared. Word on the street was that God had his hand on the newcomers—and woe be unto anyone who got in their way.

When the king heard the spies were hiding at Rahab's house, he sent soldiers to fetch them. I'm seeing half a dozen men squeeze down the narrow cobblestoned path in the red-light district. It's late at night. The torch-lit taverns are open, and the patrons are a few sheets to the wind. They yell obscenities at the king's men, but the soldiers don't react.

The guards keep walking until they stand before the wooden door of a stone building that abuts the famous Jericho walls. The lantern is unlit, leaving the soldiers to wonder if anyone is home. The captain pounds on the door. There is a shuffling inside. Rahab answers.

So the king of Jericho sent this message to Rahab: "Bring out the men who came to you" (Joshua 2:3).

Her makeup is layered and her eyes are shadowed. Her low-cut robe reveals the fringe of a lacy secret that Victoria couldn't keep. Her voice is husky from one cigarette too many. She positions a hand on her hip and holds a dirty martini with the other.

"Sorry, boys," she says, "we're booked for the night."

"We aren't here for that," the captain snaps. "We're here for the Hebrews."

"Hebrews?" She cocks her head. "I thought you were here for fun." She winks an eyelid, heavy with mascara, at a young soldier. He blushes, but the captain stays focused.

"We came for the spies. Where are they?"

She steps out onto the porch, looks to the right and left, and then lowers her voice to a whisper. "You just missed them. They snuck out before the gates were shut. If you get a move on, you can catch them."

The king's men turn and run. As they disappear around the corner, Rahab hurries up the brothel stairs to the roof, where the two spies have been hiding. She tells them the coast is clear. "The whole city is talking about you and your armies. Everyone is freaking out. The king can't sleep, and the people can't eat. They're popping Xanax like Tic Tacs. The last ounce of courage left on the morning train" (verses 8–11, Lucado Paraphrase Version.)

She said . . . "I don't know which way they went. Go after them quickly" (Joshua 2:5).

1. Read Joshua 2:1–15. What actions did Rahab take in these verses to protect the spies?

_____

_____

_____

But the woman had taken the two men and hidden them (verse 4).

2. What reasons does Rahab give for protecting the spies? Why does she say the people of Canaan are in fear of the Israelites?

_____

_____

_____

I know that the LORD has given you this land and that a great fear of you has fallen on us (verse 8).

3. Often, doing the right thing requires sacrifice. What all did Rahab sacrifice to hide the spies? What sacrifices are you currently making for the good of someone else?

_____

_____

_____

_____

4. A prostitute's house provides refuge for God's people, and God's people promise refuge for a prostitute. What does this say about

God and the way he works? What does it say about the way he cares for his people?

_____

_____

_____

_____

BOTTOM OF THE PIT

Rahab's words about the citizens' fear must have stunned the spies. They never expected to find cowards in Jericho. Even more, they never expected to find faith in a brothel. But they did. Read what Jericho's shady lady said to them:

> I know that the Lord has given you the land. . . . We have heard how the LORD dried up the water of the Red Sea . . . and what you did to the two kings . . . who were on the other side of the Jordan. . . . The LORD your God, he is God in heaven above and on earth beneath (verses 9–11).

Well, what do you know? Rahab found God. Or, better worded, God found Rahab. He spotted a tender heart in this hard city and reached out to save her. He would have saved the entire city, but no one else made the request. Then again, Rahab had an advantage over the other people. She had nothing to lose. She was at the bottom of the rung. She'd already lost her reputation, her social standing, her chance for advancement. She was at the bottom of the pit.

When Jesus heard this, he was amazed . . . [and] said, "I tell you, I have not found such great faith even in Israel" (Luke 7:9).

5. Read Joshua 2:12–24. In Rahab's conversation with the spies, she uses God's personal name, Yahweh, which is translated here as "Lord."[1] What does this say about her heart toward the one true God?

_____

_____

_____

_____

Swear to me by the LORD that you will show kindness to my family (Joshua 2:12).

6. What do Rahab and the spies negotiate in return for her kindness and protection (see verses 12–14)? What reasons does Rahab give for why she is doing this for them?

_____

_____

_____

"Our lives for your lives!" the men assured her (verse 14).

7. In verse 9, Rahab had said, "I know that the LORD has given you the land, and that the terror of you has fallen on us" (NASB). Rahab, the

When we heard of it, our hearts melted in fear (Joshua 2:11).

"enemy," had declared with assurance that the Israelites had already defeated Jericho. What did these words do for the spies' hearts? Who has God used in a surprising way to encourage you in his truth?

_____

_____

_____

8. In the end, God would provide not only for Rahab but also for the entire nation of Israel by delivering Jericho into their hands. What do you need God to provide in your life right now? How will this story of God's incredible provision bring you comfort and hope?

_____

_____

_____

God is able to bless you abundantly, so that in all things at all times, having all that you need, you will abound in every good work (2 Corinthians 9:8).

God was moving ahead of the Israelites, in the midst of the Israelites, and behind the Israelites. He prepared the way for them and provided for their every need. This same truth holds firm for us today. As Paul would write thousands of years later, "My God will meet all your needs according to the riches of his glory in Christ Jesus" (Philippians 4:19). Of course, the way God provides is often unexpected. As we see in this story, he delivered a foreign woman with a racy reputation so that she, in turn, could deliver his people. Who would have thought? Yet our Father does the same with us today. He is always going ahead of us, behind us, and operating in the midst of us to surprise us with his unfathomable provision.

❧ POINTS TO REMEMBER ❧

❖ Showing God's care for others will require sacrifice on our part.
❖ God may use an unlikely person to encourage our faith and provide for our needs.
❖ Anyone who honors and respects God becomes the object of his care and provision.

❧ PRAYER FOR THE DAY ❧

Lord, thank you for taking care of me. Just as you moved ahead of the Israelites, I know you move ahead of me. I know "you hem me in behind and before, and you lay your hand upon me" (Psalm 139:5). Forgive me when I don't trust in your provision, and help me to move this knowledge of your goodness from my head to my heart. Amen.

Day Four: Part of the Family

GOD HAS A PLACE

Maybe you can relate to Rahab. You may or may not have sold your body, but you've sold your allegiance, your affection, your attention, and your talents. You've sold out. We all have.

We've wondered—we've all wondered—what type of Promised Land life God could possibly have in store for us. *Perhaps for him or for her,* we think, *but not for us. We are too . . . soiled, dirty, afflicted. We have sinned too much. Stumbled too often. Floundered too long. We're on the garbage heap of society. No glory days for us.*

God's one-word reply for such doubt? *Rahab!*

Lest we think God's Promised Land is promised to a chosen few, he positions her story in the front of the book. The narrator gives her an entire chapter, for heaven's sake! She gets more inches of type than do the priests, the spies, or Joshua's right-hand man.

If quantity and chronology mean anything in theology, then Rahab's headline position announces this: *God has a place for the Rahabs of the world.*

1. Have you ever felt as if you were outside of God's forgiveness? If so, what made you feel that way? If not, how has God protected you from the lie that you are unforgivable?

_____

_____

_____

2. Read Numbers 14:17–19. When the first generation of Israelites failed to enter the Promised Land, Moses begged the Lord to forgive his people by reciting God's own words back to him (an interesting picture). Why does Moses say God should forgive the Israelites? On what does he base his request?

_____

_____

_____

3. Turn to Hebrews 10:12–14. What do these verses say about the power of Christ's forgiveness? What does it mean that by one sacrifice Jesus "made perfect forever those who are being made holy"?

_____

_____

As far as the east is from the west, so far has he removed our transgressions from us (Psalm 103:12).

In accordance with your great love, forgive the sin of these people, just as you have pardoned them (Numbers 14:19).

By one sacrifice he has made perfect forever those who are being made holy (Hebrews 10:14).

4. Rahab's story reveals that God's Promised Land is not promised to just a chosen few. What do the following verses say about how we receive our Promised Land from God?

Mark 16:15–16: "Jesus said to his followers, 'Go everywhere in the world, and tell the Good News to everyone. Anyone who believes and is baptized will be saved'" (NCV).

_____

_____

_____

John 14:6: "Jesus said to him, 'I am the way, the truth, and the life. No one comes to the Father except through Me'" (NKJV).

_____

_____

_____

Acts 16:30–31: "He said, 'Sirs, what must I do to be saved?' They said, 'Believe in the Lord Jesus, and you will be saved, you and your household'" (NASB).

_____

_____

_____

Romans 10:9: "If you openly declare that Jesus is Lord and believe in your heart that God raised him from the dead, you will be saved" (NLT).

_____

_____

_____

James 1:21: "Throw all spoiled virtue and cancerous evil in the garbage. In simple humility, let our gardener, God, landscape you with the Word, making a salvation-garden of your life" (MSG).

_____

_____

_____

ADOPTED CHILDREN

When we come to Christ, God not only forgives us but also adopts us. Through a dramatic series of events, we go from condemned orphans with no hope to adopted children with no fear. Just look at Rahab's story. She was a resident of Jericho, a city destined for destruction, but because of her faith God intervened and saved her and her family.

But there's more to her story, for later we read that one of Rahab's close descendants was Boaz, who married a foreigner named Ruth. They were the great-grandparents of King David, from whom descended Joseph, the husband of Mary (see Matthew 1:1–16). So, in a very real sense, Rahab became a part of God's family tree that day when salvation came to her house, for through her line came Jesus, the Son of God.

Naomi had a relative on her husband's side, a man of standing from the clan of Elimelek, whose name was Boaz (Ruth 2:1).

Like Rahab, it would be enough if God just cleansed our names, but he does more. He gives us *his* name. "You are God's children . . . God sent the Spirit of his Son into your hearts" (Galatians 4:6 NCV). It would be enough if God just set us free, but he does more. He takes us home. "And if I go and prepare a place for you, I will come again and receive you to Myself; that where I am, there you may be also" (John 14:3 NKJV).

Adoptive parents understand this more than anyone. I certainly don't mean to offend any biological parents—I'm one myself. We biological parents know well the earnest longing to have a child. But in many cases our cribs were filled easily. We decided to have a child and a child came. In fact, sometimes the child came with no decision. I've heard of unplanned pregnancies, but I've never heard of an unplanned adoption.

That's why adoptive parents understand God's passion to adopt us. They know what it means to feel an empty space inside. They know what it means to hunt, to set out on a mission, and take responsibility for a child with a spotted past and a dubious future. If anybody understands God's ardor for his children, it's someone who has rescued an orphan from despair, for that is what God has done for us.

God has adopted us. God sought us, found us, signed the papers, and took us home.

5. Read Romans 8:15–17. What do these promises say about our spiritual adoption by God?

The Spirit you received brought about your adoption to sonship (Romans 8:15).

_____

_____

_____

6. Paul tells us in Galatians 4:6 that because of our spiritual adoption, we are able to call God, "*Abba*, Father." *Abba* is an intimate, tender, folksy, pedestrian term, the warmest of the Aramaic words for "father."[2] What implications does this promise carry for your life? What does it mean that you can call God "Daddy"?

By him we cry, "Abba, Father" (verse 15).

_____

_____

_____

Suppose one of you has a hundred sheep and loses one of them. Doesn't he leave the ninety-nine in the open country and go after the lost sheep until he finds it? (Luke 15:4).

7. Read Luke 15:4–7. How does this parable describe the way that God seeks those who are lost? How does it describe how he feels when the lost join his family?

_____

_____

_____

_____

8. When God reaches us—just as he reached Rahab—we go from condemned orphans to adopted children with no fear. How has being a part of God's family driven out the fears in your life? How has it given you hope?

_____

_____

_____

_____

The message of the cross is foolishness to those who are perishing, but to us who are being saved it is the power of God (1 Corinthians 1:18).

The cross. The sacrifice Jesus made for the world on its beams covers all the sins committed before it and all the sins that follow. The power of the cross gave Rahab a fresh start and transformed her from an outcast in society to a member of God's family. The cross can do the same for us. All we have to do is receive it, accept Jesus' sacrifice for our sins, and choose to become adopted into God's family. May the reality of this truth sink in deeply today. May it change the way we see ourselves, the way we see others, and the way we see God.

❧ POINTS TO REMEMBER ❧

❖ There is no one alive who is beyond God's ability to redeem.
❖ God's forgiveness is based on his love, not on our worthiness.
❖ God not only sets us free but he also takes us into his family—into his home.

❧ PRAYER FOR THE DAY ❧

Lord, all we can say when we picture the suffering you endured on the cross is "thank you." We receive your forgiveness not because of anything we've done but all because of who you are. We accept your offer to become a part of your family. Thank you for your promise that you have gone before us to prepare a place for us—our eternal home. Amen.

Day Five: The Pattern of Grace

SHORT SUPPLY

I recently attended a fund-raiser for a ministry called Grace House. This is a transition home for women who are coming out of prison. They live under the same roof, eat at the same table, and seek the same Lord. They study the Bible. They learn a trade. Most of all, they learn to trust their new identity in Christ.

One of the residents gave her testimony. She described a life of prostitution, drugs, and alcohol. She had lost her marriage, her children, and ultimately her freedom. But then Christ found her. What struck me was the repeated rhythm of her story: "I was . . . but now . . ." "I was on drugs, but now I'm clean." "I was on the streets, but now I'm on my feet."

I was . . . but now. This is the chorus of grace. This is the work God did in the life of Rahab. "I was lost, but God found me." "I was an outcast, but now I'm part of God's family."

For many of us today, hope is in short supply. Like Rahab, we sense that the walls are going to come down—and come down soon. We need a way out. What would it take to restore our hope? Though the answers are abundant, three come quickly to mind.

The first would be a person. Not just any person. We don't need someone equally confused. We need someone who knows the way out. And from him we need some vision. We need someone to lift our spirits. We need someone to look us in the face and say, "This isn't the end. Don't give up. There is a better place than this. And I'll lead you there."

And, perhaps most important, we need direction. If we have only a person but no renewed vision, all we have is company. If he has a vision but no direction, we have a dreamer for company. But if we have a person with direction—one who can take us from our doomed city of Jericho to the place God has for us—ah, then we have one who can restore our hope.

Jesus is the One who knows the way out, and he came to this earth to guide us. He has the right vision, for he reminds us that we "are like foreigners and strangers in this world" (1 Peter 2:11 NCV). And he urges us to lift our eyes from this world around us to the heaven above us. He also has the right direction. He made the boldest claim in the history of man when he declared, "I am the way" (John 14:6 NCV).

People wondered if the claim was accurate. Jesus answered their questions by cutting a path through the underbrush of sin and death . . . and escaping alive. He's the only One who ever did. And he is the only One who can help you and me do the same.

"This son of mine was dead and is alive again; he was lost and is found." So they began to celebrate (Luke 15:24).

Jesus answered, "I am the way and the truth and the life. No one comes to the Father except through me. If you really know me, you will know my Father as well" (John 14:6–7).

1. Think about your Rahab story. How would you fill in the blanks to this statement: "I was _____, but now I am _____"? How has God led you out of the mistakes of your past and given you a new hope and a future?

_____

_____

_____

_____

2. Paul writes, "[God] made Him who knew no sin to be sin for us, that we might become the righteousness of God in Him" (2 Corinthians 5:21 NKJV). How would you paraphrase this verse? What definition of God's grace does it provide?

_____

_____

_____

The one who does not work but trusts God who justifies the ungodly, their faith is credited as righteousness (Romans 4: 5).

3. What did Rahab do to receive God's grace? What did she do to escape the destruction that was coming? According to Romans 4:4–5, how do we receive God's grace today?

_____

_____

_____

What shall we say, then? Shall we go on sinning so that grace may increase? (6:1).

4. Read Romans 6:1–4. What are some ways that we can abuse God's grace? What does Paul say about continuing in our sin so that grace may abound?

_____

_____

_____

AMPLE ROOM

The Hebrew spies, it turns out, were actually missionaries. They thought they were on a reconnaissance trip. They weren't. God needed no scouting report. His plan was to collapse the city walls like a stack of dominoes. He didn't send the men to collect data. He sent the spies to reach Rahab.

They told her to "bind this line of scarlet cord in the window" so they could identify her house (Joshua 2:18 NKJV). Without hesitation she bound the scarlet cord in the window. The spies escaped and Rahab made preparation. She told her family to get ready. She kept an eye out for the coming army. She checked (don't you know she checked!) the cord to make sure it was tied securely and dangling from the window.

This oath you made us swear will not be binding on us unless, when we enter the land, you have tied this scarlet cord in the window (Joshua 2:17–18).

When the Hebrews came and the walls fell, when everyone else perished, Rahab and her family were saved. "By faith the harlot Rahab did not perish" (Hebrews 11:31 NKJV). Her profession of faith mattered more than her profession as a harlot.

Jesus said, "There are many rooms in my Father's house" (John 14:2 NCV). Why did he make a point of mentioning the size of the house? We can answer that question as we think of the many times in life we've heard the opposite. Haven't there been occasions when we've been told, "We have no room for you here"? These are some of the saddest words on earth.

Jesus knew the sound of them. He was still in Mary's womb when the innkeeper said, "We don't have room for you." When the religious leaders accused him of blasphemy, they proclaimed, "We don't have room for a self-proclaimed Messiah." When he was hung on the cross, the message was one of utter rejection. "We don't have room for you in this world."

But every so often, Jesus is welcomed. Every so often, someone like Rahab throws open the door of his or her heart and invites him to stay. And to that person Jesus gives a great promise. "It doesn't matter if your past is a checkered one. Or if your peers share your faith. Or if your pedigree is one of violence or rebellion. I came to seek and save the lost, and there is ample space for you in my Father's house."

My Father's house has many rooms; if that were not so, would I have told you that I am going there to prepare a place for you? (John 14:2).

5. Read the climactic conclusion to Rahab's story in Joshua 6:20–25. What happens to Rahab and her family? Why did Joshua say they must rescue her?

_____

_____

_____

Joshua said . . . "Go into the prostitute's house and bring her out and all who belong to her, in accordance with your oath to her." . . . They brought out her entire family and put them in a place outside the camp of Israel (Joshua 6:22–23).

6. "The gospel doesn't make bad people good; it makes dead people alive."[3] How does this quote speak poignantly to the culture we live in today? In what ways does our culture have a hard time understanding the idea of grace?

_____

_____

_____

7. Joshua and the Israelites accepted Rahab, and she and her family dwelt among them and became a part of them. How have you allowed God's grace to give you a fresh start? In what ways are you embracing your fellow believers in Christ?

_____

_____

_____

_____

But because of his great love for us, God, who is rich in mercy, made us alive with Christ even when we were dead in transgressions—it is by grace you have been saved (Ephesians 2:4–5).

8. Read Ephesians 2:4–8. In this passage, Paul lays the foundation of grace that Jesus gave to us. Which of his words speak the most to you today? Why?

_____

_____

_____

_____

_____

_____

_____

We don't drop scarlet cords from our windows. But we trust the crimson thread of Christ's blood. We don't prepare for the coming of the Hebrews, but we do live with an eye toward the second coming of our Joshua—Jesus Christ. Ultimately, we will all see what the people of Asunción, Paraguay, are discovering. Our mess will become music, and God will have a heaven full of rescued Rahabs in his symphony. That'll be me on the tuba. And you? What will you be playing? One thing is for sure. We will all know "Amazing Grace" by heart.

❧ POINTS TO REMEMBER ❧

❖ Jesus provides the way from sin and despair to hope and a future.
❖ Jesus clothed himself in our sin—and in the death we rightly deserved—so that we could be clothed in his righteousness and his life.
❖ The richness of God's grace is expressed in his gift of salvation through Christ Jesus.

❧ PRAYER FOR THE DAY ❧

Sweet Jesus, thank you for your grace. We abuse it, fail to comprehend it, and forget its beauty, yet you continue to lavish it on us. Help us to understand it more, live by it more, and give it to others more. Amen.

❧ WEEKLY MEMORY VERSE ❧

For by grace you have been saved through faith, and that not of yourselves; it is the gift of God.
EPHESIANS 2:8 (NKJV)

For Further Reading

Selections throughout this lesson were taken from *Great House of God* (Nashville: Thomas Nelson, 1997); *When Christ Comes* (Nashville: Thomas Nelson, 1998); *Traveling Light* (Nashville: Thomas Nelson, 2001); *Great Day Every Day* (Nashville: Thomas Nelson, 2007); *Max on Life* (Nashville: Thomas Nelson, 2010); *Before Amen* (Nashville: Thomas Nelson, 2014); and *Glory Days* (Nashville: Thomas Nelson, 2015).

Notes

1. Earl Radmacher, Ronald B. Allen, H. Wayne House, eds., *Nelson's New Illustrated Bible Commentary* (Nashville: Thomas Nelson, 1999), p. 276.
2. The research of Joachim Jeremias led him to write, "Abba was an everyday word, a homely, family word. . . . No Jew would have dared to address God in this manner. Jesus did it always, in all His prayers which are handed down to us, with one single exception, the cry from the cross" (Joachim Jeremias, *The Prayers of Jesus,* London: SCM Press, 1967, p. 57). Some scholars have disagreed with Jeremias. Even so, the invitation to pray "Abba" is reinforced by Jesus' instruction to become like children.
3. Tullian Tchividjian, *Surprised by Grace: God's Relentless Pursuit of Rebels* (Wheaton, Ill.: Crossway, 2010).

LESSON 3

ABIGAIL

BEAUTY IN THE MIDST OF THE BEASTS

Ernest Gordon groans in the Death House of Chungkai, Burma. He listens to the moans of the dying and smells the stench of the dead. Pitiless jungle heat bakes his skin and parches his throat. Had he the strength, he could wrap one hand around his bony thigh. But he has neither the energy nor the interest. Diphtheria has drained both, and he can't walk or feel his body.

Ernest shares a cot with flies and bedbugs and awaits a lonely death in a Japanese prisoner-of-war camp. How harsh the war has been on him. He entered World War II in his early twenties, a robust Highlander in Scotland's Argyle and Sutherland Brigade. But then came the capture by the Japanese, months of backbreaking labor in the jungle, daily beatings, and slow starvation. Scotland seems forever away. Civility, even farther.

The Allied soldiers behave like barbarians, stealing from each other, robbing dying colleagues, fighting for food scraps. Servers shortchange rations so they can have extra for themselves. The law of the jungle has become the law of the camp. Ernest is happy to bid it *adieu*. Death by disease trumps life in Chungkai.

But then something wonderful happens. Two new prisoners, in whom hope still stirs, are transferred to the camp. Although they are also sick and frail, they heed a higher code. They share their meager meals and volunteer for extra work. They cleanse Ernest's ulcerated sores and massage his atrophied legs. They give him his first bath in six weeks. His strength slowly returns and, with it, his dignity.

Their goodness proves contagious, and Ernest contracts a case. He begins to treat the sick and share his rations. He even gives away his few belongings. Other soldiers do likewise. Over time, the tone of the camp softens and brightens. Sacrifice replaces selfishness. Soldiers hold worship services and Bible studies.

Truly I tell you, whatever you did for one of the least of these brothers and sisters of mine, you did for me (Matthew 25:40).

Where, O death, is your victory?
Where, O death, is your sting?
(1 Corinthians 15:55).

Twenty years later, when Ernest serves as chaplain of Princeton University, he describes the transformation with these words: "Death was still with us—no doubt about that. But we were slowly being freed from its destructive grip. . . . Selfishness, hatred . . . and pride were all anti-life. Love . . . self-sacrifice . . . and faith, on the other hand, were the essence of life . . . gifts of God to men. . . . Death no longer had the last word at Chungkai."[1]

Selfishness, hatred, and pride—you don't have to go to a POW camp to find them. A dormitory will do just fine. As will the boardroom of a corporation or the bedroom of a marriage or the backwoods of a county. The code of the jungle is alive and well. *Every man for himself. Get all you can, and can all you get. Survival of the fittest.*

Does the code contaminate your world? Do personal possessive pronouns dominate the language of your circle? *My* career, *my* dreams, *my* stuff. I want things to go *my* way on *my* schedule. If so, you know how savage this giant can be. Yet every so often, a diamond glitters in the mud. A comrade shares, a soldier cares, or Abigail—stunning Abigail—stands on your trail.

1. Where in your life do you see this "code of the jungle"—the code of selfishness, hatred, and pride—the most? What issues does this cause for a believer in Christ?

   _____

   _____

   _____

   _____

   _____

2. In your relationships, how have you worked to be like the two hope-filled prisoners in this story who treated others with kindness? What effects have you seen?

   _____

   _____

   _____

   _____

Let each of you look out not only for his own interests, but also for the interests of others (Philippians 2:4 NKJV).

Selfishness. We are all born with it. As King David wrote, "Surely I was sinful at birth, sinful from the time my mother conceived me" (Psalm 51:5). Look no further than the evening news or a two-year-old to see it. Even in our attempts to do "good" we are often selfish. We want our good deeds to be noticed on Instagram. We want to help only when it's convenient. We expect our service to be returned in kind. To not live for self takes supernatural help. It takes the work of the only human who entered our savage world and never tripped over his own ego. He taught us a new code: "The Son of Man did not come to be served, but to serve, and to give his life as a ransom for many" (Matthew 20:28).

❧ PRAYER FOR THE WEEK ❧

God, in our own strength we can't put you first. We can't put others first. Only through you in us can our lives be selfless. So today, we pray that you will be bigger in us so that we can become smaller (see John 3:30). Thank you for working in our hearts. Amen.

$\mathcal{D}$ay One: The Only Refuge

THE BRUTE OF CARMEL

Abigail lived during the days of David and was married to Nabal, whose name means "fool" in Hebrew. He lived up to the definition. Think of him as the Saddam Hussein of the territory. He owned cattle and sheep and took pride in both. He kept his liquor cabinet full, his date life hot, and motored around his hometown of Carmel in a stretch limo. His NBA seats were front row, his jet was Lear, and he was prone to hop over to Vegas for a weekend of Texas Hold 'em.

Half a dozen linebacker-size security guards followed him wherever he went. He needed the protection. He was "churlish and ill-behaved—a real Calebite dog. . . . He is so ill-natured that one cannot speak to him."[2] He learned people skills in the local zoo. He never met a person he couldn't anger or a relationship he couldn't spoil.

Nabal's world revolved around one person—Nabal. He owed nothing to anybody and laughed at the thought of sharing with anyone. Especially David.

David played a Robin Hood role in the wilderness. He and his soldiers protected the farmers and shepherds from brigands and Bedouins. Israel had no highway patrol or police force, so David and his mighty men met a definite need in the countryside. They guarded with enough effectiveness to prompt one of Nabal's shepherds to say, "Night and day they were a wall around us the whole time we were herding our sheep near them" (1 Samuel 25:16).

1. Let's get to know the characters of David, Nabal, and Abigail in 1 Samuel 25. What are some of the descriptions you find about Nabal?

Whoever wants to become great among you must be your servant, and whoever wants to be first must be your slave—just as the Son of Man did not come to be served, but to serve (Matthew 20:26–28).

A certain man in Maon, who had property there at Carmel, was very wealthy. He had a thousand goats and three thousand sheep (1 Samuel 25:2).

[He] was surly and mean in his dealings—he was a Calebite (verse 3).

What picture does the writer give us about his personality? In what ways does he act foolishly?

_____

_____

_____

_____

His wife's name was Abigail. She was an intelligent and beautiful woman (1 Samuel 25:3).

2. What are some of the descriptions you find of Abigail? How do you see her live out these descriptions through her actions?

_____

_____

_____

These men were very good to us. They did not mistreat us, and the whole time we were out in the fields near them nothing was missing. Night and day they were a wall around us the whole time we were herding our sheep near them (verses 15–16).

3. Look at the servant's words in 1 Samuel 25:14–16. Based on these verses, how would you describe David and his men? What does this say about David's heart?

_____

_____

_____

4. The Bible has much to say about the dangers of not acting with wisdom. How do the following verses describe a fool? How do these descriptions relate to Nabal?

Psalm 14:1: "Fools say in their hearts, 'There is no God.' They are corrupt, and their actions are evil; not one of them does good!" (NLT).

_____

_____

_____

Proverbs 10:14: "Wise people store up knowledge, but the mouth of the foolish is near destruction" (NKJV).

_____

_____

_____

Proverbs 20:3: "Keeping away from strife is an honor for a man, but any fool will quarrel" (NASB).

_____

_____

_____

Proverbs 29:9: "If a wise man has an argument with a fool, the fool only rages and laughs, and there is no quiet" (ESV).

Ecclesiastes 7:9: "Do not be quickly provoked in your spirit, for anger resides in the lap of fools."

A King on the Run

David had been driven into this role through the actions of King Saul, who by this point had effectively and systematically isolated him from every source of stability. His half-dozen assassination attempts had ended David's military career. His pursuit had driven a wedge in David's marriage. After David's wife, Michal, helped him escape, Saul demanded an explanation from her. "I had to," she lied. "He threatened to kill me if I didn't help him" (1 Samuel 19:17 TLB). David never trusted his wife again. They stayed married but slept in different beds.

David had raced from Saul's court to Samuel's house. But no sooner had he arrived than someone had told Saul that he was there. David had fled to Jonathan, but there was nothing his friend could do for him. Jonathan could not leave the court in the hands of a madman—he had to stay with his father. David could hear the twine popping on the lifeline.

No place in the court.

No position in the army.

No wife, no priest, no friend.

Nothing to do but run.

But during this desperate time in David's life, the word *refuge* surfaces as one his favorites. Circle its appearances in the book of Psalms, and you'll count as many as forty-plus instances in some versions. Although David has nowhere to turn, he knows that God is his refuge and that he is not alone. And from the recesses of a cave in that wilderness a sweet voice floats: "Be merciful to me, O God, be merciful to me! For my soul trusts in You; and in the shadow of Your wings I will make my refuge" (Psalm 57:1 NKJV).

5. Check out some of David's backstory in 1 Samuel 18:6–9, 19:11–18, 22:1–2, and 23:14. Why was Saul after David?

Saul told his son Jonathan and all the attendants to kill David (1 Samuel 19:1).

Jonathan said to David, "Go in peace, for we have sworn friendship with each other in the name of the LORD, saying, 'The LORD is witness between you and me, and between your descendants and my descendants forever.'" Then David left, and Jonathan went back to the town (20:42).

David . . . went to Jonathan and asked, "What have I done? What is my crime? How have I wronged your father, that he is trying to kill me?"
(1 Samuel 20:1).

6. Have you ever felt, like David, that you were being attacked unfairly? How did you react to the situation? What was the outcome?

7. David wrote a number of psalms as he was on the run from the king. According to the following verses, what does David do in response to Saul's barbaric behavior?

Psalm 59:14–16: "[My enemies] come back at night. Like dogs they growl and roam around the city. They wander about looking for food, and they howl if they do not find enough. But I will sing about your strength. In the morning I will sing about your love. You are my defender, my place of safety in times of trouble" (NCV).

Psalm 52:7–9: "'Here is the man who did not make God his strength, but trusted in the abundance of his riches, and strengthened himself in his wickedness.' But I am like a green olive tree in the house of God; I trust in the mercy of God forever and ever. I will praise You forever, because You have done it; and in the presence of Your saints I will wait on Your name, for it is good" (NKJV).

Psalm 57:1–3, 7: "Be gracious to me, O God, be gracious to me, for my soul takes refuge in You; and in the shadow of Your wings I will take refuge until destruction passes by. I will cry to God Most High, to God who accomplishes *all things* for me. He will send from heaven and save me; He reproaches him who tramples upon me. God will send forth His lovingkindness and His truth. . . . My heart is steadfast, O God, my heart is steadfast; I will sing, yes, I will sing praises!" (NASB).

8. Who or what do you turn to as a refuge before turning to God? What does it look like to take refuge in God when someone else hurts or attacks you?

_____

_____

_____

_____

_____

_____

_____

_____

_____

_____

_____

Nabal rejected David. Saul threatened David. But what had David done? He had humbly served the king and protected Nabal's men—and this was how he was repaid? He had trusted in God—and this was what he got in return? David had reasons to reject God and take his own path. But instead, he pressed into God. He knew the Lord was the only constant good in a world poisoned by the pride and power of men like Saul and Nabal. We must do the same. We must keep doing good, keep trusting God, keep pressing into him more. He is our refuge, and when we spend time in the shelter of his wings, we find our wounds healed and our souls restored.

> The LORD is good and his love endures forever; his faithfulness continues through all generations (Psalm 100:5).

❧ POINTS TO REMEMBER ☙

❖ Fools think only of themselves and treat others unfairly, while wise people seek God and treat others with kindness.
❖ Trusting God even when we are treated unfairly allows us to keep our focus off our circumstances and on God's protection.
❖ How we respond to mistreatment reveals the state of our relationship with God.

❧ PRAYER FOR THE DAY ☙

Lord, you are our refuge, an ever-present help in times of trouble. Today we pray that you would wrap your arms around us. Give us peace where we are anxious and rest where we are weary. We love you, Lord. In Jesus' name, amen.

Day Two: Wild West in the Ancient East

God-Seeking Misfits

All those who were in distress or in debt or discontented gathered around [David], and he became their commander. About four hundred men were with him (1 Samuel 22:2).

Wilderness survivors find refuge in God's presence. They also discover community among God's people. In David's case, his brothers and other relatives soon join him. Then others begin to arrive—those who are in trouble or in debt or are just discontented—until David is the leader of about 400 men.

Not what you'd call a corps of West Point cadets. In trouble, in debt, or discontent. Quite a crew. Misfits, yes. Dregs from the barrel, no doubt. Rejects. Losers. Dropouts. But who is David to turn them away? He's no candidate for archbishop. He's a magnet for marginal people. So David creates a community of God-seeking misfits, and God forges a mighty group out of them. "They came to David day by day to help him, until it was a great army, like the army of God" (1 Chronicles 12:22 NKJV).

David and his band of misfits journey from place to place as they avoid the soldiers King Saul has sent to kill them. Eventually, they find themselves in the Desert of Paran, where they settle in and start protecting the land from those brigands and Bedouins. But David is not the only powerhouse in the region, for, as it turns out, much of the property is owned by none other than the wealthy Nabal.

Now Samuel died, and all Israel assembled and mourned for him; and they buried him at his home in Ramah. Then David moved down into the Desert of Paran (25:1).

The two men are soon cohabiting the territory with the harmony of two bulls in the same pasture. Both are strong and strong-headed. It is just a matter of time before they collide.

1. David sought refuge in God while he was on the run from Saul, but he also offered refuge to others. Who is a refuge for you? What makes that person a refuge?

   _____

   _____

   _____

   _____

This inheritance is kept in heaven for you, who through faith are shielded by God's power (1 Peter 1:4–5).

2. Who in your life would say you are a refuge for them? How can you become more of a "safe place" for others to seek refuge?

   _____

   _____

   _____

3. David created a community of "misfits"—a place where outsiders and rebels felt like they belonged. Today, God calls those of us in the church to be a safe place for outsiders. In Matthew 25:35–40, what does Jesus infer about how the church should look at the "misfits" of the world?

_____

_____

_____

For I was hungry and you gave me something to eat, I was thirsty and you gave me something to drink, I was a stranger and you invited me in (Matthew 25:35).

4. Read Ephesians 4:15. Are you part of a godly community that is building itself up in love? Is it a safe place for people to find refuge? Why or why not?

_____

_____

_____

Speaking the truth in love, we will grow to become in every respect the mature body of him who is the head, that is, Christ (Ephesians 4:15).

TROUBLE BREWS AND ERUPTS

For David and his band of misfits, trouble begins to brew shortly after the harvest. With sheep sheared and hay gathered, it is time to bake bread, roast lamb, and pour wine. It's time to take a break from the furrows and flocks and enjoy the fruit of the labor. As we pick up the story, Nabal's men are doing just that.

David hears of the gala and thinks his men deserve an invitation. After all, they've protected the man's crops and sheep, patrolled the hills, and secured the valleys. They deserve a bit of the bounty. So David sends ten men to Nabal with this request: "We come at a happy time, so be kind to my young men. Please give anything you can find for them and for your son David" (1 Samuel 25:8 NCV).

Boorish Nabal scoffs at the thought. "Who is David, and who is the son of Jesse?" he asks. "There are many servants nowadays who break away each one from his master. Shall I then take my bread and my water and my meat that I have killed for my shearers, and give it to men when I do not know where they are from?" (25:10–11 NKJV). Nabal pretends he's never heard of David, lumping him in with runaway slaves and vagabonds.

Such insolence infuriates the messengers, and they turn on their heels and hurry back to David with a full report. David doesn't need to hear the news twice. He tells the men to form a posse. Or, more precisely, "Strap on your swords!" (25:13 MSG).

Four hundred men mount up and take off. Eyes glare. Nostrils flare. Lips snarl. Testosterone flows. David and his troops thunder down on Nabal, the scoundrel, who obliviously drinks beer and eats barbecue with his buddies. The road rumbles as David grumbles, "May God do

While David was in the wilderness, he heard that Nabal was shearing sheep. So he sent ten young men and said to them, "Go up to Nabal at Carmel and greet him in my name. Say to him: 'Long life to you! Good health to you and your household! And good health to all that is yours!'" (1 Samuel 25:4–6).

About four hundred men went up with David, while two hundred stayed with the supplies (verse 13).

his worst to me if Nabal and every cur in his misbegotten brood aren't dead meat by morning!" (25:22 MSG).

Hang on. It's the Wild West in the Ancient East.

5. Look at 1 Samuel 25:10–13. It's obvious from these verses that Nabal has a hot temper and prideful heart, but how would you describe David's reaction? Was it God-honoring or self-honoring? Explain your thoughts.

6. Nabal and David were both strong and strong-headed—"two bulls in the same pasture." Describe a situation in your life when you were around two strong leaders who didn't get along. Why was there conflict? How was the conflict handled?

7. Good leaders are needed in every community in which you find yourself involved, whether it's your workplace, church, small group, or family. According to the following verses, what does healthy leadership look like?

2 Timothy 2:15–16: "Make every effort to give yourself to God as the kind of person he will approve. Be a worker who is not ashamed and who uses the true teaching in the right way. Stay away from foolish, useless talk, because that will lead people further away from God" (NCV).

2 Timothy 2:1, 3–5: "Be strong in the grace that is in Christ Jesus. . . . Suffer hardship with me, as a good soldier of Christ Jesus. No soldier in active service entangles himself in the affairs of everyday life, so that he may please the one who enlisted him as a soldier. Also if anyone competes as an athlete, he does not win the prize unless he competes according to the rules" (NASB).

Titus 1:7: "An elder is a manager of God's household, so he must live a blameless life. He must not be arrogant or quick-tempered; he must not be a heavy drinker, violent, or dishonest with money" (NLT).

_____

_____

_____

_____

Titus 1:8–9: "He must enjoy having guests in his home, and he must love what is good. He must live wisely and be just. He must live a devout and disciplined life. He must have a strong belief in the trustworthy message he was taught" (NLT).

_____

_____

_____

_____

8. Read Titus 3:1–2 and 1 Peter 5:5. How does God want us to support our leaders so that our community remains healthy?

_____

_____

_____

_____

Remind the people to be subject to rulers and authorities (Titus 3:1).

You who are younger, submit yourselves to your elders (1 Peter 5:5).

Community. We were made for it. From the very beginning, God, after creating Adam, proclaimed, "It is not good for the man to be alone" (Genesis 2:18). But with community comes stress. Tension among leaders, prideful hearts who won't submit, socially awkward misfits, quick tempers and cutting tongues . . . they all exist because sin exists. For this reason, we need to frequently turn to the Word of God as a guide for how to get along. We need to pray for our leaders and ask God to help us love others well. When problems surface and feathers ruffle, we must not lose heart but remember that God loves his bride—the church. He is transforming her, unifying her, and using her as a refuge for the broken. He will never forsake her.

Christ loved the church and gave himself up for her (Ephesians 5:25).

⁓ Points to Remember ⁓

❖ When we respond in faith by offering refuge to those who are marginalized, we are serving Jesus.
❖ Godly character, discipline, and training make us effective leaders—especially during times of conflict.
❖ What is right in God's eyes must supersede our own self-centered desires.

Day Three: The Peacemaker Appears

BRAINS AND BEAUTY

One of the servants told Abigail . . . "See what you can do, because disaster is hanging over our master and his whole household" (1 Samuel 25:14, 17).

The escalating tensions between Nabal and David have led to a boiling point. David has ordered his men to equip their swords, and now his army—400 strong—is on its way to teach Nabal a lesson in respect. It seems the only way for the two powerhouses to determine supremacy in the region is to duke it out.

But then, into the midst of the chaos, beauty appears. A daisy lifts her head in the desert. A swan lands at the meat packing plant. A whiff of perfume floats through the men's locker room. Abigail, the wife of Nabal, stands on the trail. And she is a striking contrast to her ill-behaved husband. Whereas he is churlish, brutish, and mean, she is "intelligent and good-looking" (1 Samuel 25:3 MSG).

Brains *and* beauty. Abigail puts both to work. When she learns of Nabal's crude response, she springs into action. With no word to her husband, she gathers gifts and races to intercept David. As David and his men descend a ravine, she takes her position, armed with "two hundred loaves of bread, two skins of wine, five sheep dressed out and ready for cooking, a bushel of roasted grain, a hundred raisin cakes, and two hundred fig cakes . . . all loaded on some donkeys" (verse 18 MSG).

Abigail acted quickly. . . . She told her servants, "Go on ahead; I'll follow you" (verses 18–19).

1. Review 1 Samuel 25:18–20. What was Abigail's immediate response to her servant's warning about David? What can you gather from the text about her demeanor?

   _____

   _____

   _____

2. What actions of Abigail in this passage would you consider to be wise?

   _____

   _____

   _____

3. Abigail took time to encourage David in verses 28–30. What does she say? What does she believe about the future of Israel? How do you think these words sounded to David, especially given the position he was in?

_____

_____

_____

The LORD your God will certainly make a lasting dynasty for my lord, because you fight the LORD's battles (1 Samuel 25:28).

4. Which traits of this "wife of noble character" do you wish to model more in your own life? How do you think exhibiting those traits would affect your relationships?

_____

_____

_____

STOPPED IN THEIR TRACKS

David's 400 men rein in their rides when they see Abigail. Some gape at the food, while the others gawk at the female. She's good lookin' with good cookin', a combination that stops any army. (Picture a neck-snapping blonde showing up at boot camp with a truck full of burgers and ice cream.)

Abigail's no fool. She knows the importance of the moment. She stands as the final barrier between her family and sure death. Falling at David's feet, she issues a plea worthy of a paragraph in Scripture. "On me, my lord, on me let this iniquity be! And please let your maidservant speak in your ears, and hear the words of your maidservant" (1 Samuel 25:24 NKJV).

She doesn't defend Nabal but agrees that he is a scoundrel. She begs not for justice but forgiveness, accepting blame when she deserves none. "Please forgive the trespass of your maidservant" (25:28 NKJV). She offers the gifts from her house and urges David to leave Nabal to God and avoid the dead weight of remorse.

When Abigail saw David, she quickly got off her donkey and bowed down before David with her face to the ground (1 Samuel 25:23).

5. Look again at Abigail's words to David in 1 Samuel 25:23–31. What is her physical demeanor as she delivers this message? How does this demonstrate her wisdom?

_____

_____

She fell at his feet and said . . . "Pay no attention, my lord, to that wicked man Nabal" (verses 24–25).

6. Read Proverbs 31:10–31. This well-known passage describes the "wife of noble character." Which traits of this woman does Abigail possess, and how do you see these traits surface?

_____

_____

_____

A wife of noble character who can find? She is worth far more than rubies (Proverbs 31:10).

What does the LORD your God ask of you but to fear the LORD your God, to walk in obedience to him (Deuteronomy 10:12).

7. The Bible says that to be wise like Abigail, we must "fear the LORD" (Deuteronomy 10:12). This means respecting him, obeying him, submitting to his discipline, and worshiping him in awe. What do the following verses say about fearing God?

Psalm 33:8: "Let all the earth fear the LORD; let all the people of the world revere him."

_____

_____

_____

_____

_____

_____

Psalm 34:9: "O fear the LORD, you His saints; for to those who fear Him there is no want" (NASB).

_____

_____

_____

_____

_____

Proverbs 1:7: "The fear of the LORD is the beginning of knowledge, but fools despise wisdom and instruction" (NKJV).

_____

_____

_____

_____

_____

Jeremiah 5:23–24: "The people . . . are stubborn and have turned against me. They have turned aside and gone away from me. They do not say to themselves, 'We should fear the LORD our God, who gives us autumn and spring rains in their seasons, who makes sure we have the harvest at the right time'" (NCV).

_____

_____

_____

_____

_____

_____

Matthew 10:28: "Don't be afraid of those who want to kill your body; they cannot touch your soul. Fear only God, who can destroy both soul and body in hell" (NLT).

_____

_____

_____

_____

8. What does it look like to "fear the Lord" in your life? How do you see the Lord guiding you to make wise decisions when you trust in him and submit to him?

_____

_____

_____

_____

_____

Abigail didn't fear her foolish husband. She didn't fear David's 400-person army. She feared *the Lord*. How else would she have had the clarity of mind and guts to do what she did? And because she feared God, when tempers were flaring, she reflected the peace of God. When words were cutting, she spoke in the grace of God. If you are struggling to do the same, remember this promise from James 1:5: "If any of you lacks wisdom, you should ask God, who gives generously to all without finding fault, and it will be given to you." Even in asking for wisdom, you will demonstrate you fear God and desire to place him above your heart.

The peace of God, which transcends all understanding, will guard your hearts and your minds in Christ Jesus (Philippians 4:7).

⤜ Points to Remember ⤛

❖ To be wise we must "fear the Lord," or show him the respect he deserves through worship, honor, and devotion.
❖ Fearing the Lord minimizes our fear of those who have the potential to harm us.
❖ When tempers flare around us, centering ourselves on God's purposes will allow us to have his peace to act wisely.

⤜ Prayer for the Day ⤛

Lord God, you tell us in your Word that when we ask for wisdom, you will grant it. So today, we ask for more. In all our relationships, in all our decisions, in all our interactions, give us your wisdom and understanding. We want to reflect you in all we do. Amen.

Day Four: Humility Saves the Day

A CLOSE CALL

Abigail's words fall on David like July sun on ice. He melts. "Blessed be God, the God of Israel," he says to her. "He sent you to meet me! And blessed be your good sense! Bless you for keeping me from murder and taking charge of looking out for me" (1 Samuel 25:32–33 MSG).

It's a close call, as David readily admits. "As God lives," he continues, "the God of Israel who kept me from hurting you, if you had not come as quickly as you did, stopping me in my tracks, by morning there would have been nothing left of Nabal but dead meat" (verse 34 MSG).

David accepts the gifts that Abigail has brought. "Return home in peace," he tells her. "I've heard what you've said and I'll do what you've asked" (verse 35 MSG). So David returns to camp, and Abigail returns to Nabal.

When she arrives, she finds Nabal too drunk for conversation. So she waits until the next morning to describe how close David came to camp and Nabal came to death. What happens next is surprising. "Right then and there he had a heart attack and fell into a coma. About ten days later God finished him off and he died" (verses 37–38 MSG).

Do not be quickly provoked in your spirit, for anger resides in the lap of fools (Ecclesiastes 7:9).

When Abigail went to Nabal, he was in the house holding a banquet like that of a king (1 Samuel 25:36).

1. Based on this passage, what effect did Abigail's wise words have on David? How did he react to her overall efforts to bring peace?

_____

_____

_____

Blessed are the peacemakers, for they will be called children of God (Matthew 5:9).

2. In what situations in the past has God called you to be a peacemaker? Were the results similar or different from what Abigail experienced in this passage? Explain.

_____

_____

_____

_____

3. Who is someone in your life—perhaps a leader like David—whom you can encourage today? Take some time to ask God to identify that person and what you can say to him or her. Write down what God puts on your heart and share it with that person.

_____

_____

_____

4. What do the following verses say about how God wants us to treat our leaders?

Titus 3:1: "Remind the believers to yield to the authority of rulers and government leaders, to obey them, to be ready to do good" (NCV).

---

1 Peter 2:17–18: "Honor all people, love the brotherhood, fear God, honor the king. Servants, be submissive to your masters with all respect, not only to those who are good and gentle, but also to those who are unreasonable" (NASB).

---

1 Peter 5:5: "You who are younger must accept the authority of the elders. And all of you, dress yourselves in humility as you relate to one another, for 'God opposes the proud but gives grace to the humble'" (NLT).

THE POWER OF THE MEEK

When David learns of Nabal's death and Abigail's sudden availability, he thanks God for the first and takes advantage of the second. Unable to shake the memory of the pretty woman in the middle of the road, he proposes, and she accepts. David gets a new wife, Abigail gets a new home, and we get a great principle: beauty can overcome barbarism.

Meekness saved the day that day. Abigail's willingness to humble herself reversed a river of anger in David. We are called to do the same—to humble ourselves and be peacemakers in this world. And for our model we need look no further than Christ, who "humbled himself and was fully obedient to God, even when that caused his death—death on a cross" (Philippians 2:8 NCV).

Christ abandoned his reputation. No one in Nazareth saluted him as the Son of God. He did not stand out in his elementary-classroom photograph, demanded no glossy page in his high-school annual. Friends knew him as a woodworker, not a star hanger. His looks turned no heads; his position earned him no credit. In the great stoop we call

When David heard that Nabal was dead, he said, "Praise be to the LORD." . . . Then David sent word to Abigail, asking her to become his wife (1 Samuel 25:39–40).

Jesus said to them, "A prophet is not without honor except in his own town" (Mark 6:4).

Christmas, Jesus abandoned heavenly privileges and aproned earthly pains. God hunts for those who will do likewise—Abigails through whom he can deliver Christ into the world.

Nabal's story shows us that success sabotages the memories of the successful. An old fable tells of an elephant lumbering across a wooden bridge suspended over a ravine. As the big animal crossed over the worn-out structure, it creaked and groaned under the elephant's weight. When he reached the other side, a flea that had nestled itself in the elephant's ear proclaimed, "Boy, did we shake that bridge!"[3]

What a flea-brained declaration! The elephant had done all the work. But don't we do the same? The man who begged for help in medical school ten years ago is too busy to worship today. Back when the family struggled to make ends meet, they leaned on God for daily bread. Now that there is an extra car in the garage and a jingle in the pocket, they haven't spoken to him in a while. Success begets amnesia.

However, as Abigail's story reveals, humility has the power to overcome pride. Apologies can disarm arguments. Contrition can defuse rage. Olive branches do more good than battle-axes ever will. "Soft speech can break bones" (Proverbs 25:15 NLT).

Praise the LORD, my soul, and forget not all his benefits (Psalm 103:2).

5. As you review this story, in what ways do you see Abigail demonstrating humility?

_____

_____

_____

When the LORD your God has brought my lord success, remember your servant (1 Samuel 25:31).

6. Abigail asked for forgiveness from David and then asked for all the blame due to Nabal to fall on her. It's a beautiful picture of the power of humility. What do the following verses say that humility will do in our lives?

2 Chronicles 34:27: "Because your heart was responsive and you humbled yourself before God . . . because you humbled yourself before me and tore your robes and wept in my presence, I have heard you, declares the LORD."

_____

_____

_____

Jeremiah 9:24: "If people want to brag, let them brag that they understand and know me. Let them brag that I am the LORD, and that I am kind and fair, and that I do things that are right on earth" (NCV).

_____

_____

_____

Luke 14:11: "Whoever exalts himself will be humbled, and he who humbles himself will be exalted" (NKJV).

_____

_____

_____

James 4:10: "Humble yourselves in the presence of the Lord, and He will exalt you" (NASB).

_____

_____

_____

7. What are some ways that you can model Christ's humility today?

_____

_____

_____

_____

8. Notice in this story that David also responds with humility. How do you see his heart change? Who in your world has nurtured humility in you? Explain.

_____

_____

_____

_____

_____

David accepted from her hand what she had brought him and said, "Go home in peace. I have heard your words and granted your request" (1 Samuel 25:35).

We live in a world where we all are little kings of our own kingdoms. We want our way and we want it now. Humility looks like a foreigner in our selfish society. It stands out, goes against, and contrasts the norm just like Abigail. Abigail goes against the selfish hostility surrounding her. When Abigail opens her mouth in this story, the tone shifts from dark to light. She understands the power of humility, because behind that humility is the power of God. Only when we allow the grace of God to shift our eyes off our own kingdoms and onto the real kingdom can true humility begin to grow.

But seek first his kingdom and his righteousness (Matthew 6:33).

❧ POINTS TO REMEMBER ❧

❖ How we treat our leaders—regardless of whether those leaders are good or unreasonable—is a reflection of God's grace in us.
❖ Wise words and a humble attitude can divert others from sin and disaster.
❖ God uses those who humble themselves to provide opportunities for reconciliation—though sometimes at the expense of their reputation.

‿ PRAYER FOR THE DAY ‿

Lord Jesus, we are so naturally selfish. Please continue to chisel away at our pride and shape our hearts into ones that take after yours. Thank you for Abigail's story. May we, like her, humble ourselves before you and before others. Amen.

*D*ay Five: The Perfect Gift

GRACE CHANGES LIVES

Let us . . . [fix] our eyes on Jesus, the pioneer and perfecter of faith. For the joy set before him he endured the cross (Hebrews 12:1–2).

Abigail teaches us so much. The contagious power of kindness. The strength of a gentle heart. Her greatest lesson, however, is to take our eyes from her beauty and set them on someone else's. She lifts our thoughts from a rural trail to a Jerusalem cross. Abigail never knew Jesus. She lived a thousand years before his sacrifice. Nevertheless, her story prefigures his life, for her grace prefigures the grace that Jesus gave to us.

God's grace is a perfect personal gift that he has given just for us. "There has been born *for you* a Savior, who is Christ the Lord" (Luke 2:11 NASB, emphasis added). An angel spoke these words. Shepherds heard them first. But what the angel said to them, God says to anyone who will listen. "There has been born *for you* . . ."

Jesus is the gift. He himself is the treasure. Grace is precious because he is. Grace secures us because he will. Just as the grace Abigail displayed to David changed their lives, so the grace Jesus bestows on us changes our lives. The gift is the Giver.

To discover grace is to discover God's utter devotion to you, his stubborn resolve to give you a cleansing, healing, purging love that lifts the wounded back to their feet. Does he stand high on a hill and bid you climb out of the valley? No. He bungees down and carries you out. Does he build a bridge and command you to cross it? No. He crosses the bridge and shoulders you over. "You did not save yourselves; it was a gift from God" (Ephesians 2:8 NCV).

Let your conversation be always full of grace, seasoned with salt, so that you may know how to answer everyone (Colossians 4:6).

The story of Abigail and David shows us that when we allow God's grace to seep into the crusty cracks of our lives, it softens hearts and changes lives. So let God's grace bubble to the surface of your heart like a spring in the Sahara—in words of kindness and deeds of generosity. As you do, you will find that it changes not only other lives but your life as well.

1. The climactic moment of Abigail's story occurs when she falls before David, takes the blame for her husband's actions—though she is innocent—and pleads for his mercy. Read Isaiah 53:5. How do her actions compare to what Christ did for us?

   _____

   _____

   _____

   But he was pierced for our transgressions, he was crushed for our iniquities; the punishment that brought us peace was on him, and by his wounds we are healed (Isaiah 53:5).

2. "Just as the grace Abigail displayed to David changed their lives, so the grace Jesus bestows on us changes our lives." How has grace changed your life?

   _____

   _____

   _____

3. Take some time to meditate on Philippians 2:4–11. What words stand out to you from these verses? How can you have the mindset of Jesus in your relationships with others?

   _____

   _____

   _____

   In your relationships with one another, have the same mindset as Christ Jesus (Philippians 2:5).

4. Abigail was willing to sacrifice her life for her household. Christ was willing to sacrifice his life for the world. According to Romans 12:1, what should that compel us to do as Christ-followers? How do you live out the words of this verse in your own life?

   _____

   _____

   _____

   Offer your bodies as a living sacrifice, holy and pleasing to God (Romans 12:1).

A CHANGE OF HEARTS

The barbarism we see in Nabal is still alive and well today on the planet earth. We could not deny our sin problem any more than Quasimodo could deny his hump. Our heart problem is uNIVersal. And personal. Just measure your life against the standards set forth in the Ten Commandments and you'll see how unruly is your heart. There's a bit of Nabal in each of us.

A holy and perfect God cannot overlook these sins as just "innocent mistakes." But Abigail's story reveals what he can do—and *did*

All have sinned and fall short of the glory of God (Romans 3:23).

do—to respond to our sinful condition. We find it throughout the New Testament: "The good shepherd lays down his life for the sheep" (John 10:11); "This is my body given for you" (Luke 22:19); "Christ died for our sins" (1 Corinthians 15:3); "Jesus gave himself for our sins" (Galatians 1:4 NCV); "Christ redeemed us from the curse of the Law, having become a curse for us" (3:13 NASB).

Just as Abigail placed herself between David and Nabal, Jesus placed himself between God and us. Just as Abigail volunteered to be punished for Nabal's sins, Jesus allowed heaven to punish him for yours and mine. Just as Abigail turned away the anger of David, Christ shielded us from the wrath of God. Though healthy, he took our disease upon himself. Though diseased, we who accept his offer are pronounced healthy.

The result? More than just pardoned, we are declared innocent. We enter heaven not with healed hearts but with *his* heart.

God presented Christ as a sacrifice of atonement (Romans 3:25).

5. Just as Abigail was a mediator on behalf of Nabal, Christ is a mediator on behalf of us. Hebrews 7:26–28 and 9:6–7 tell us a bit about the role of a mediator. According to these verses, what was the purpose of the high priests in the Old Testament?

Such a high priest truly meets our need—one who is holy, blameless, pure, set apart from sinners, exalted above the heavens (Hebrews 7:26).

_____

_____

_____

6. Read Hebrews 9:22. The sacrifices the high priest performed always involved the shedding of blood for the people's sin. What is the significance of blood?

Without the shedding of blood there is no forgiveness (9:22).

_____

_____

_____

7. Turn to Hebrews 9:11–15. Before Jesus, the high priest functioned as a mediator between the people and God, making blood sacrifice for the forgiveness of sin. Why do these verses say that Jesus is the *ultimate* high priest?

_____

_____

_____

8. What promise are we given in Hebrews 7:25? How does picturing Christ as our mediator give us peace and assurance for this life and the life to come?

Therefore he is able to save completely those who come to God through him (7:25).

_____

_____

_____

Abigail was a mediator who reconciled David and Nabal. Likewise, Jesus is our mediator who reconciles us to God, for "he gave his life to purchase freedom for everyone" (1 Timothy 2:5–6 NLT). Christ stood in between God's anger and our punishment. Something remotely similar happened in the story of Ernest Gordon and the Chungkai prison camp that I told at the beginning of this lesson.

As I mentioned, the camp had been transformed with the arrival of two prisoners who held to a higher code than just "survival of the fittest." Their goodness and mercy proved contagious, and soon all the prisoners were displaying these traits. Then, one evening after work detail, a Japanese guard announced that a shovel was missing. The officer kept the Allies in formation, insisting that someone had stolen it.

Screaming in broken English, the guard demanded that the guilty man step forward. He shouldered his rifle, ready to kill one prisoner at a time until a confession was made. Just then, a Scottish soldier broke ranks, stood stiffly at attention, and said, "I did it." The officer unleashed his anger and beat the man to death. When the guard was finally exhausted, the prisoners picked up the man's body and their tools and returned to camp. Only then were the shovels recounted. The Japanese soldier had made a mistake. No shovel was missing after all.[4]

Greater love has no one than this: to lay down one's life for one's friends (John 15:13).

What kind of person would take the blame for something he didn't do? Who does that? When you find the adjective, attach it to Jesus. "God has piled all our sins, everything we've done wrong, on him, on him" (Isaiah 53:6 MSG). God treated his innocent Son like the guilty human race. His Holy One like a lying scoundrel. His Abigail like a Nabal.

Christ lived the life we could not live and took the punishment we could not take to offer the hope we cannot resist. His sacrifice begs us to ask this question: *If he so loved us, can we not love each other?* Having been forgiven, can we not forgive? Having feasted at the table of grace, can we not share a few crumbs? "My dear, dear friends, if God loved us like this, we certainly ought to love each other" (1 John 4:11 MSG).

Do you find your Nabal world hard to stomach? Then do what David did: stop staring at Nabal. Shift your gaze to Christ. Look more at the Mediator and less at the troublemakers. "Don't let evil get the best of you; get the best of evil by doing good" (Romans 12:21 MSG).

[Abigail] bowed down with her face to the ground and said, "I am your servant and am ready to serve you" (1 Samuel 25:41).

One prisoner can change a camp. One Abigail can save a family. Be the beauty amidst your beasts and see what happens.

❧ POINTS TO REMEMBER ❧

❖ God's grace in us points others to him and changes lives.
❖ God's grace cleanses, heals, and provides us with the strength we need to stand as a new person bearing the heart of Christ.
❖ Jesus was punished for our sins, and he shields those who turn to him for salvation from the wrath of God.

❧ PRAYER FOR THE DAY ☙

Jesus, because of your sacrifice, we can rest in the security of salvation. Thank you, Lord, for sitting at the right hand of the Father and interceding for us, as unworthy as we are. We are forever grateful. In your name we pray, amen.

❧ WEEKLY MEMORY VERSE ☙

For there is one God and one mediator between God and mankind, the man Christ Jesus, who gave himself as a ransom for all people.
1 TIMOTHY 2:5–6

For Further Reading

Selections throughout this lesson were taken from *It's Not About Me* (Nashville: Thomas Nelson, 2004); *Facing Your Giants* (Nashville: Thomas Nelson, 2006); *Cure for the Common Life* (Nashville: Thomas Nelson, 2006); *3:16—The Numbers of Hope* (Nashville: Thomas Nelson, 2007); and *Grace* (Nashville: Thomas Nelson, 2012).

Notes
1. Ernest Gordon, *To End All Wars: A True Story About the Will to Survive and the Courage to Forgive* (Grand Rapids: Zondervan, 2002), pp. 105–106, 101.
2. Hans Wilhelm Hertzberg, *First and Second Samuel*, trans. J. S. Bowden (Philadelphia: Westminster John Knox Press, 1964), pp. 199–200.
3. Anthony de Mello, *Taking Flight: A Book of Story Meditations* (New York: Doubleday, 1988), p. 99.
4. Gordon, *To End All Wars*, pp. 101–102.

LESSON 4

ESTHER

TOUCHING THE KING'S HEART

MANY YEARS AGO, WHEN MY DAUGHTERS ANDREA AND SARA were young, our family went desk hunting. I needed a new one for the office, and I'd promised Andrea and Sara desks for their rooms. Sara was especially enthused. Whenever she came home from school, she would play school. I never did that as a kid. I tried to forget the classroom activities, not rehearse them.

So off to the store we went. When my wife, Denalyn, bought furniture, she preferred one of two extremes—so antique it's fragile, or so new it's unpainted. This time we opted for the latter and entered a store of in-the-buff furniture.

Andrea and Sara succeeded quickly in making their selections, and I set out to do the same. Somewhere in the process Sara learned we weren't taking the desks home that day. This news disturbed her deeply. I explained the piece had to be painted, and they would deliver the desk in about four weeks. I might as well have said four millennia.

Her eyes filled with tears, "But, Daddy, I wanted to take it home today." Much to her credit, she didn't stomp her feet and demand her way. She did, however, set out on an urgent course to change her father's mind. Every time I turned a corner she was waiting on me.

"Daddy, don't you think we could paint it ourselves?"

"Daddy, I just want to draw some pictures on my new desk."

"Daddy, please, let's take it home today."

After a bit she disappeared, only to return, arms open wide and bubbling with a discovery. "Guess what, Daddy? It'll fit in the back of the car!"

You and I know that a seven-year-old had no clue what would or wouldn't fit in a vehicle, but the fact she had measured the trunk with her arms softened my heart. The clincher, though, was the name she called me: "Daddy."

The Lucado family took a desk home that day.

I heard Sara's request for the same reason God hears ours. Her desire was for her own good. What dad wouldn't want his child to spend more time writing and drawing? Sara wanted what I wanted for her—she only wanted it sooner. When we agree with what God wants, he hears us as well (see 1 John 5:14).

Sara's request was heartfelt. God, too, is moved by our sincerity. The "earnest prayer of a righteous man has great power" (James 5:16 TLB). But most of all, I was moved to respond because Sara called me "Daddy." Because she is my child, I heard her request. Because we are God's children, he hears ours. The King of creation gives special heed to the voice of his family. He is not only willing to hear us; he loves to hear us. He even tells us what to ask him.

Jesus tells how to begin. "When you pray, pray like this. 'Our Father who is in heaven, hallowed be thy name. Thy kingdom come.'" When you say, "Thy kingdom come," you are inviting the Messiah himself to walk into your world. "Come, my King! Take your throne in our land. Be present in my heart. Be present in my office. Come into my marriage. Be Lord of my family, my fears, and my doubts."

This is no feeble request. It's a bold appeal for God to occupy every corner of your life. Who are you to ask such a thing? Who are you to ask God to take control of your world? You are his child, for heaven's sake! "So let us come boldly to the very throne of God and stay there to receive his mercy and to find grace to help us in our times of need" (Hebrews 4:16 TLB).

1. Tell about a time in your life when you knew God had heard a desire of your heart. How did God answer that request?

   _____

   _____

   _____

   _____

2. "I was moved to respond because Sara called me 'Daddy.' Because she is my child, I heard her request." Why can it be difficult to picture God as our Father?

   _____

   _____

   _____

   _____

A. W. Tozer once wrote, "What comes to mind when we think of God is the most important thing about us."[1] If we see God as our good Father, we can be who we were created to be: his children. And as his children, we can joyfully and fearlessly approach him with our requests, questions, and concerns, knowing he loves us. Our prayer life becomes rich and, most of all, relational. But if the picture that comes to mind when we think of God is negative, our prayer life suffers, and this prevents us from approaching the throne of God with boldness. God wants us to know him not just as Father but also as Daddy (see Romans 8:15).

The Spirit you received brought about your adoption to sonship (Romans 8:15).

⸻ PRAYER FOR THE WEEK ⸻

God, sometimes it's hard for us to see you as a good Father. And because of that, our conversations with you struggle. Help us to see you the way you want us to see you so that our prayers align with your heart. Amen.

Day One: A Drama Fit for Hollywood

BEHIND THE SCENES

A wonderful illustration of this kind of boldness God is seeking is in the story of Hadassah. Although her language and culture are an atlas apart from ours, she can tell you about the power of a prayer to a king. There are a couple of differences, though. Her request was not to her father, but to her husband, the king. Her prayer wasn't for a desk, but for the delivery of her people. And because she entered the throne room, because she opened her heart to the king, he changed his plans, and millions of people in 127 different countries were saved.

This is what happened during the time of Xerxes, the Xerxes who ruled over 127 provinces stretching from India to Cush (Esther 1:1).

Oh, how I'd love for you to meet Hadassah. But since she lived in the fifth century BC, such an encounter is not likely. We'll have to be content with reading about her in the book that bears her name—her *other* name—the book of Esther.

And what a book it is! Hollywood would have a challenge matching the drama of this story . . . the evil Haman who demanded that all pay him homage . . . the gutsy Mordecai who refused to bow before Haman . . . Mordecai's great words to Esther that she may have been chosen queen for "such a time as this" . . . and Esther's conviction to save her people. "If I perish, I perish," she resolved.

1. This "Hollywood drama" we know as the book of Esther was written after the temple in Jerusalem had been destroyed and the

After affliction and harsh labor, Judah has gone into exile. She dwells among the nations; she finds no resting place (Lamentations 1:3).

Babylonians had taken almost all of Judah's inhabitants into exile. Read Lamentations 1:1–3. What does the author say about the Jewish people during this time? What is his tone behind the words?

_____

_____

_____

The LORD will scatter you among all nations, from one end of the earth to the other (Deuteronomy 28:64).

2. Turn to Deuteronomy 28:63–67. These words came to pass during the time of Esther. What had God promised would happen to his people if they didn't follow his commands? What do these verses say about the state of the people's hearts?

_____

_____

_____

3. Esther lived during the reign of the Persian Empire, which had overthrown the Babylonian Empire. As exiles in a foreign land, how do you think the Jews were viewed?

_____

_____

_____

_____

4. On top of being a foreigner, Esther was a woman—and women in that culture were seen as inferior, dominated, and owned by men. So, before even looking at our story, what does all of this tell you about our main character and how she saw herself?

_____

_____

_____

_____

SETTING THE STAGE

This is what Cyrus king of Persia says: "The LORD . . . has appointed me to build a temple for him at Jerusalem in Judah. Any of his people among you may go up" (2 Chronicles 36:23).

Let's review the central characters, starting with the one who seemingly held all the power on earth. Xerxes was the king of Persia and the absolute monarch over the land from India to Ethiopia. His official title was *shahanshah*. While this can be translated "emperor," it actually carries a bit loftier meaning—"king of kings." Xerxes was the grandson of Cyrus the Great, who the Bible tells us allowed the Jews to return to Jerusalem, and the son of Darius the Great, who was responsible for making Persia the largest empire in the world.

One of the first matters Xerxes had to address after assuming the throne was crushing a revolt that had broken out in Babylon. In years past, both Cyrus and Darius had officiated at a festival in which the ruler grasped the hands of the statue of Marduk, the patron god of the city. For the Babylonians, this ensured their continued prosperity. But Xerxes had little time or patience for such ceremonies—and apparently little diplomacy.

Instead, he opted to do away with this ritual by melting down the statue. As you might imagine, this didn't sit well with the Babylonians, who quickly revolted when the new king assumed the throne. They would soon come to learn that when Xerxes raised an eyebrow, the destiny of the world would change. Xerxes crushed the revolt in Babylon, and then one in Egypt, and then invaded Greece. Such was the power and temperament of the mighty king who would become known as "Xerxes the Great."

In many respects Xerxes symbolized the power of God—the true "KING OF KINGS AND LORD OF LORDS" (Revelation 19:16)—for he guides the river of life and doesn't even raise an eyebrow. Yet while our God is patient and loving, and invites us to come into his presence, the subjects of Xerxes knew he was a man to be feared. And fear him they did.

5. The first character introduced in our drama is Xerxes (or in some translations King Ahasuerus, his name in Hebrew). Read Esther 1:1–9. What is the setting for this drama that will take place? What is the king doing when the book opens?

_____

_____

_____

_____

On his robe and on his thigh he has this name written: KING OF KINGS AND LORD OF LORDS (Revelation 19:16).

6. What can you gather about King Xerxes's character based on these verses?

_____

_____

_____

_____

At that time King Xerxes reigned from his royal throne in the citadel of Susa, and in the third year of his reign he gave a banquet for all his nobles and officials (Esther 1:2–3).

7. In many respects, Xerxes symbolizes the power of God in the land. How is God showing his strength in the following verses? What are the key differences between the way Xerxes and God flex their muscles?

Exodus 14:17–18: "My great glory will be displayed through Pharaoh and his troops, his chariots, and his charioteers. When my glory is displayed through them, all Egypt will see my glory and know that I am the LORD!" (NLT).

_____

_____

_____

Judges 7:22: "When the three hundred blew the trumpets, the LORD set every man's sword against his companion throughout the whole camp; and the army fled to Beth Acacia, toward Zererah, as far as the border of Abel Meholah, by Tabbath" (NKJV).

Isaiah 14:26–27: "This is the plan, planned for the whole earth, and this is the hand that will do it, reaching into every nation. God-of-the-Angel-Armies has planned it. Who could ever cancel such plans? His is the hand that's reached out. Who could brush it aside?" (MSG).

Matthew 19:26: "Jesus looked at them and said, 'For mortals it is impossible, but for God all things are possible'" (NRSV).

Romans 1:20: "His invisible attributes, namely, his eternal power and divine nature, have been clearly perceived, ever since the creation of the world, in the things that have been made" (ESV).

Hebrews 1:3: "The Son reflects the glory of God and shows exactly what God is like. He holds everything together with his powerful word. When the Son made people clean from their sins, he sat down at the right side of God, the Great One in heaven" (NCV).

8. The main character of our story is a Jewish woman in captivity. Knowing this—and knowing the sad state of Israel—how do you think God is setting up a perfect stage to display his glory?

Oftentimes, God is glorified more when life gets hard. We see this throughout the Bible. When the Israelites were in Egyptian captivity, God showed his glory. When Gideon only had 100 men to defeat an overwhelming enemy, God showed his glory. When there was no room in the inn, God displayed his glory. He does the same in our lives today. It's not that God needs a black backdrop to shine brighter. However, because we are human, sometimes it takes everything falling out from under us before we are willing to see and hear from God. So, if you're going through a hard time—like the Jews in our story—perhaps God is setting the stage in your heart, destroying all that had played a lead role in your life so that he can shine brighter.

The Word became flesh and made his dwelling among us. We have seen his glory, the glory of the one and only Son (John 1:14).

⤙ POINTS TO REMEMBER ⤚

❖ God displays his power and glory through world events, through leaders on this earth, and through his Son, Jesus.
❖ God is often glorified when times are difficult and when resolving those difficulties is beyond the control of his people.
❖ The way we view God will determine how we respond when life is difficult.

⤙ PRAYER FOR THE DAY ⤚

God, your Word shows us that you are mighty and able to save us from anything we face on this earth. Please forgive us when we get caught up in our own glory or in the glory of those around us. We want to see how big you are—to see your glory. Destroy anything in our hearts today that rivals that glory in our lives. Amen.

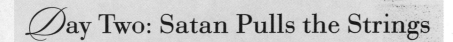

*D*ay Two: Satan Pulls the Strings

A DANGEROUS EGOMANIAC

Xerxes is certainly the one who holds the power. Yet in the story told in Esther, we don't get the sense that he is always the one pulling the strings. For that we turn to Haman, the king's right-hand man whose name sounds like hangman (which you will soon see as more than just a curious coincidence). Read every word about the man and you'll find

King Xerxes honored Haman son of Hammedatha, the Agagite (Esther 3:1).

nothing good about him. He is an insatiable egotist who wants the worship of every person in the kingdom.

Haman, we read, was an Agagite (see Esther 3:1), or one who was descended from Agag, the king of a nation that was hostile to Israel. In 1 Samuel 15:7–9, we read how King Saul had spared Agag's life in disobedience to God's command. When Samuel found out, he had Agag brought before him and put to death (see verses 32–33). Now that the Jews were the minority in Persia, Haman decided to exterminate them once and for all. He convinced Xerxes the world would be better with a holocaust and set a date for the genocide of all of Abraham's children.

Haman is a servant of hell and a picture of the devil himself, who has no higher aim than to have every knee bow as he passes. Satan also has no other plan than to persecute the promised people of God. He comes to "steal and kill and destroy" (John 10:10), and "he is filled with anger, because he knows he does not have much time" (Revelation 12:12 NCV).

In this case, Satan hopes to destroy the Jews, thereby destroying the lineage of Jesus. For Haman, the massacre is a matter of expediency. For Satan, it is a matter of survival. He will do whatever it takes to impede the presence of Jesus in the world.

But Saul and the army spared Agag and the best of the sheep and cattle (1 Samuel 15:9).

1. Read Esther 3:1–6. What can you discern about Haman's personality from these verses? Why did he become enraged when not everyone in the kingdom bowed down to him?

_____

_____

_____

_____

All the royal officials at the king's gate knelt down and paid honor to Haman, for the king had commanded this concerning him (Esther 3:2).

2. The tension between Haman's people (the Amalekites) and Esther's people (the Jews) had gone back for hundreds of years. Read 1 Samuel 15:1–3. Why did God's anger burn against the Amalekites? What did God command Saul to do as a result?

_____

_____

_____

_____

Dispatches were sent . . . to destroy, kill and annihilate all the Jews (verse 13).

3. Read Esther 3:7–15. What did Haman's anger against the Jews provoke him to do? How did he deceive King Xerxes through the request he made of him?

_____

_____

_____

_____

4. Turn to Psalm 36:1–4. How do these verses describe the condition of Haman's heart? How did his pride drive him to make evil plans?

_____

_____

_____

_____

_____

In their own eyes they flatter themselves too much to detect or hate their sin (Psalm 36:2).

THE LURE OF SELF-IMPORTANCE

Satan used pride to puff up Haman's heart and compel him to plot atrocities against God's people. Pride is a familiar tactic in his arsenal that we see him using as far back as the dawn of creation. There, in the Garden of Eden, his first promise of prestige was whispered to Eve with a hiss, a wink, and a snakish grin.

God had said, "Of every tree of the garden you may freely eat; but of the tree of the knowledge of good and evil you shall not eat, for in the day that you eat of it you shall surely die" (Genesis 2:16-17 NKJV). Standing in the shadow of that very tree, Satan knew what to offer Eve to convince her to disobey the order. It wasn't pleasure. It wasn't health. It wasn't prosperity. It was . . . well, read his words and look for his lure: "God knows that if you eat the fruit from that tree, you will learn about good and evil and you will be like God!" (3:5 NCV).

The words found a soft spot.

"You will be like God . . ." Eve stroked her chin as she replayed the promise. The snake pulled back the curtain to the throne room and invited Eve to take a seat. Put on the crown. Pick up the scepter. Put on the cape. See how it feels to have power. See how it feels to have a name. See how it feels to be in control!

Eve swallowed the hook. The temptation to be like God eclipsed her view of God . . . and the crunch of an apple echoed in the kingdom. Centuries later, Haman would take the same bait. "King Xerxes promoted Haman . . . over all the other nobles, making him the most powerful official in the empire" (Esther 3:1 NLT). The power went to Haman's head so completely that he could not stand the thought of even one man not bowing down to him.

The serpent still hisses his lies to us today. "You are so good. You are so wonderful. People need to recognize this fact and give you the praise you deserve." The Bible is clear we must capture every such thought and make it obedient to Christ (see 2 Corinthians 10:5). We must resist any exaggerated ideas of our own importance (see Romans 12:3). We must make the cross of our Lord Jesus Christ our own reason for bragging (see Galatians 6:14).

As we do, we will come to understand that pride doesn't please God . . . and we will avoid the terrible consequences that come from leading a pride-filled life.

When pride comes, then comes disgrace (Proverbs 11:2).

When the woman saw that the fruit of the tree was good for food and pleasing to the eye, and also desirable for gaining wisdom, she took some and ate it (Genesis 3:6).

We demolish arguments and every pretension that sets itself up against the knowledge of God (2 Corinthians 10:5).

81

"The days are coming,"
declares the LORD, "when I will
raise up for David a righteous
Branch (Jeremiah 23:5).

5. Turn to Jeremiah 23:5–6. What does this prophecy say about Jesus? In the Bible, how do we see Satan use individuals such as Haman to try to destroy God's people and prevent the fulfillment of this prophecy? (See, for example, Exodus 1:8–10.)

_____

_____

_____

_____

6. What do the following passages of Scripture say about Satan's nature and the ways in which he operates in this world?

Ezekiel 28:17–18: "Your heart was filled with pride because of all your beauty. Your wisdom was corrupted by your love of splendor. . . . You defiled your sanctuaries with your many sins and your dishonest trade" (NLT).

_____

_____

_____

John 8:44: "[Satan] was a murderer from the beginning, and does not stand in the truth, because there is no truth in him. When he lies, he speaks out of his own character, for he is a liar" (ESV).

_____

_____

_____

2 Corinthians 4:3–4: "If our gospel is veiled, it is veiled to those who are perishing, whose minds the god of this age has blinded, who do not believe, lest the light of the gospel of the glory of Christ, who is the image of God, should shine on them" (NKJV).

_____

_____

_____

2 Corinthians 11:14–15: "For Satan disguises himself as an angel of light. Therefore it is not surprising if his servants also disguise themselves as servants of righteousness, whose end will be according to their deeds" (NASB).

_____

_____

_____

1 Peter 5:8: "Control yourselves and be careful! The devil, your enemy, goes around like a roaring lion looking for someone to eat" (NCV).

_____

_____

_____

_____

7. What tactics have you seen the enemy use against you? How do these verses help you recognize his strategies and see them for what they truly are?

_____

_____

_____

_____

_____

8. What do the following verses say about the power we have over Satan? What do they say we should do if we are feeling attacked by evil?

Ephesians 6:10–11: "Be strong in the Lord and in the strength of his power. Put on the whole armor of God, so that you may be able to stand against the wiles of the devil" (NRSV).

_____

_____

_____

_____

James 4:7–8: "Let God work his will in you. Yell a loud _no_ to the Devil and watch him scamper. Say a quiet _yes_ to God and he'll be there in no time" (MSG).

_____

_____

_____

_____

1 Peter 5:9: "Resist [the devil], steadfast in the faith, knowing that the same sufferings are experienced by your brotherhood in the world" (NKJV).

_____

_____

_____

_____

1 John 4:4: "You belong to God, my dear children. You have already won a victory over those people, because the Spirit who lives in you is greater than the spirit who lives in the world" (NLT).

_____

_____

_____

_____

_____

_____

_____

_____

_____

_____

Put on the full armor of God, so that when the day of evil comes, you may be able to stand your ground (Ephesians 6:13).

To focus too much on the devil takes away from the power and safety we have in Christ. But to disregard him completely takes away from the warning in Scripture for us to be sober-minded and watchful against his schemes. A balance is needed. We need to arm ourselves but remember the devil is a defeated foe. He is defeated *now* in our lives through the victory we have in Christ, and he will be defeated *forever* after the return of Christ. "And the devil, who deceived them, was thrown into the lake of burning sulfur" (Revelation 20:10). There is a day coming when all evil will be vindicated and destroyed forever! Until then, we must remain *watchful*, remembering that the demons flee at the presence of Christ in us. And we must also remain *hopeful*, remembering the beautiful ending that is to come.

POINTS TO REMEMBER

❖ Satan will do everything in his power to impede the presence and impact of Jesus in the world.
❖ Satan builds up our own pride as a way to attack us and destroy our relationship with God.
❖ Pride is a weapon of destruction, but the work of our Lord Jesus Christ on the cross is a defense against evil.

PRAYER FOR THE DAY

Jesus, you have already won victory over the enemy—and you live within us! Therefore we know that we have nothing to fear. Today we pray that you will help us stand in the full armor of God so we can be armed and protected against all of the enemy's schemes. Let us not fall prey to lies or deception, but enable us to resist his temptations. Amen.

Day Three: For Such a Time as This

THE NEW MISS PERSIA

There are two more important players in the story: Esther and Mordecai. When the book opens, Esther has just become queen by winning a Miss Persia contest. It appears the former queen—a woman named Vashti— had quickly fallen out of the king's favor when she refused to be paraded in front of his friends. The sordid episode occurred during a seven-day party at the palace, in which the guests were allowed "to drink with no restrictions" (Esther 1:8). On the seventh day, "when King Xerxes was in high spirits from wine," he decided it would be a good idea to summon Vashti "to display her beauty to the people" (verses 10–11).

Vashti decided it was *not* a good idea and refused to appear. Furious, the king consulted with his . . . lawyers. They quickly advised the king to do some damage control by sending her into exile, for fear the "women of the nobility . . . will respond to all the king's nobles in the same way" (verse 18). They also told Xerxes to hold a royal beauty pageant in order to choose Vashti's replacement. As you might expect, this, of course, pleased the king.

Esther would end up winning this contest and, in virtually one day, go from obscurity to royalty. In more ways than one, she should remind us of ourselves. Like Esther we are residents of the palace—Esther, the bride of Xerxes, and we, the bride of Christ. We both have access to the throne of the king, and we both have a counselor to guide and teach us. Our counselor is the Holy Spirit. Esther's counselor was Mordecai, the final player in this tale.

1. Read Esther 1:10–22. In addition to his own pride, why else does the king punish Vashti (see verses 17–20)? What clear message was he sending to women? How do you think this would have made Esther feel as she moved into the palace?

   _____

   _____

   _____

   _____

2. Turn to Esther 2:1–18. What do you learn about Esther's past and her upbringing? Why is it significant that Mordecai is her cousin?

   _____

   _____

   _____

King Xerxes . . . commanded the seven eunuchs who served him . . . to bring before him Queen Vashti, wearing her royal crown, in order to display her beauty to the people and nobles (Esther 1:10–11).

Vashti is never again to enter the presence of King Xerxes. Also let the king give her royal position to someone else who is better than she (verse 19).

The queen's conduct will become known to all the women, and so they will despise their husbands (verse 17).

85

*Esther won the favor of everyone
who saw her* (Esther 2:15).

3. What recurring theme do you find in verses 9, 15, and 17? How did this quality in Esther serve her well in the Persian court?

_____

_____

_____

4. Considering Esther's upbringing, her Jewish roots, and the thousands of other women in the king's harem, the odds of Esther becoming queen looked slim. Yet she won the favor of everyone. Just a coincidence? Not at all. Look up the following verses and write down what each says about the favor of God.

Psalm 5:12: "For You, O LORD, will bless the righteous; with favor You will surround him as with a shield" (NKJV).

_____

_____

_____

Psalm 84:11: "The LORD God is like a sun and shield; the LORD gives us kindness and honor. He does not hold back anything good from those whose lives are innocent" (NCV).

_____

_____

_____

Proverbs 3:34: "The LORD mocks the mockers but is gracious to the humble" (NLT).

_____

_____

_____

2 Corinthians 9:8: "God is able to make all grace abound to you, so that having all sufficiency in all things at all times, you may abound in every good work" (ESV).

_____

_____

_____

Ephesians 2:8–9: "For by grace you have been saved through faith; and that not of yourselves, it is the gift of God; not as a result of works, so that no one may boast" (NASB).

_____

_____

_____

_____

A PICTURE OF THE HOLY SPIRIT

Mordecai had adopted Esther as his daughter, and it was he who urged Esther to keep her Jewish nationality a secret when she became queen. It was also Mordecai who discovered Haman's plot to exterminate the Jews and persuaded Esther to talk to Xerxes about the impending massacre. You may wonder why she would need any encouragement.

Mordecai must have wondered the same thing. But consider the message he got from Esther: "No man or woman may go to the king in the inner courtyard without being called. There is only one law about this: Anyone who enters must be put to death unless the king holds out his gold scepter. Then that person may live. And I have not been called to go to the king for thirty days" (Esther 4:11 NCV). As strange as it may sound to us, not even the queen could approach the king without an invitation. To enter his throne room uninvited was to risk a visit to the gallows. But Mordecai convinces her to take the risk.

If you wonder why I see Mordecai as a picture of the Holy Spirit, just watch how he next encourages her to do what is right. He tells Esther that just because she lives in the king's palace, she should not think that out of all the Jewish people she alone will escape. He tells her that if she remains quiet at this time, someone else will help save the Jewish people, but she and her family will all die. Then he adds: "And who knows, you may have been chosen queen for just such a time as this" (Esther 4:14 NCV).

5. Read Esther 2:19–23 and 4:1–14. What do these verses tell us about Mordecai's loyalties? What do they tell us about his integrity? About his boldness?

_____

_____

_____

6. Mordecai is a "picture of the Holy Spirit" and prompted Esther to do what was right. What do the following verses tell us about the role of the Holy Spirit in our lives?

John 14:26: "The Helper will teach you everything and will cause you to remember all that I told you. This Helper is the Holy Spirit whom the Father will send in my name" (NCV).

_____

_____

_____

John 16:8–10: "When [the Holy Spirit] comes, he will convict the world of its sin, and of God's righteousness, and of the coming

Esther had not revealed her nationality and family background, because Mordecai had forbidden her to do so (Esther 2:10).

Do not think that because you are in the king's house you alone of all the Jews will escape (4:13).

judgment. The world's sin is that it refuses to believe in me. Righteousness is available because I go to the Father" (NLT).

John 16:13–14: "When the Friend comes, the Spirit of the Truth, he will take you by the hand and guide you into all the truth there is. He won't draw attention to himself, but will make sense out of what is about to happen and, indeed, out of all that I have done and said. He will honor me; he will take from me and deliver it to you" (MSG).

Romans 8:26: "The Spirit helps us in our weakness; for we do not know how to pray as we ought, but that very Spirit intercedes with sighs too deep for words" (NRSV).

Titus 3:5–6: "[God] saved us, not because of works done by us in righteousness, but according to his own mercy, by the washing of regeneration and renewal of the Holy Spirit, whom he poured out on us richly through Jesus Christ our Savior" (ESV).

7. How do you see the favor of God not only on Esther's life but also on the lives of the Jewish people through Mordecai?

8. As Christians, the Holy Spirit indwelling us is proof of God's favor on our lives. How have you seen the Spirit protect you lately?

Although the book of Esther never mentions God by name, the word *favor* pops up frequently. Commentators believe the Hebrew word for *favor* is used regularly "to describe the character of God" and "could be a subtle way of suggesting the presence of the Lord without mentioning his name."[2] The word can be translated "loyal love," and this is the type of love we find at the center of God's relationship with Israel. The people had done nothing to deserve God's favor, yet he chose them and never let them go. In Esther, we see that God was still with Israel, even in captivity. Before Haman's edict to destroy the Jews was even a thought, God had his players in place: Mordecai, the messenger and encourager; and Esther, the link to the king. God's loyal love never ceased. Israel couldn't outrun it, and neither can we.

Now the king was attracted to Esther more than to any of the other women, and she won his favor and approval more than any of the other virgins (Esther 2:17).

❧ POINTS TO REMEMBER ❧

❖ We are the bride of Christ with access to the King and a Counselor to guide and train us.
❖ God is gracious to the humble, and his favor and protection rest on his children.
❖ The Holy Spirit prompts us to do what is right, and he teaches us the truth about who God is, what God wants of us, and how we can live as his people.

❧ PRAYER FOR THE DAY ❧

Father, thank you for your merciful favor and for your loyal love that never lets us go. Today, we pray that your loyal love will define everything we are and everything we do. In Jesus's name, amen.

Day Four: Taking the Plunge

DISAGREEING WITH GOD

I have to wonder how we would respond to a request like the one made to Esther. How would we react if we were asked to put our necks on the line to save someone else? The truth is that even when the circumstances are less dire, we don't always like to obey God. Sometimes we disagree with the intent behind what God is asking us to do. We don't *want* God to show mercy to someone we don't think *deserves* God's mercy.

Jesus Christ laid down his life for us. And we ought to lay down our lives for our brothers and sisters (1 John 3:16).

But Jonah ran away from the LORD and headed for Tarshish (Jonah 1:3).

The LORD provided a huge fish to swallow Jonah, and Jonah was in the belly of the fish three days and three nights (verse 17).

From inside the fish Jonah prayed to the LORD his God (2:1).

The LORD commanded the fish, and it vomited Jonah onto dry land (verse 10).

But to Jonah this seemed very wrong, and he became angry (4:1).

Just consider Jonah. Like Esther, God raised him up for "such a time as this" to save a nation of people who were doomed to destruction. "Get up," God said to him, "go to the great city of Nineveh, and preach against it, because I see the evil things they do" (Jonah 1:2). Jonah, however, had no desire to go to that heathen city. So instead he hopped on another boat while God wasn't looking . . . or so he thought.

Jonah was sailing in the opposite direction when he looked over his shoulder and saw clouds brewing. God had followed him onto the ocean. The storm overtook the boat, and the crew ultimately was forced to throw Jonah overboard to calm the seas. There, God would put his wayward prophet into a fish's belly to bring him back to his senses.

For three days God left Jonah in the belly of the fish, surrounded by gastric juices and sucked-in seaweed. For three days Jonah pondered his choices. For three days he came to the same conclusion: *there are no choices.* From where he sits (or floats) there are two exits—and neither is appealing. But then again, neither is Jonah. He blew it as a preacher. He was a flop as a fugitive. At best he's a coward. At worst a traitor. And what he's lacked all along he now has in abundance—guts.

So Jonah does the only thing he can do: he prays. He says nothing about how good he is, but a lot about how good God is. He doesn't even ask for help, but help is what he gets. Before he can say *amen,* the belly convulses, the fish belches, and Jonah ends up flying over the surf and landing big-eyed and repentant on the beach. (Which just goes to show that you can't keep a good man down.)

Why did Jonah resist the Lord's call? "I knew that you are a God who is kind and shows mercy," he would later say to the Lord. "You don't become angry quickly, and you have great love. I knew you would choose not to cause harm" (Jonah 4:2 NCV). Jonah didn't want to warn the Ninevites because he didn't believe they were worthy of mercy. He disagreed with God. But God rejected Jonah's opinion by forgiving the Ninevites and saving them from destruction.

1. Read Jonah 1:1–17. In what ways are God's call to Jonah and his call to Esther similar? In what ways are they different?

2. What is the biggest faith risk that God has asked you to take? In what ways were you tempted to respond like Jonah?

3. Read Jonah 2:1–10. Even before God delivered Jonah from the fish's belly, he was already praising the Lord for delivering him. How did God respond to Jonah's faith? What does this teach you about God?

_____

_____

_____

_____

In my distress I called to the LORD, and he answered me (Jonah 2:1).

4. Read Jonah 3:1–6. How did the people of Nineveh respond to Jonah's message? What does this say about the way God will use us for his purposes in spite of what we want?

_____

_____

_____

_____

When Jonah's warning reached the king of Nineveh, he rose from his throne, took off his royal robes, covered himself with sackcloth and sat down in the dust (3:6).

APPROACHING THE KING

Esther faced a challenge similar to the one Jonah faced. God had called her, through Mordecai, to save an entire people from certain destruction. So, how did Esther respond to this challenge? Unlike Jonah, "Esther put on her royal robes and stood in the inner courtyard of the king's palace, facing the king's hall" (Esther 5:1 NCV). She saw the greater purpose, accepted the risk, and went boldly before the king to seek his favor and his protection for the Jewish people.

On the third day Esther put on her royal robes and stood in the inner court of the palace (Esther 5:1).

Picture the scene. Can't you see Esther walking into the throne room? She's right off the cover of *Mademoiselle* magazine. Now picture King Xerxes sitting there, flipping through his copy of *Car and Chariot*. On either side of him is a burly-chested guard. Behind him is a chattering eunuch. Ahead of him is a long day of cabinet meetings and royal red tape. He lets out a sigh and sinks down into his throne . . . and out of the corner of his eye, he sees Esther.

"When the king saw Queen Esther standing in the courtyard, he was pleased" (5:2 NCV). Let me give you my translation of that verse: "When the king saw Queen Esther standing in the courtyard he said, 'a-*hubba-hubba-hubba*.'" He held out to her the gold scepter in his hand, which was a rod about five feet long that had an ornamental ball at the end. The scepter indicated the Persian king's absolute authority in the land, and by holding it out to Esther, he was indicating that she had found favor in his eyes.[3]

He was pleased with her and held out to her the gold scepter that was in his hand. So Esther approached and touched the tip of the scepter (verse 2).

Esther went forward and touched the end of it, which indicated her desire to be heard. "What is it, Queen Esther?" the king replied. "What do you want to ask me? I will give you as much as half of my kingdom" (verse 3 NCV). So far, it appeared Esther's plan was working.

Esther sent this reply to Mordecai: "Go, gather together all the Jews who are in Susa, and fast for me" (Esther 4:15).

5. Read Esther 4:15–5:8. Mordecai's words cause Esther to spring into action, but notice her first plan of action is to fast. In the Bible, we find that people often went into a time of fasting and prayer before making important decisions. What does this tell you about Esther's view of God? What was the very real danger in approaching the king?

_____

_____

_____

_____

6. How did Xerxes respond when Esther approached him? In what ways is this similar to the way that God responds when we approach him with our requests?

_____

_____

_____

_____

7. Why do you think Esther held two banquets (with Haman as their guest) instead of directly asking the king to spare her people? What strategy was she employing to make the king more favorable to her request? What was the purpose in inviting Haman?

_____

_____

_____

_____

Let us then approach God's throne of grace with confidence, so that we may receive mercy and find grace (Hebrews 4:16).

8. Read Hebrews 4:16. Regardless of whether we choose to obey God like Esther, or run away from him like Jonah, why are we able to approach the King of Kings with confidence? How are you approaching him today with your requests?

_____

_____

_____

When God calls us to do something, we have the choice of running from him (like Jonah) or obeying him (like Esther). When God calls us, let's consider why. As Mordecai said to Esther, "If you remain silent at this time, relief and deliverance for the Jews will arise from another place" (Esther 4:14). Mordecai knew that God didn't need Esther to work out his sovereign plan—and he doesn't need us to fulfill his purposes either. But God, in his mercy, extended an invitation to Esther to join in his work, trust in him completely, and do something truly courageous that would forever be remembered by God's people. God does the same when he extends invitations for us to join in his work. And when he does, he always provides the help and support we need. Like Xerxes, he extends

We are God's handiwork, created in Christ Jesus to do good works, which God prepared in advance for us to do (Ephesians 2:10).

his scepter of authority to us and gives us the power and strength we need to accomplish the task before us.

⧼ POINTS TO REMEMBER ⧽

❖ God will fulfill his purposes in spite of what we do, but he invites us to participate in what he is already going to accomplish.
❖ When we see God's greater purpose and accept the tasks he has called us to undertake, we will experience his favor and his protection.
❖ As God's beloved children, we can approach him with confidence, knowing that he is ready and willing to listen to our requests.

⧼ PRAYER FOR THE DAY ⧽

Lord God, thank you for the opportunities you give us each day to partner with you in this world and accomplish your purposes. Thank you that, because of Jesus Christ, we can approach your throne with confidence in making our requests. Today we pray that you would give us the ears to hear your voice and respond with faith. Amen.

Day Five: The Throne of Grace

SATAN'S PLANS COLLAPSE

What follows in the rest of the story is the rapid collapse of Satan's deck of cards. Haman schemes to string up Mordecai, the only man who won't grovel at his feet. Esther plans to throw a couple of banquets for Xerxes and Haman. At the end of the second banquet Xerxes begs Esther to ask for something. Esther looks sort of sheepishly at the floor and says, "Well, now that you mention it, there is one eensy weensy favor I've been wanting to ask."

Esther proceeds to inform the king about the raging anti-Semite who was hell-bent on killing her friends like rats, which meant that Xerxes was about to lose his bride if he didn't act soon—and you don't want that, do you, honey? Xerxes demands the name of the murderer. Haman looks for the exits. Esther spills the beans. Xerxes loses his cool.

The king storms out the door to take a Prozac, only to return to find Haman at the feet of Esther. Haman is begging for mercy, but the king

Queen Esther answered, "If I have found favor with you, Your Majesty, and if it pleases you, grant me my life—this is my petition. And spare my people—this is my request. For I and my people have been sold to be destroyed, killed and annihilated" (Esther 7:3–4).

So they hanged Haman on the gallows he had prepared for Mordecai. Then the king's wrath subsided (verse 10 NKJV).

thinks he's making a move on the queen. Before Haman has a chance to explain, he's headed to the same gallows he'd built for Mordecai. Haman gets Mordecai's rope. Mordecai gets Haman's job. Esther gets a good night's sleep. The Jews live to see another day.

And we get a dramatic reminder of what happens when we approach our King.

1. Read Esther 5:9–7:10. What range of emotions does Haman experience in this passage? How do his plans for Mordecai ultimately backfire?

   _____

   _____

   _____

   _____

2. How does Esther break the news to the king about Haman's plot? How does Haman react? How does the king then react?

   _____

   _____

   _____

   _____

The king's edict granted the Jews in every city the right to assemble and protect themselves; to destroy, kill and annihilate the armed men of any nationality or province who might attack them and their women and children, and to plunder the property of their enemies (Esther 8:11).

3. Read Esther 8:1–17. After Haman is hanged on the gallows that he himself had ordered to be constructed, what did Esther request for her people? What rights did Xerxes grant to the Jewish people as a result of Esther's words?

   _____

   _____

   _____

   _____

4. King Xerxes not only says yes to Esther's request to save her people, but he also puts a crown on the head of Mordecai and blesses her family. When was a time that God gave you even more than you requested? What did this show you about God?

   _____

   _____

   _____

   _____

NEVER TURNED AWAY

Come to me, all you who are weary and burdened, and I will give you rest (Matthew 11:28).

Esther is able to save her people because of her willingness to approach Xerxes, the "king of kings," with her requests. When Jesus comes to earth, he reveals what happens when we are likewise willing to approach God, the true Kings of Kings, with our requests. The Gospels are filled with stories of people from all classes of society and walks of life who are willing to approach Jesus and tell him their needs. And Jesus never turns them away.

One such individual who boldly approaches Jesus with a request is a man named Jairus. He is the leader of the local synagogue, which makes him the most important person in the community. In many ways, he is the senior religious leader, the highest-ranking professor, the mayor, and the best-known citizen all rolled in one. Jairus has it all. Job security. A guaranteed welcome at the coffee shop. A pension plan. Golf every Thursday and an annual all-expenses-paid trip to the national convention.

One of the synagogue leaders, named Jairus, came, and when he saw Jesus, he fell at his feet (Mark 5:22).

Who could ask for more? Yet Jairus does. He *has* to ask for more. In fact, he would trade the whole package of perks and privileges for just one assurance—that his daughter will live. So Jairus seeks an audience with the King of Kings. And when he finds Jesus, he falls at the Lord's feet and says again and again, "My daughter is dying. Please come and put your hands on her so she will be healed and will live" (Mark 5:22–23 NCV).

Jairus doesn't barter, negotiate, or make excuses. He just approaches the King of Kings and pleads for mercy. And how does Jesus respond? He holds out the golden scepter of heaven to him. He stops what he is doing and travels with Jairus back to his house.

So Jesus went with him (verse 24).

On the way, news arrives that Jairus's daughter has died. Here's where the story gets moving. Jesus goes from being led to leading. When he arrives at the home, he literally throws the mourners out! He picks them up by collar and belt and sets them sailing. The Lord of Life then takes the girl's hand and instructs her to stand up. At once, the girl stands up straight and begins walking around.

Immediately the girl stood up and began to walk around. . . . At this they were completely astonished (Mark 5:42).

Jairus is amazed. The people are amazed. And we receive a lesson about the authority of Christ. We also learn that when we boldly approach the throne of God's grace, we can be confident that the King of Kings will hear us and meet our needs.

5. Read Mark 5:21–24. What has Jesus just been doing when Jairus approaches him? What does this show about Christ's willingness to always help people?

_____

_____

_____

_____

6. Read Mark 5:35–43. What do the emissaries say to Jesus? How does Jesus respond?

_____

_____

_____

_____

Overhearing what they said, Jesus told him, "Don't be afraid; just believe" (Mark 5:36).

7. At this point, Jairus certainly believed that there was no hope Jesus could still fulfill his request. But what does Jesus say to him? What does he ask Jairus to do?

_____

_____

_____

_____

8. When have you approached God but the answer did not seem to come in the time or the way you expected? In what way did you lose hope that your request would be answered? What did you learn in the end about trusting in God always?

_____

_____

_____

_____

_____

_____

When Mordecai left the king's presence, he was wearing royal garments of blue and white (Esther 8:15).

There are so many truths that we can discover in the story of Esther. Like her, we have been plucked out of obscurity and given a place in the palace. Like her, we have been given royal robes—she was dressed in cloth, we are dressed in righteousness. And like Esther, we have the privilege of making our request to the King of Kings.

That's what my daughter Sara did those many years ago when she embarked on her urgent quest to change my mind about the desk. When she met me at every corner in the store and pleaded with me to take home the desk that same day. And while her request wasn't as dramatic as Esther's, it changed her father's plans.

By the way, the living parable of Sara and her desk didn't stop at the store. On the way home, she realized that my desk was still at the store. "I guess you didn't beg, did you, Daddy?" (We have not because we ask not.) When we unloaded her desk she invited me to christen it with her by drawing a picture. I made a sign that read, "Sara's desk." She made a sign that read, "I love my Daddy." (Worship is the right response to answered prayer.)

My favorite part of the story is what happened the next day. I shared this account in my Sunday sermon. A couple from our church dropped by and picked the desk up, telling us they would paint it. When they returned it a couple of days later, it was covered with angels. And I was reminded that when we pray for God's kingdom to come, it comes! All the hosts of heaven rush to our aid.

The LORD has established his throne in heaven, and his kingdom rules over all (Psalm 103:19).

❧ POINTS TO REMEMBER ❧

❖ When we approach the throne of God with our requests, we can be confident that he will hear us and not turn us away.

❖ God's invitation to join in his work is an opportunity for us to see him accomplish great things in this world and see evil defeated.

❖ Through our faith in God, he not only answers our prayers but also blesses us beyond our expectations.

❧ PRAYER FOR THE DAY ❧

Lord, thank you for not only being the King of Kings and Creator of the UNIVerse but also our loving heavenly Father. Today, we ask that you would help us to trust you as a Father who only wants the very best for his children. Thank you that we can always approach you with our requests, and thank you for always hearing our prayers and answering them. We love you, Lord. Amen.

❧ WEEKLY MEMORY VERSE ❧

So let us come boldly to the throne of our gracious God. There we will receive his mercy, and we will find grace to help us when we need it most.
Hebrews 4:16 (NLT)

ℱor Further Reading

Selections throughout this lesson were taken from *No Wonder They Call Him Savior* (Nashville: Thomas Nelson, 1986); *The Applause of Heaven* (Nashville: Thomas Nelson, 1990); *He Still Moves Stones* (Nashville: Thomas Nelson, 1993); *Just Like Jesus* (Nashville: Thomas Nelson, 1998); *The Great House of God* (Nashville: Thomas Nelson, 1997); *Traveling Light* (Nashville: Thomas Nelson, 2001); and *A Love Worth Giving* (Nashville: Thomas Nelson, 2002).

Notes

1. A. W. Tozer, *The Knowledge of the Holy* (San Francisco: HarperOne, 1978).
2. Earl Radmacher, Ronald B. Allen, H. Wayne House, eds., *Nelson's New Illustrated Bible Commentary* (Nashville: Thomas Nelson, 1999), p. 606.
3. Geoffrey W. Bromiley, *International Standard Bible Encyclopedia*, entry for "scepter" (Grand Rapids: Wm. B. Eerdmans, 1988).

LESSON 5

MARY, THE MOTHER OF JESUS

MORE THAN A CHRISTMAS STORY

THE PINT-SIZE JOSEPH SCURRIES ACROSS THE CHURCH STAGE. He is wearing sandals, a robe, and his best attempt at an anxious face. He raps on the door his dad built for the children's Christmas play, and then shifts from one foot to the other, partly because he's supposed to act nervous. Mostly because he is exactly that.

The innkeeper answers. He too wears a tow sack of a robe and a towel turned turban. An elastic band secures a false beard to his face. He looks at Joseph and chokes back a giggle. Just a couple of hours ago the two boys were building a front-lawn snowman. Their moms had to tell them twice to get dressed for the Christmas Eve service.

Here they stand. The innkeeper crosses his arms. Joseph waves his. He describes a donkey ride from Nazareth, five days on the open road, a census here in Bethlehem, and, most of all, a wife. He turns and points in the direction of a pillow-stuffed nine-year-old girl.

She waddles onto center stage with one hand on the small of her back and the other mopping her brow. She limps with her best portrayal of pregnant pain, though, if pressed, she would have no clue about the process of childbirth.

She plays up the part. *Groan. Sigh.* "Joseph, I need help!"

The crowd chuckles.

Joseph looks at the innkeeper.

The innkeeper looks at Mary.

And we all know what happens next. Joseph urges. The innkeeper shakes his head. His hotel is packed. Guests occupy every corner. There is no room at the inn.

I think some dramatic license could be taken here. Rather than hurry to the next scene, let Joseph plead his case. "Mr. Innkeeper, think twice about your decision. Do you know whom you are turning away? That's God inside that girl! You're closing the door on the King of the universe. Better reconsider. Do you really want to be memorialized as the person who turned out heaven's child into the cold?"

And let the innkeeper react. "I've heard some desperate appeals for a room, but God inside a girl? *That* girl? She has pimples and puffy ankles, for goodness' sake! Doesn't look like a God-mother to me. And you don't look too special yourself there . . . uh . . . what was your name? Oh yeah, Joe. Good ol' Joe. Covered head to toe with road dust. Take your tale somewhere else, buddy. I'm not falling for your story. Sleep in the barn for all I care!"

The innkeeper huffs and turns. Joseph and Mary exit. The choir sings "Away in a Manger" as stagehands wheel out a pile of hay, a feed trough, and some plastic sheep. The audience smiles and claps and sings along. They love the song, the kids, and they cherish the story. But most of all, they cling to the hope. The Christmas hope that God indwells the everydayness of our world.

1. No fanfare. No fireworks. Just the slamming doors of rejection, a tired donkey, and an even more tired pregnant teenager. Why do you think God preordained the Christmas story to look so humble?

_____

_____

_____

_____

2. We take special time during the Christmas season to celebrate the incarnation—God made flesh—but God indwelling "the everydayness of our world" is an everyday reason to worship. Think about your day. What about the splendor of the incarnation can affect every detail of your day—monotonous or new, big or small? (Get specific!)

_____

_____

_____

_____

The most earth-shattering miracle of the Bible is also the quietest: God becoming man. When accepted, this miracle changes our identity, our heart, our future—everything. Yet oftentimes we forget the magnitude of this miracle. Maybe in our busy routines we, like the innkeeper,

I stand at the door and knock. If anyone hears my voice and opens the door, I will come in (Revelation 3:20).

This is how we know that [God] lives in us: We know it by the Spirit he gave us (1 John 3:24).

don't make much room for it, and we miss out on the promises of the incarnation. We depend on our own power instead of the promised power of Christ in us. We face our fears alone, forgetting that God is with us. The miracle of Christ coming to earth was not a one-time miracle. It's an everyday miracle offering us everyday promises. So let's make room for it, remember it, and ask God to help us rely on it.

You will receive power when the Holy Spirit comes on you (Acts 1:8).

❧ PRAYER FOR THE WEEK ❧

Lord, we cannot thank you enough for becoming man and dwelling among us. May the truth of this bring joy, peace, and hope to our everyday lives. Amen.

Day One: An Ordinary Couple

NORMAL AND UNNOTICED

The story drips with normalcy. This isn't Queen Mary or King Joseph. The couple doesn't caravan into Bethlehem with camels, servants, purple banners, and dancers. Mary and Joseph have no tax exemption or political connection. They have the clout of a migrant worker and the net worth of a minimum wage earner. Not subjects for a PBS documentary.

God sent the angel Gabriel to Nazareth, a town in Galilee, to a virgin pledged to be married to a man named Joseph (Luke 1:26–27).

Not candidates for welfare either. Joseph and Mary would celebrate the birth of Jesus with a temple offering of two turtledoves, which the Gospels tell us was the gift of the poor (see Luke 2:22–24). Their life is difficult but not destitute. Joseph has the means to pay taxes. They inhabit the populous world between royalty and rubes.

If she cannot afford a lamb, she is to bring two doves or two young pigeons (Leviticus 12:8).

They are, well, *normal*. Normal has calluses like Joseph, stretch marks like Mary. Normal stays up late with laundry and wakes up early for work. Normal drives the car pool wearing a bathrobe and slippers. Normal is Norm and Norma, not Prince and Princess.

Norm sings off-key. Norma works in a cubicle and struggles to find time to pray. Both have stood where Joseph stood and have heard what Mary heard. Not from the innkeeper in Bethlehem but from the coach in middle school or the hunk in high school or the foreman at the plant. "We don't have room for you . . . time for you . . . a space for you . . . a job for you . . . interest in you. Besides, look at you. You are too slow . . . fat . . . inexperienced . . . late . . . young . . . old . . . pigeon-toed . . . cross-eyed . . . hackneyed. You are too . . . ordinary."

But then comes the Christmas story—Norm and Norma from Normal, Ohio, plodding into ho-hum Bethlehem in the middle of the night. No one notices them. No one looks twice in their direction. The innkeeper won't even clean out a corner in the attic. Trumpets don't blast, bells don't sound, and angels don't toss confetti. Aren't we glad they didn't?

While they were there, the time came for the baby to be born, and she gave birth to her firstborn, a son. She wrapped him in cloths and placed him in a manger, because there was no guest room available for them (Luke 2:6–7).

1. Read the story of Jesus' birth as told in Luke 2:1–7. What details in this story point to Mary and Joseph's humble state?

   _____

   _____

   _____

2. Why do you think God chose two very normal and humble people to be the parents of the King of Kings? What does this say about his nature?

   _____

   _____

   _____

This is the name by which he will be called: The LORD Our Righteous Savior (Jeremiah 23:6).

3. Many of the Jews in Mary and Joseph's day were expecting the promised Messiah to have earthly clout—a literal earthly kingdom—because of prophecies such as Jeremiah 23:5–6. What was God telling the world through the humble birth of Jesus about the difference between earthly kingdoms and his spiritual kingdom?

   _____

   _____

   _____

   _____

He has brought down rulers from their thrones but has lifted up the humble (Luke 1:52).

4. Read Luke 1:46–55. In this song of worship and praise, Mary proclaims many of the wonders of God's upside-down kingdom. What are some verses in her song that teach us the opposite of what the world promotes?

   _____

   _____

   _____

ORDINARY LIKE US

Joseph and Mary didn't have the advantage we have: ultrasound. When Denalyn was pregnant with each of our three daughters, we took full advantage of the technology. The black-and-white image on the screen looked more like Doppler radar than a child. But as the doctor moved the instrument around Denalyn's belly, he took inventory. "There's the head, the feet, the torso . . . well, everything looks normal."

Mary's doctor would have made the same announcement. Jesus was an ordinary baby. There is nothing in the story to imply that he levitated over the manger or walked out of the stable. Just the opposite. He "dwelt among us" (John 1:14 NKJV). John's word for *dwelt* traces its origin to *tabernacle* or *tent*. Jesus did not separate himself from his creation. Rather, he pitched his tent right in the middle of the neighborhood.

What if Joseph and Mary had shown up in furs with a chauffeur, bling-blinged and high-muckety-mucked? What if God had decked out Bethlehem like Hollywood on Oscar night: red carpet, flashing lights, with angels interviewing the royal couple? "Mary, Mary, you look simply divine." Had Jesus come with such whoop-de-do, we would have read the story and thought, *My, look how Jesus entered their world.* But since he didn't, we can read the story and dream.

Might Jesus be born in our world? Our everyday world? Isn't that what we indwell? Not a holiday world. Or a red-letter-day world. No, we live an ordinary life. We have bills to pay, beds to make, and grass to cut. Our faces won't grace any magazine covers, and we aren't expecting a call from the White House. We qualify for a modern-day Christmas story. God enters the world through folks like us and comes on days like today.

The splendor of the first Christmas is the lack thereof. What no rabbi dared to dream, God did. "The Word became flesh" (John 1:14 NKJV). The Artist became oil on his own palette. The Potter melted into the mud on his own wheel. God became an embryo in the belly of a village girl. Christ in Mary. God in Christ. The Word of God entered the world with the cry of a baby. His family had no cash or connections or strings to pull. Jesus, the Maker of the universe, the one who invented time and created breath, was born into a family too humble to swing a bed for a pregnant mom-to-be.

Will God really dwell on earth with humans? The heavens, even the highest heavens, cannot contain you (2 Chronicles 6:18).

The virgin will conceive and give birth to a son, and will call him Immanuel (Isaiah 7:14).

5. Joseph and Mary were average, working-class, ordinary people, and yet God used them to usher in the greatest story ever told. How does knowing this truth encourage your everyday, ordinary life?

_____

_____

_____

6. Read John 1:14, and then sit in the truth of this verse for a while. In the Old Testament, God dwelt among his people in the tabernacle. In the New Testament, he dwelt among them in human skin. What does this say about the God we serve?

_____

_____

_____

7. Paraphrase the following verses in your own words, and then write down the common theme running through each verse.

2 Corinthians 13:5: "Examine yourselves, to see whether you are in the faith. Test yourselves. Or do you not realize this about yourselves, that Jesus Christ is in you?—unless indeed you fail to meet the test!" (ESV).

_____

_____

_____

Galatians 2:20: "I was put to death on the cross with Christ, and I do not live anymore—it is Christ who lives in me. I still live in my body, but I live by faith in the Son of God who loved me and gave himself to save me" (NCV).

_____

_____

_____

Colossians 1:27: "To them God willed to make known what are the riches of the glory of this mystery among the Gentiles: which is Christ in you, the hope of glory" (NKJV).

_____

_____

_____

Now you are the body of Christ, and each one of you is a part of it (1 Corinthians 12:27).

8. When Christ dwells in us, our ordinary identity suddenly becomes extraordinary. Our natural life suddenly becomes supernatural. Read John 1:12, 1 Corinthians 12:27, and 1 Peter 2:9. How do these verses speak to you personally about your extraordinary identity in Christ?

_____

_____

_____

He made himself nothing by taking the very nature of a servant, being made in human likeness (Philippians 2:7).

God was not above growing inside of an average teenage girl. He was not above breathing his first breath in an animal stable. (Talk about a stinky first breath.) He was not above touching the leper, talking to the tax collector, blessing the prostitute. From day one, God "made himself nothing" (Philippians 2:7), revealing to the world that the real kingdom is not about wealth but the poor in spirit. It's about the ordinary folk who think more highly of God than they do of themselves. It's about the humble folk who put God first and others before themselves. So, if you think you're ordinary, you're in good company. God loves to use ordinary for his kingdom. And when he does, ordinary becomes extraordinary.

POINTS TO REMEMBER

❖ Jesus entered the world—his creation—through ordinary people and became part of the fabric of human life.
❖ When Christ dwells in us, our ordinary identity becomes extraordinary.
❖ The kingdom of God appears in humble folk who put God first and others before themselves.

PRAYER FOR THE DAY

Lord, thank you for being a God who wants to dwell among and inside his people. As sinful and ordinary as we are, you still choose to live in our hearts. Today, allow your presence in us to take over everything we do and everything we are. We love you. Amen.

Blessed are the poor in spirit, for theirs is the kingdom of heaven (Matthew 5:3).

Day Two: A Lesson in Trust

A BREED APART

Some things only a mom can do. Only a mother can powder a baby's behind with one hand and hold the phone with the other. Only a mom can discern which teen is entering the door just by the sound of the key in the lock. Only a mom can spend a day wiping noses, laundering enough socks for the Yankees, balancing a checkbook down to $1.27, and still mean it when she thanks God for her kids. Only a mom.

Some things only a mom can fix. Like Hamburger Helper without the hamburger. Like the cabinet door her husband couldn't and his bruised ego when he found out that she could. Broken shoelace? Broken heart? Breaking out on your face? Breaking up with your sweetheart? Moms can handle that. Some things only a mom can fix.

Some things only a mom can know. The time it takes to drive from piano lesson to Little League practice? She knows. How many pizzas you need for a middle school sleepover? Mom knows. How many Weight Watcher points are left in the day and days are left in the semester? Mom can tell you. She knows.

We men usually don't. The kids are usually clueless. Moms are a breed apart. The rest of us can only wonder . . . only ponder. And if we've ever

She speaks with wisdom, and faithful instruction is on her tongue (Proverbs 31:26).

wondered such thoughts about mothers, how much more have we wondered them about the most famous mother of all: Mary. To bear a baby is one thing, but to carry God? What is *that* like?

Mary was pledged to be married to Joseph, but before they came together, she was found to be pregnant through the Holy Spirit (Matthew 1:18).

1. Read Matthew 1:18–19. Before Joseph and Mary consummate their marriage, the angel tells them they have conceived through the Holy Spirit. What does Joseph initially decide to do? What feelings do you think Mary wrestled with as she thought of Joseph's stress and the reaction of their small town of Nazareth?

_____

_____

_____

"I am the LORD's servant," Mary answered. "May your word to me be fulfilled" (Luke 1:38).

2. Turn to Luke 1:26–45. What were Mary's reactions to the news from the angel? What are your initial observations about her personality?

_____

_____

_____

3. After the angel's visit, Luke says that Mary hurried to see her cousin. Why did she hurry? What do you think staying with Elizabeth did for Mary emotionally and spiritually?

_____

_____

_____

At that time Mary got ready and hurried to a town in the hill country of Judea (verse 39).

4. "Mary's journey into the Judean hill country was no leisurely stroll . . . the hill country was bleak . . . it was an area fit for fugitives, rebels, and hermits but certainly not for a pregnant woman."[1] What does this say about Mary's relationship with Elizabeth? Do you have an "Elizabeth" in your life? What does she do to encourage you?

_____

_____

_____

A WILLING SERVANT

Like Mary, you and I are *indwelt* by Christ. Find that hard to believe? How much more did Mary? The line beneath her picture in the high-school annual did not read, "Aspires to be the mother of God." No. No one was more surprised by this miracle than she was.

And no one was more passive than she was. God did everything. Mary didn't volunteer to help. What did she have to offer? Advice? "From my perspective, a heavenly choir would add a nice touch." Yeah, right. She offered no assistance. And she offered no resistance. She could have. "Who am I to have God in my womb? I'm not good enough," she could have said. Or, "I've got other plans. I don't have time for God in my life."

Mary didn't say such words. Nor did she refuse God's calling on her life out of fear. Instead, she believed the angel when he said, "Do not be afraid, Mary, you have found favor with God" and replied, "Behold, the bondslave of the Lord; may it be done to me according to your word" (Luke 1:30, 38 NASB). If Mary is our measure, God seems less interested in talent and more interested in trust.

We will never know what it was like for Mary to give birth to the Son of God. But we can learn a great deal from her example. We can learn not to try to "assist" God when he calls, assuming our part is as important as his. We can learn not to resist, thinking we are too bad or too busy. Even more, we can learn not to miss out on the reason we were placed on earth—to be so pregnant with heaven's child that he lives through us. To be so full of him that we could say with Paul, "It is no longer I who live, but Christ lives in me" (Galatians 2:20 NKJV).

5. Take a moment to reread Mary's response to the angel in Luke 1:38. What does she call herself in this verse? What does this imply about her heart toward God?

_____

_____

_____

The angel went to her and said, "Greetings, you who are highly favored! The Lord is with you." Mary was greatly troubled at his words and wondered what kind of greeting this might be (Luke 1:28–29).

6. Read Luke 1:11–22. How was Zechariah's reaction to the angel different from Mary's reaction? When was the last time God presented you with a seemingly impossible task or situation? Was your reaction more like Mary's or Zechariah's? Explain.

_____

_____

_____

Zechariah asked the angel, "How can I be sure of this? I am an old man and my wife is well along in years" (verse 18).

7. After living with a mute husband, Elizabeth joyfully proclaimed Mary was blessed. Why was Mary blessed? Turn to Galatians 3:9 and John 20:29. How do these verses relate to Elizabeth's words in Luke 1:45?

_____

_____

_____

Those who rely on faith are blessed (Galatians 3:9).

Blessed are those who have not seen and yet have believed (John 20:29).

8. Mary was favored in God's eyes because of her trust, not because of her talents. In your relationship with God, do you believe that he

accepts you based on your faith, or do you struggle with earning his love through your talents? Explain your thoughts.

_____

_____

_____

_____

His master replied, "Well done, good and faithful servant! You have been faithful with a few things; I will put you in charge of many things" (Matthew 25:21).

The angel opened his heavenly decree by saying that Mary was God's "favored one." Don't we want to be called the same? Don't we want to rest in the assurance that God sees us and approves of us? The good news the angel announced to Mary about God coming to earth gives us the rest for which our souls long. By trusting in the words of the angel—by trusting the Son of God has come—we are also given unmerited favor. Like Mary, we too can proclaim, "He has looked on the humble estate of his servant" (Luke 1:48 ESV). May our trust in Christ be one that not only saves us but also defines everything we do, say, and think.

—◦ POINTS TO REMEMBER ◦—

❖ God is more interested in our trust than in our talent.
❖ When we are full of Christ, he lives through us.
❖ Our trust in Christ defines everything we do, say, and think.

—◦ PRAYER FOR THE DAY ◦—

God, thank you for Mary's example of trust. Thank you for the favor you give us through the gift of your Son. Today, we ask that you increase our trust in you. Give us humility to be used by you and live our lives as your servants, just as Mary was willing. Amen.

Day Three: The Inaugural Miracle

ANGELIC COMMITTEE

He will command his angels concerning you (Psalm 91:11).

Let's pretend you are an angel. (That may be a stretch for some of you, but let's give it a try.) You are an angel in the era before the Messiah. God has not yet come to the earth, but he soon will and that's where you come in. You receive notice that you've been given a special assignment.

A once-in-an-eternity opportunity. You've been asked to serve on a special committee. Quite an honor, don't you think?

Michael chairs the heavenly task force. "Let's begin by choosing the first miracle the Messiah will perform," he states. "Now, this first miracle is crucial. It's the lead-off proclamation. It's the vanguard demonstration. It must be chosen carefully."

"Must be powerful," someone volunteers.

"Unforgettable," chimes another.

"We are in agreement, then," affirms Michael. "The first miracle of God on earth must have clout. Any ideas?"

Angelic creativity begins to whir.

"Have him raise a person from the dead."

"Feed every hungry person a meal."

"Remove disease from the planet!"

"I know!" you say. All the other angels turn to look at you. "What if he rids the earth of all evil? I mean, with one great swoop all the bad is gone and just the good remains."

"Not bad," says Michael. "It's settled, then. The first miracle will obliterate evil from the earth!" Wings rustle with approval, and you smile with pride.

Sound far-fetched? Maybe, but the story is not without a couple of threads of truth. One is that Jesus *did* have a plan. The mission of Christ was planned. I doubt if a committee ever existed, but a plan did. But, as it would turn out, that plan would change because of a simple request made by his mother, Mary.

1. Have you ever "held a committee" to give God a suggestion? What ideas, as of late, have you passed along to God, expecting him to obey?

_____

_____

_____

_____

2. Throughout Scripture, we find that God does not work the way we think he should. Read God's words to Isaiah in Isaiah 55:8–9. According to this passage, how much higher, better, clearer are God's ways than our own?

_____

_____

_____

3. Read Paul's words in 1 Corinthians 1:27. What does this tell us about the way God operates in our world?

_____

_____

Michael, the great prince who protects your people (Daniel 12:1).

"For my thoughts are not your thoughts, neither are your ways my ways," declares the LORD. "As the heavens are higher than the earth, so are my ways higher than your ways and my thoughts than your thoughts" (Isaiah 55:8–9).

God chose the foolish things of the world to shame the wise (1 Corinthians 1:27).

Be transformed by the renewing of your mind (Romans 12:2).

4. God, in his kindness, transforms our minds to think more like him so that we will grow in our trust that his ways are higher. What does the apostle Paul say about this transformation in Romans 12:2 and 1 Corinthians 2:16?

We have the mind of Christ (1 Corinthians 2:16)

_____

_____

_____

_____

_____

A Low-Key Affair

On the third day a wedding took place at Cana in Galilee. Jesus' mother was there, and Jesus and his disciples had also been invited to the wedding (John 2:1–2).

The plot is almost too simple. Jesus and his disciples are at a wedding. A common wedding. The bride wasn't the daughter of an emperor. The groom wasn't a prince. Were it not for the fact that the family invited Mary and Jesus to the wedding, the event would have been lost in time. But because Jesus always goes where he is invited, he and his disciples traveled to Cana for their first excursion.

The guests were happy and celebrating. But someone had underestimated the size of the crowd or the appetite of the guests or the depth of the wine vats or the number of friends Jesus would bring. As a result, the bride and groom ran out of wine. All the stores were closed, so Jesus, at his mother's urging, transformed six jugs of water into six jugs of wine.

That's it. That's the lead-off hitter for Jesus' miracles on earth. Pretty low-key, don't you think? Certainly doesn't have the punch of calling a person from the dead or the flair of straightening a crippled leg. Or does it? Maybe there is more to this than we think.

A wedding in the day of Christ was no small event. It usually began with a sundown ceremony at the synagogue. People would then leave the synagogue and begin a long, candlelight procession through the city. After the processional, the couple didn't go on a honeymoon. They would go home to a party. For several days there would be gift-giving, speech-making, food-eating, and . . . wine-drinking. Food and wine were taken seriously. It was considered an insult to the guests if the host ran out of food or wine.

When the wine was gone, Jesus' mother said to him, "They have no more wine" (verse 3).

Mary was one of the first to notice the wine had run out. She went to her son and pointed out the problem: "They have no more wine." Jesus' response? "Dear woman, why come to me? My time has not yet come" (John 2:3–4 NCV). Jesus was aware of the plan. He had a place and a time for his first miracle. And this wasn't it.

About now the angelic committee on the miracles of the Messiah let out a collective sigh of relief. "Whew, for a minute there, I thought he was going to blow it. Could you imagine Jesus inaugurating his ministry with a water-to-wine miracle?"

5. Read John 2:1–11. What are your initial observations about Mary in this story—her words, her personality, her actions?

_____

_____

_____

_____

6. Jesus chose for his first miracle to be at a wedding feast among his friends and family. What does this tell us about the kind of God we serve?

_____

_____

_____

_____

_____

The kingdom of heaven is like a king who prepared a wedding banquet for his son. He sent his servants to those who had been invited to the banquet to tell them to come (Matthew 22:2–3).

7. In Jesus' initial response to Mary, he said, "My hour has not yet come" (John 2:4). What did Jesus mean when he said this? Why do you think Mary continued with her request in spite of this initial response?

_____

_____

_____

_____

_____

8. Mary didn't stop after Jesus said it was not time for him to reveal his power. Maybe the reason can be traced to something in his tone. Maybe Jesus gave Mary a look that only a mother would notice. Regardless, Mary believed Jesus would respond. Do you likewise trust that Jesus hears your requests? Do you trust that he will respond?

_____

_____

_____

_____

His mother said to the servants, "Do whatever he tells you" (John 2:5).

Suggesting plans to God is a normal human response. It's normal because we just naturally want to be in control. Our desire for control stretches all the way back to Adam and Eve. But God wants to break this Adam nature in us and remind us of our Christ nature. Jesus is in us. His mind is in us. Struggle with trusting that God's ways are higher? Then tell him! We can ask him to help us think with the mind of Christ. When we do, we will find that he will respond to us in miraculous ways. He will begin turning our desire for control into trust, just as he turned the water into wine.

If any of you lacks wisdom, you should ask God, who gives generously to all (James 1:5).

⤳ POINTS TO REMEMBER ⤶

- ❖ God does not work according to our plans . . . in fact, his perspective is far beyond our ability to dictate his plan.
- ❖ God transforms our minds so that we can grow to trust in him and his plans.
- ❖ When we struggle with trusting God, we can ask him to help us think with the mind of Christ.

⤳ PRAYER FOR THE DAY ⤶

Lord, please forgive us when we don't trust in you. Although we can't always comprehend your ways, help us trust you in the same way that Mary trusted you. Even more, help us to trust you like Jesus trusted you. Thank you for hearing us and responding to us. We love you. Amen.

*D*ay Four: Lessons from Cana

A CHANGE IN PLANS

At first, it appeared that Jesus was going to stick with the plan. But as he heard Mary and looked into the faces of the wedding party, he reconsidered. The significance of the plan was slowly eclipsed by his concern for the people. Timing was important, but people were even more so. As a result, he changed his plan to meet the needs of some friends.

Incredible. The schedule of heaven was altered so some friends wouldn't be embarrassed. The inaugural miracle was motivated not by tragedy or famine or moral collapse but by concern for friends who were in a bind.

Jesus said to the servants, "Fill the jars with water" (John 2:7).

Now, if you're an angel on the committee of messianic miracles, you don't like this one bit. No, sir. You don't like this move on the part of Jesus. Everything about it is wrong. Wrong time. Wrong place. Wrong miracle. But if you're a human who has ever been embarrassed, you like this very much. Why? Because it tells you that what matters to you matters to God.

You probably think that's true when it comes to the big stuff. When it comes to the major-league difficulties like death, disease, sin, and disaster—you know that God cares. But what about the smaller things? What about grouchy bosses or flat tires or lost dogs? What about broken dishes, late flights, toothaches, or a crashed hard drive? Do these matter to God?

I'm glad you asked. Let me tell you who you are. *You are God's child.* "The Father has loved us so much that we are called children of God. And we really are his children" (1 John 3:1 NCV). As a result, if something is important to us, it's important to God.

Jesus didn't change the water to wine to impress the crowd—they didn't even know he did it. He didn't do it to get the wedding master's attention—that man actually thought the groom was being generous. So, why *did* Jesus do it? What motivated his first miracle? He performed this first miracle because his mother asked him to do so. He did it because what bothered her and his friends also bothered him. If it hurts the child, it hurts the father.

From this, we learn that we can tell God what hurts. We can talk to him and know he won't push us away. He won't think our request is silly. Does God care about the little things in our lives? You better believe it. If it matters to us, it matters to him.

Are not five sparrows sold for two pennies? Yet not one of them is forgotten by God. Indeed, the very hairs of your head are all numbered. Don't be afraid; you are worth more than many sparrows (Luke 12:6–7).

1. "[Mary's] prominence in asking Jesus to help when the wine ran out may indicate that she was in some way related to the family holding the wedding."[2] On top of this, hospitality in Mary's day was a sacred duty. Given this, what emotions and/or thoughts do you think flooded Mary's mind when the feast ran out of wine?

   _____

   _____

   _____

   _____

   _____

2. Jesus knew the thoughts and emotions of his mother. Even though the problem wasn't catastrophic, he knew, in his mom's head, that it was. Jesus likewise knows all your thoughts and concerns. What does David say about this in Psalm 139:2–4?

   _____

   _____

   _____

You know when I sit and when I rise; you perceive my thoughts from afar. You discern my going out and my lying down; you are familiar with all my ways (Psalm 139:2–3).

3. Do you ever keep concerns from God that feel too petty to bring to him? If so, what types of concerns do you tend to harbor? Why do you feel you can't bring them to God? Or, if you do hand them over to God, why do you feel you have the freedom to do so?

   _____

   _____

   _____

   _____

In every situation, by prayer and petition, with thanksgiving, present your requests to God (Philippians 4:6).

4. What is the danger in not sharing your small concerns with God—in believing you can only go to him with the "big issues" in life?

_____

_____

_____

_____

_____

THE PROPER CHANNEL

There is something else we can learn from this first miracle of Jesus. Look at how Mary reacted when faced with this problem at the wedding, for her solution poses a practical plan for untangling life's knots. "When the wine was gone, Jesus' mother said to him, 'They have no more wine'" (John 2:3 NCV). That's it. That's all she said. She didn't go ballistic. She simply assessed the problem and gave it to Christ.

For my nickel, Mary appears too seldom in Scripture. After all, who knew Jesus better than she did? She carried him for nine months. Breast-fed him for more. She heard his first words and witnessed his first steps. She was the ultimate authority on Jesus. So on the rare occasion she speaks, we perk up.

Notice that Mary wasn't bossy. She didn't say, "Jesus, they are out of wine, so here is what I need you to do. Go down to the grove at the corner, accelerate the growth of some Bordeaux grapes, and turn them into wine." She didn't try to fix the problem herself.

[Jesus] told them, "Now draw some out and take it to the master of the banquet." They did so, and the master of the banquet tasted the water that had been turned into wine. He did not realize where it had come from, though the servants who had drawn the water knew. Then he called the bridegroom aside and said, "Everyone brings out the choice wine first and then the cheaper wine after the guests have had too much to drink; but you have saved the best till now" (John 2:8–10).

Nor was she critical. "If only they had planned better, Jesus. People just don't think ahead. What is society coming to? The world is going over the cliff! Help, Jesus, help!" She didn't blame the host. She didn't blame Jesus. "What kind of Messiah are you? If you truly were in control, this never would have happened!"

Nor did she blame herself. "It's all my fault, Jesus. Punish me. I failed as a friend. Now the wedding is ruined. The marriage will collapse. I am to blame." None of this. Mary didn't whine about the wine. She simply looked at the knot, assessed it, and took it to the right person. "I've got one here I can't untie, Jesus." Problem presented. Prayer answered. Crisis avoided. All because Mary entrusted the problem to Jesus.

There is another version of this story. In it, Mary never involved Jesus. She took the master of the feast to task for poor planning. He took exception to her accusations. Mary stormed out of the party. The groom overheard the argument and lost his temper. The bride told her groom to forget marriage. If he couldn't manage his anger, he sure couldn't manage a home. By the end of the day, the guests left sad, the marriage was ended before it began, and Jesus shook his head and said, "I could've helped if only I'd been asked."

Call to me and I will answer you and tell you great and unsearchable things you do not know (Jeremiah 33:3).

That version of the story isn't in the Bible, but the principle surely exists in life. We can only wonder: *How many disasters would be averted if we would go first, in faith, to Jesus?* The punch line is clear: take your problem to Jesus.

5. What does Mary tell the servants to do in John 2:5? How do these words reflect her secure faith in Jesus?

_____

_____

_____

_____

6. Peter writes, "Cast all your anxiety on [Christ] because he cares for you" (1 Peter 5:7). What types of anxieties does this verse say we can bring to Jesus? How does Mary obey the words of this verse through her actions?

_____

_____

_____

_____

_____

Therefore I tell you, do not worry about your life (Matthew 6:25).

7. Notice in this story that when Mary brought her request to Christ, she wasn't bossy, she wasn't critical, and she didn't try to blame herself for the problem. When you are stressed with a problem, do you tend to follow her example? If not, which of these other tendencies best describes the way you handle problems?

_____

_____

_____

_____

_____

_____

8. What is one problem that you need to take straight to Jesus today?

_____

_____

_____

Commit your way to the LORD; trust in him and he will do this (Psalm 37:5).

When Peter wrote about casting all our anxieties on Christ, he didn't say cast some anxiety. He didn't say cast only the anxiety that we feel is worth giving to him. We are to cast it all. Why? Because he cares for us. That's it. He loves us. He's a good Father, and good fathers do not consider the requests of their children to be burdens. No, good fathers delight in their children—they delight in just being in relationship with their children. When we, like Mary, go straight to God with our problems, the Lord not only addresses our need, but in the process our relationship with him is strengthened.

"If you then, though you are evil, know how to give good gifts to your children, how much more will your Father in heaven give the Holy Spirit to those who ask him! (Luke 11:13).

⟋ POINTS TO REMEMBER ⟍

- ❖ God is interested in and responds to the needs of people.
- ❖ We can talk to God about anything and know that he is listening.
- ❖ When problems arise, we need to take them immediately to Jesus—for he delights in caring for us.

⟋ PRAYER FOR THE DAY ⟍

Father, help us to always take our concerns directly to you before we turn to anyone or anything else. Thank you for caring for us. Thank you for carrying our burdens. Amen.

Day Five: The Heartache of Goodbye

A CHALLENGING STATEMENT

The gospel is full of rhetorical challenges that test our faith and buck against human nature. "It is more blessed to give than to receive" (Acts 20:35). "For whoever wants to save their life will lose it, but whoever loses their life for me will save it" (Luke 9:24). "A prophet is not without honor except in his own town" (Mark 6:4).

But no statement is as confusing or frightening as the one in Matthew 19:29: "And all those who have left houses, brothers, sisters, father, mother, children, or farms to follow me will get much more than they left, and they will have life forever" (NCV).

The part about leaving land and fields I can understand. It is the other part that causes me to cringe. It's the part about leaving mom and dad, saying goodbye to brothers and sisters, placing a farewell kiss on a son or daughter. It is easy to parallel discipleship with poverty or public disgrace, but leaving my family? Why do I have to be willing to leave those I love? Can sacrifice get any more sacrificial than that?

"Woman, behold your son."

Mary is older now. The hair at her temples is gray. Wrinkles have replaced her youthful skin. Her hands are calloused. She has raised a houseful of children. And now she beholds the crucifixion of her first-born. One wonders what memories she conjures up as she witnesses his torture. The long ride to Bethlehem. A baby's bed made from cow's hay. Fugitives in Egypt. At home in Nazareth. Panic in Jerusalem. Carpentry lessons. Dinner table laughter.

Everyone who has left houses or brothers or sisters or father or mother or wife or children or fields for my sake will receive a hundred times as much and will inherit eternal life. But many who are first will be last, and many who are last will be first (Matthew 19:29–30).

When Jesus saw his mother there, and the disciple whom he loved standing nearby, he said to her, "Woman, here is your son" (John 19:26).

Then the morning Jesus came in from the shop early, his eyes firmer, his voice more direct. He had heard the news. "John is preaching in the desert." He took off his nail apron, dusted off his hands, and with one last look said goodbye to his mother. They both knew it would never be the same again. In that last look they shared a secret, the full extent of which was too painful to say aloud.

Mary learned that day the heartache that comes from saying goodbye. From then on she was to love her son from a distance, on the edge of the crowd, outside of a packed house, on the shore of the sea. Maybe she was even there when the enigmatic promise was made, "All those who have left . . . mother . . . to follow me."

1. Read Matthew 19:23–30. In this passage, Jesus tells the disciples how hard it is for a wealthy person to enter the kingdom of God. Why do you think that is?

_____

_____

_____

_____

Truly I tell you, it is hard for someone who is rich to enter the kingdom of heaven (Matthew 19:23).

2. Jesus then goes on to say the confusing, maybe even frightening, words of Matthew 19:29. How do Jesus' words about leaving family for his sake connect with his prior statement about a wealthy man not entering the kingdom of God?

_____

_____

_____

3. Jesus was saying that if we put our trust in riches or in people—even if that is our own family—we've missed the "eye of the needle." We've missed the key to the kingdom of God, which is trusting in him. Who or what do you find yourself tempted to trust in more than Christ?

_____

_____

_____

_____

It is easier for a camel to go through the eye of a needle than for someone who is rich to enter the kingdom of God (verse 24).

4. After spending thirty years together, Mary had to say goodbye to her oldest son when he began his public ministry. To watch him walk away was no doubt one of her hardest goodbyes. Have you ever had to say goodbye to someone or something for the sake of God's greater plan? If so, what was it? How did a greater good come out of it?

_____

_____

THE SON A MOTHER NEEDS

Still another said, "I will follow you, Lord; but first let me go back and say goodbye to my family." Jesus replied, "No one who puts a hand to the plow and looks back is fit for service in the kingdom of God" (Luke 9:61–62).

Mary wasn't the first one to be called to say goodbye to loved ones for the sake of the kingdom. Joseph was called to be an orphan in Egypt. Hannah sent her firstborn son away to serve in the temple. Daniel was sent from Jerusalem to Babylon. Abraham was sent to sacrifice his own son. The Bible is bound together with goodbye trails and stained with farewell tears.

In fact, it seems goodbye is all too prevalent in the Christian's vocabulary. Missionaries know it well. Those who send them know it too. The doctor who leaves the city to work in the jungle hospital has said it. So has the Bible translator who lives far from home. Those who feed the hungry, those who teach the lost, those who help the poor all know the word *goodbye*.

What kind of God would put people through such agony? What kind of God would give us families and then ask us to leave them? What kind of God would give us friends and then ask us to say goodbye to them?

A God who knows that the deepest love is built not on passion and romance but on a common mission and sacrifice. A God who knows that we are only pilgrims and that eternity is so close that any "goodbye" is in reality a "see you tomorrow." *A God who did it himself.*

"Woman, behold, your son!" (John 19:26 NASB).

[Jesus said] to the disciple, "Here is your mother." From that time on, this disciple took her into his home (John 19:27).

John fastened his arm around Mary a little tighter. Jesus was asking him to be the son that a mother needs and that in some ways he never was. Jesus looked at Mary. His ache was from a pain far greater than that of the nails and thorns. In their silent glance they again shared a secret. And he said goodbye.

5. As Christians, we, like Jesus, are called to sacrifice. Sometimes that means sacrificing time with people we love or the comforts of this world. What do the following passages tell us about the sacrifice that comes with following Jesus?

Luke 9:24: "Whoever wishes to save his life will lose it, but whoever loses his life for My sake, he is the one who will save it" (NASB).

_____

_____

_____

John 15:12–14: "This is my commandment: Love each other in the same way I have loved you. There is no greater love than to lay down one's life for one's friends. You are my friends if you do what I command" (NLT).

_____

_____

_____

Philippians 3:8: "Not only those things, but I think that all things are worth nothing compared with the greatness of knowing Christ Jesus my Lord. Because of him, I have lost all those things, and now I know they are worthless trash. This allows me to have Christ" (NCV).

Hebrews 13:16: "Make sure you don't take things for granted and go slack in working for the common good; share what you have with others. God takes particular pleasure in acts of worship—a different kind of 'sacrifice'—that take place in kitchen and workplace and on the streets" (MSG).

---

6. Any "goodbye" is in reality a "see you tomorrow." Read Paul's words in Philippians 3:20. According to this verse, how should we view our time here on earth?

Our citizenship is in heaven. And we eagerly await a Savior from there, the Lord Jesus Christ (Philippians 3:20).

---

7. How does seeing ourselves as "citizens of heaven" affect the way we hold on to people or possessions?

By faith he made his home in the promised land like a stranger in a foreign country (Hebrews 11:9).

---

8. From the day the angel announced the holy conception to Mary, she knew Jesus was not hers to claim. She knew she would have to say goodbye so that a greater glory could come. Take a moment to read about that greater glory in Romans 8:11. What promise does Paul say impregnates us because of Christ's agonizing death?

He who raised Christ from the dead will also give life to your mortal bodies (Romans 8:11).

The story of Mary in the Bible reveals just how close Christ will come to us. The first stop on his itinerary was a womb. Where will God go to touch the world? Look deep within Mary for an answer. Better still, look

Grow in the grace and knowledge of our Lord and Savior Jesus Christ (2 Peter 3:18).

deep within yourself. What he did with Mary, he offers to you! He issues a Mary-level invitation to all his children: "If you'll let me, I'll move in!"

Proliferating throughout Scripture is this preposition *in*. Jesus lives *in* his children. To his apostles, Christ declared, "I am in you" (John 14:20 NCV). Paul's prayer for the Ephesians was "that Christ may dwell in your hearts through faith" (3:17). John was clear that "the one who keeps God's commands live in him, and he in them" (1 John 3:24). The sweetest invitation comes from Christ: "If anyone hears my voice and opens the door, I will come in and eat with him, and he with me" (Revelation 3:20 ESV).

Christ grew in Mary until he had to come out. Christ will grow in you until the same occurs. He will come out in your speech, in your actions, in your decisions. Every place you live will be a Bethlehem, and every day you live will be a Christmas. You, like Mary, will deliver Christ into the world. God in us! Have we sounded the depth of this promise?

God was with Adam and Eve, walking with them in the cool of the evening.

God was with Abraham, even calling the patriarch his friend.

God was with Moses and the children of Israel. Parents could point their children to the fire by night and cloud by day; God is with us, they could assure.

Between the cherubim of the ark, in the glory of the temple, God was with his people. He was with the apostles. Peter could touch God's beard. John could watch God sleep. Multitudes could hear his voice. God was with them!

Do you not know that your bodies are temples of the Holy Spirit, who is in you, whom you have received from God? You are not your own; you were bought at a price (1 Corinthians 6:19–20).

But he is in you. You are a modern-day Mary. Even more so. He was a fetus in her, but he is a *force* in you. He will do what you cannot. Imagine a million dollars being deposited into your checking account. To any observer you look the same, except for the goofy smile, but are you? Not at all! With God in you, you have a million resources that you did not have before!

Can't stop drinking? Christ can. And he lives within you.

Can't stop worrying? Christ can. And he lives within you.

Can't forgive the jerk, forget the past, or forsake your bad habits? Christ can! And he lives within you.

Paul knew this. "For this purpose also I labor, striving according to His power, which mightily works within me" (Colossians 1:29 NASB).

Like Mary, you and I are indwelt by Christ.

⟿ POINTS TO REMEMBER ⟿

❖ Trusting in God means putting him before everything we hold dear.
❖ Sacrificing for the sake of Christ draws us into intimate relationship with him.
❖ Sacrificing in the name of Jesus is an act of worship that is pleasing to God.

❧ PRAYER FOR THE DAY ❧

*Thank you, Jesus, for the sacrifice you made on our behalf on the cross.
We are honored by your willingness to put our salvation before your
personal needs. May we face hardship and sacrifice for your sake with the
joy of knowing we are expressing our love and worship for you. Amen.*

❧ WEEKLY MEMORY VERSE ❧

*The Word became human and made his home among us.
He was full of unfailing love and faithfulness. And we have seen his glory,
the glory of the Father's one and only Son.*
JOHN 1:14 (NLT)

For Further Reading

Selections throughout this lesson were taken from *No Wonder They Call Him Savior* (Nashville: Thomas Nelson, 1986); *He Still Moves Stones* (Nashville: Thomas Nelson, 1993); *A Gentle Thunder* (Nashville: Thomas Nelson, 1995); *Next Door Savior* (Nashville: Thomas Nelson, 2003); *Max on Life* (Nashville: Thomas Nelson, 2010); *Before Amen* (Nashville: Thomas Nelson, 2014); and *More to Your Story* (Nashville: Thomas Nelson, 2016).

Notes
1. Earl Radmacher, Ronald B. Allen, H. Wayne House, eds., *Nelson's New Illustrated Bible Commentary* (Nashville: Thomas Nelson, 1999), p. 1250.
2. Ibid., p. 1315.

LESSON 6

THE SAMARITAN WOMAN

FROM OUTCAST TO EVANGELIST

I HAD DRIVEN BY THE PLACE COUNTLESS TIMES. Daily I passed the small plot of land on the way to my office. Daily I told myself, *Someday I need to stop there.*

Today, that "someday" came. I convinced a tight-fisted schedule to give me thirty minutes, and I drove in. The intersection appears no different from any other in San Antonio: a Burger King, a Rodeway Inn, a restaurant. But turn northwest, go under the cast-iron sign, and you will find yourself on an island of history that is holding its own against the river of progress.

The name on the sign? *Locke Hill Cemetery.*

As I parked, a darkened sky threatened rain. A lonely path invited me to walk through the two-hundred-plus tombstones. The fatherly oak trees arched above me, providing a ceiling for the solemn chambers. Tall grass, still wet from the morning dew, brushed my ankles.

The tombstones, though weathered and chipped, were alive with yesterday. *Ruhet in herrn* accents the markers that bear names like Schmidt, Faustman, Grundmeyer, and Eckert.

Ruth Lacey is buried there. She was born in the days of Napoleon. Died more than a century ago. I stood on the same spot where a mother wept on a cold day many decades past. The tombstone read simply, "Baby Boldt—Born and died December 10, 1910." Eighteen-year-old Harry Ferguson was laid to rest in 1883 under these words, "Sleep sweetly, tired young pilgrim." I wondered what wearied him so.

Then I saw it. It was chiseled into a tombstone on the northern end of the cemetery. The stone marks the destination of the body of Grace Llewellen Smith. No date of birth is listed, no date of death. Just the names of her two husbands, and this epitaph: "*Sleeps, but rests not. Loved, but was loved not. Tried to please, but pleased not. Died as she lived—alone.*"

I stared at the marker and wondered about Grace Llewellen Smith. I wondered about her life. I wondered if she'd written the words . . . or just lived them. I wondered if she deserved the pain. I wondered if she was bitter or beaten. I wondered if she was plain. I wondered if she was beautiful. I wondered why some lives are so fruitful while others are so futile.

I also wondered how many Grace Llewellen Smiths are out there. How many people will die in the loneliness in which they are living? The homeless in Atlanta. The happy-hour hopper in LA. A bag lady in Miami. The preacher in Nashville. Any person who doubts whether the world needs him. Any person who is convinced that no one really cares. Any person who has been given a ring, but never a heart; criticism, but never a chance; a bed, but never rest.

These are the victims of futility. And unless someone intervenes, unless something happens, the epitaph of Grace Smith will be theirs. That's why the story of the Samaritan woman told in John 4 is so significant. It's the story of another tombstone. But this time, the tombstone doesn't mark the death of a person—it marks the birth.

1. It's easy to read Grace Llewellen Smith's epitaph and feel pity for her, but the truth is that most of us have felt at least some of the sentiments on her gravestone at some point in our lives—*unlovable, lonely, failure, striving for acceptance, restless.* Which of the words on her gravestone do you relate to the most? Why?

   _____

   _____

   _____

   _____

2. Who or what intervened in your past feelings of loneliness, failure, rejection, or lack of peace? How have you intervened for someone else?

   _____

   _____

   _____

As we will see in the story of the Samaritan woman, our struggle for significance—and the feelings of futility that come when we look to others to fill our emptiness—are symptoms of our need for the Savior. Our basic human need to belong . . . to feel loved . . . can lead us into situations where we rely on people who don't deserve our trust or do things that ultimately destroy our self-worth. God created a hunger for significance within us, and it was his intention to have a relationship with us. Only when we turn to his Son, Jesus, and rely on him alone to meet our needs will we find the satisfaction our souls have been craving.

He satisfies the longing soul (Psalm 107:9 NKJV).

⟶ PRAYER FOR THE WEEK ⟵

Lord, we see our own inadequacy to meet our needs for significance and purpose. Thank you for wanting to have a relationship with us. Thank you for intervening and meeting our deepest needs through the Lord Jesus. We are grateful that you allow us to cling to you and that you are the solution for our emptiness. Amen.

Day One: A Woman on the Fringe

EXPECTATIONS CHANGED

Her eyes squint against the noonday sun. Her shoulders stoop under the weight of the water jar. Her feet trudge, stirring dust on the path. She keeps her eyes down so she can dodge the stares of the others.

She is a Samaritan; she knows the sting of racism. She is a woman; she's bumped her head on the ceiling of sexism. She's been married to five men. *Five.* Five different marriages. Five different beds. Five different rejections. She knows the sound of slamming doors.

She knows what it means to love and receive no love in return. Her current mate won't even give her his name. He only gives her a place to sleep. If there is a Grace Llewellen Smith in the New Testament, it is this woman. The epitaph of insignificance could have been hers. And it would have been, except for an encounter with a stranger.

On this particular day, she came to the well at noon. Why hadn't she gone in the early morning with the other women? Maybe she had. Maybe she just needed an extra draw of water on a hot day. Or maybe not. Maybe it was the other women she was avoiding. A walk in the hot sun was a small price to pay in order to escape their sharp tongues.

"Here she comes."

"Have you heard? She's got a new man!"

"They say she'll sleep with anyone."

"Shhh. There she is."

So she came to the well at noon. She expected silence. She expected solitude. Instead, she found one who knew her better than she knew herself.

Jesus learned that the Pharisees had heard that he was gaining and baptizing more disciples than John—although in fact it was not Jesus who baptized, but his disciples. So he left Judea and went back once more to Galilee. Now he had to go through Samaria. So he came to a town in Samaria called Sychar, near the plot of ground Jacob had given to his son Joseph. Jacob's well was there (John 4:1–6).

1. Read the beginning of the Samaritan woman's story in John 4:1–14. What are some of the key characteristics you observe about her in this passage?

_____

_____

_____

It was about the sixth hour (John 4:6 NKJV).

2. In verse 6 we read that this story took place at the "sixth hour," which was noon. Customarily, women would draw water when the sun was not high in the sky, yet here we see the Samaritan woman drawing water during the heat of the day. Why did she do this? In what ways can you relate to her desire to avoid the "water drawing hour"?

_____

_____

_____

_____

The Samaritan woman said to him, "You are a Jew and I am a Samaritan woman. How can you ask me for a drink?" (For Jews do not associate with Samaritans) (verse 9).

3. What does John tell us in verse 9 about the relationship between the Jews and Samaritans? What does the fact that later Jesus' disciples were "surprised to find him talking with a woman" tell you about male and female relations at the time?

_____

_____

_____

_____

4. The Samaritan woman had experienced the sting of racism, had been forced to deal with sexism, and knew what it meant to love but receive no love in return. Which of these can you relate to the most in your life? Why?

_____

_____

_____

_____

LIVING WATER

Jesus, tired as he was from the journey, sat down by the well (verse 6).

He was seated on the ground: legs outstretched, hands folded, back resting against the well. His eyes were closed. She stopped and looked at him. She looked around. No one was near. She looked back at him. He was obviously Jewish. What was he doing here? His eyes opened and hers ducked in embarrassment. She went quickly about her task.

Maybe it was the bags under her eyes or the way she stooped that made Jesus forget how weary he was. *How strange that she should be here at midday*. He sensed her discomfort at seeing him there and asked for water. But she was too streetwise to think that all he wanted was a drink. "Since when does an uptown fellow like you ask a girl like me for water?" She wanted to know what he really had in mind. Her intuition was partly correct. He was interested in more than water. He was interested in her heart.

They talked. Who could remember the last time a man had spoken to her with respect?

He told her about a spring of water that would quench not the thirst of the throat but of the soul. He told her, "The water I give will become a spring of water gushing up inside that person, giving eternal life" (John 4:14 NCV). Jesus offered this woman not a singular drink of water but a perpetual artesian well!

Shortly after this event, Jesus would proclaim to the people, "Let anyone who is thirsty come to me and drink" (7:37 NCV). Some of the most incredible invitations are found in the pages of the Bible. You can't read about God without finding him issuing invitations. He invited Eve to marry Adam, the animals to enter the ark, David to be king, Mary to birth his Son, the disciples to fish for men, the adulterous woman to start over, and Thomas to touch his wounds.

God is a God who invites. God is a God who calls. God is a God who opens the door and waves his hand, pointing pilgrims to a full table. God is a God who quenches people's thirst. But his invitation is not just for a meal or a cup of water. It is for *life*. An invitation to come into his kingdom and take up residence in a tearless, graveless, painless world.

Who can come? As the story of the Samaritan woman at the well reveals, whoever wishes to do so. The invitation is at once universal and personal.

5. In John 4:9 we learn that the Samaritan woman is hesitant to speak with Jesus. Describe a time when your own shame made you hesitant to speak with Jesus.

_____

_____

_____

_____

6. Why do you think Jesus asked the Samaritan woman for a drink? Was he just seeking to quench his thirst, or do think there was a greater purpose behind his request?

_____

_____

_____

_____

When a Samaritan woman came to draw water, Jesus said to her, "Will you give me a drink?" (John 4:7).

Let anyone who is thirsty come to me and drink. Whoever believes in me, as Scripture has said, rivers of living water will flow from within them (7:37–38).

The Son of Man came to seek and to save the lost (Luke 19:10).

If you knew the gift of God and who it is that asks you for a drink, you would have asked him and he would have given you living water (John 4:10).

7. After Jesus asks the woman for water, he tells her that she should be the one asking him for water. How does Jesus describe this water (see verses 10 and 14)?

_____
_____
_____
_____
_____

With joy you will draw water from the wells of salvation (Isaiah 12:3).

8. Read John 7:37–39 and Isaiah 12:3. Based on these passages of Scripture, what does "living water" represent? What was the real invitation Jesus was offering the woman? How has Jesus given you life that is like living water?

_____
_____
_____
_____
_____

Blessed are those who hunger and thirst for righteousness, for they will be filled (Matthew 5:6).

The thirst of the Samaritan woman in the heat of the day reflected the thirst of her soul in the heat of her shame. She had gone from one man to the next. Maybe she had been forced to do so. Maybe she was destitute. Or maybe her soul was thirsty. Perhaps she was desperate for love, desperate for stability, desperate for . . . life. Each of us can relate to her plight. Our souls are thirsty, and yet we turn to food, drink, and the things of this world to fulfill that desire—but those things never satisfy. Instead, we must let Jesus' invitation to the woman be an invitation for us. Only he can satisfy our deepest thirst, for in him is life, real living-water life.

❧ POINTS TO REMEMBER ❧

❖ The barriers that get in the way of us reaching for God do not keep him from reaching out to us.
❖ Jesus treats us with respect and meets us where we are—in our sin and in our emptiness.
❖ Jesus personally invites us to an abundant life in his kingdom . . . but we must accept his invitation and surrender our lives to him.

❧ PRAYER FOR THE DAY ❧

Jesus, thank you for the invitation of salvation. Thank you that your Spirit fills us and flows through us like living water. Forgive us when we turn to other people or things for satisfaction, for we know that only in you are we quenched. We love you. Amen.

Day Two: A Life Revealed

BEHIND THE MASK

The Samaritan woman was certainly intrigued by Jesus' offer. "Sir," she said, "give me this water so that I won't get thirsty and have to keep coming here to draw water."

"Go, call your husband and come back."

Her heart must have sunk. Here was a Jew who didn't care if she was a Samaritan. Here was a man who didn't look down on her as a woman. Here was the closest thing to gentleness she'd ever seen. And now he was asking her about . . . *that*.

Anything but that. Maybe she considered lying. "Oh, my husband? He's busy." Maybe she wanted to change the subject. Perhaps she wanted to leave—but she stayed. And she told the truth. "I have no husband." (Kindness has a way of inviting honesty.)

You probably know the rest of the story. I wish you didn't. I wish you were hearing it for the first time. For if you were, you'd be wide-eyed as you waited to see what Jesus would do next. Why? Because you've wanted to do the same thing.

You've wanted to take off your mask. You've wanted to stop pretending. You've wondered what God would do if you opened your cobweb-covered door of secret sin.

This woman wondered what Jesus would do. She must have wondered if the kindness would cease when the truth was revealed. *He will be angry. He will leave. He will think I'm worthless.* If you've had the same anxieties, then get out your pencil. You'll want to underline Jesus' answer.

"You're right. You have had five husbands and the man you are with now won't even give you a name."

No criticism? No anger? No what-kind-of-mess-have-you-made-of-your-life lectures? No. It wasn't perfection that Jesus was seeking; it was honesty.

1. Read John 4:15–18. Why do you think Jesus asked the Samaritan woman to call her husband, given the fact he knew every detail about her?

_____

_____

_____

_____

_____

The woman said to him, "Sir, give me this water so that I won't get thirsty and have to keep coming here to draw water." He told her, "Go, call your husband and come back." "I have no husband," she replied (John 4:15–17).

Jesus said to her . . . "You have had five husbands, and the man you now have is not your husband" (verses 17–18).

2. How did Jesus respond to the woman when she said that she had no husband? How did his words speak truth to her rather than condemnation?

_____

_____

_____

Therefore, there is now no condemnation for those who are in Christ Jesus, because through Christ Jesus the law of the Spirit who gives life has set you free from the law of sin and death (Romans 8:1–2).

3. In Romans 8:1 Paul states, "There is therefore now no condemnation for those who are in Christ Jesus" (NRSV). What does this truth tell you about how Jesus sees you? Do you have an easy time or a hard time accepting this truth? Explain.

_____

_____

_____

4. Is there a sin in your life you have held back because of your fear of God's reaction? If so, what do you feel Jesus is calling you to do today to expose that sin to the light?

_____

_____

_____

A GAPING HOLE

"Sir," the woman said, "I can see that you are a prophet. Our ancestors worshiped on this mountain, but you Jews claim that the place where we must worship is in Jerusalem" (John 4:19–20).

The woman was amazed. "I can see that you are a prophet," she said. Translation? "There is something different about you. Do you mind if I ask you something?"

Then she asked a question that revealed the gaping hole in her soul. "Where is God? My people say he is on the mountain. Your people say he is in Jerusalem. I don't know where he is."

I'd give a thousand sunsets to see the expression on Jesus' face as he heard those words. Did his eyes water? Did he smile? Did he look up into the clouds and wink at his Father? Of all the places to find a hungry heart . . . *Samaria.*

Talk about a wall, ancient and tall. "Jews," John wrote in his Gospel, "refuse to have anything to do with Samaritans" (John 4:9 NLT). It's why the woman had said to Jesus, "I am surprised that you ask me for a drink, since you are a Jewish man and I am a Samaritan woman" (NCV). The two cultures had hated each other for a thousand years. The feud involved claims of defection, intermarriage, and disloyalty to the temple.

Hatred stirs up conflict, but love covers over all wrongs (Proverbs 10:12).

The Samaritans had been blacklisted by the Jews. Their beds, utensils—even their spittle—were considered unclean. No orthodox Jew would travel into the region. Most Jews would gladly double the length of their trips rather than go through Samaria.

Jesus, however, played by a different set of rules. He spent the better part of a day on the turf of a Samaritan woman, drinking water from her ladle, discussing her questions. He stepped across the cultural taboo as if it were a sleeping dog in the doorway.

Why did he do this? Because he loves to break down walls.

5. Read John 4:19–24. When the Israelites were in the wilderness, they worshiped in a movable tent called the tabernacle. When Israel became a nation, Solomon built a fixed temple in Jerusalem, and it became the location where the people would worship. Read Numbers 9:15–17 and 2 Chronicles 6:41–7:1. Why would the Jews and the Samaritans associate the place of worship with God's presence?

Fire came down from heaven and consumed the burnt offering and the sacrifices, and the glory of the LORD filled the temple (2 Chronicles 7:1).

_____

_____

_____

_____

6. After Assyria conquered the nation of Israel, the Jews who survived began to marry Gentiles in the surrounding nations. These racially mixed Jews were the Samaritans, and "pure" Jews wanted nothing to do with them and would not allow them to worship in the temple. So the Samaritans built a separate temple. To what can you compare this scene today? How have you seen hatred divide the church in our time?

The king of Assyria brought people from Babylon, Kuthah, Avva, Hamath and Sepharvaim and settled them in the towns of Samaria to replace the Israelites (2 Kings 17:24).

_____

_____

_____

_____

7. The woman's question about the place of worship revealed her search for the presence of God. Little did she know that the presence of God was not bound by the walls of humankind. Read Acts 7:48–50. What does this passage say about the presence of God?

Heaven is my throne, and the earth is my footstool (Acts 7:49).

_____

_____

_____

8. Jesus said, "A time is coming and has now come when the true worshipers will worship the Father in the Spirit and in truth" (John 4:23). What did Jesus mean? How would the Samaritan woman embody the type of worshiper God was seeking?

_____

_____

_____

_____

Your beauty should not come from outward adornment . . . [but] that of your inner self, the unfading beauty of a gentle and quiet spirit, which is of great worth in God's sight (1 Peter 3:3–4).

The Samaritan woman lived in a world where the exterior was elevated higher than the interior. Her physical appearance, her physical relationships with men, the physical place she worshiped . . . all these things are what others judged, because that's what they thought mattered the most. But Jesus saw things differently. He saw past her exterior and through her relationships with men—and he rebuked the worshipers who were caught up with *where* they worshiped instead of *whom* they worshiped. Jesus didn't come to condemn people's exteriors but to transform their interiors. He was in search of worshipers who had interiors soft enough for this transformation. The Samaritan woman's humble honesty and search for God revealed that she was ready for this transformation. Little did she know that her heart was primed for true worship—a worship led by the Spirit of Jesus and fixed on his truth.

POINTS TO REMEMBER

- ❖ Jesus knows our condition, speaks the truth about our situation, and extends kindness to us without condemnation.
- ❖ Jesus calls us to expose our sin to the light so we can find healing and transformation in him.
- ❖ Jesus loves to break down walls that keep us from him and from each other.

PRAYER FOR THE DAY

Lord, we know that nothing is hidden from you. Thank you for bringing our sins to the light and for extending your grace, mercy, and forgiveness to us when we fall short of your standard. We praise you, God, for your love and kindness. We praise you for accepting us even in our sinful condition and for meeting us right where we are. Amen.

Nothing in all creation is hidden from God's sight (Hebrews 4:13).

Day Three: The Walls That Divide

WALLS IN OUR WORLD

The story of the Samaritan woman forces us to ask if any walls bisect *our* world. If there are any places in our lives in which we stand on one side, and on the other stands . . . the person we've learned to disregard, perhaps even disdain. Or the teen with the tats. Or the boss with the bucks. Or the immigrant with the hard-to-understand accent. Or that person who stands on the opposite side of your political fence. Or maybe even the beggar who sits outside our church door every week.

During Jesus' ministry, we see that he often sought to break down the walls that divided people. In fact, it was the topic of one of his best-known parables. Here's how we might tell it today. One day, an affluent white was driving home from his downtown office. Since the hour was late and he was tired, he took the direct route, which led through the roughest part of the city. Wouldn't you know it—he ran out of gas. As the man was walking to the convenience store, he was mugged and left for dead on the sidewalk.

A few minutes later, a preacher drove by on the way to an evening church service. He saw the man on the sidewalk and started to help, but then he realized it would be too dangerous to stop. Soon after, a respected seminary professor came by and saw the man. But he too decided it was best not to get involved. Finally, a Hispanic immigrant driving a beat-up truck saw the man, stopped, and took him to the hospital. He paid the bill and went on his way.

A man was going down from Jerusalem to Jericho, when he was attacked by robbers. They stripped him of his clothes, beat him and went away, leaving him half dead (Luke 10:30).

1. How many barriers—both cultural and spiritual—do you see Jesus breaking down to reach this Samaritan woman?

_____

_____

_____

_____

A priest happened to be going down the same road, and when he saw the man, he passed by on the other side. So too, a Levite, when he came to the place and saw him, passed by on the other side (verses 31–32).

2. Read Luke 10:30–37. What barriers between people did Jesus challenge in this story?

_____

_____

_____

But a Samaritan, as he traveled, came where the man was; and when he saw him, he took pity on him (verse 33).

3. Who were the men who passed by the injured man without stopping? Why do you think they just passed him by?

_____

_____

_____

_____

4. What did the Samaritan do "above and beyond" to show the love of God to the injured man in spite of their cultural differences?

_____

_____

_____

Then he put the man on his own donkey, brought him to an inn and took care of him (verse 34).

No Excuse for Prejudice

[Jesus asked,] "Which of these three do you think was a neighbor to the man who fell into the hands of robbers?" The expert in the law replied, "The one who had mercy on him" (Luke 10:36–37).

I altered the characters but not Jesus' question: "Which . . . was a neighbor to the man?" (Luke 10:36). The answer? The man who responded with kindness. Neighborliness, then, is not defined by where we live but how we love. Our neighbor is not just the person in the next house but the one who needs our help. Our neighbor may be the person we've been taught not to love. For the Jew in the days of Jesus, it was a Samaritan.

For an Israeli today, it is a Palestinian. For an Arab, a Jew. For a black male, how about a pickup-driving, gun-toting, tobacco-chewing, ballcap-wearing redneck? For the Hispanic poor, how about the Hispanic affluent?

Jesus' story about the Good Samaritan and his interaction with the woman at the well show us that Christians have no excuse for prejudice. The prejudice of pagans can be explained, but in the case of a Christian, there is no explanation. No justification. We will never cross a cultural barrier greater than the one Jesus did. He learned our language, lived in our world, ate our food . . . but most of all, took on our sins.

We love because he first loved us (1 John 4:19).

Given this, how can we, who have been loved so much, not do the same for others? Those who find it hard to reach across racial differences should think twice. Unless they are Jews, a foreigner died on the cross for their sins.

5. It is tragic that the men who refused to help in Jesus' parable were the ones who were seen at the time as being the most religious. What is the difference between being religious and being a neighbor to others? How do people in the church today fall into the same trap of building up walls that divide?

_____

_____

_____

_____

We, who are many, are one body (1 Corinthians 10:17).

6. Read 1 Corinthians 10:16–17. Sometimes the thickest walls are within the church—the barriers that exist between believers. How have you seen division within the church? How does Paul say we should view others in the body of Christ?

_____

_____

_____

7. Who is someone (or even a group of people) whom you have a hard time viewing as your "neighbor"? What makes it so difficult to see them that way?

_____

_____

_____

8. Read John 1:1–14. What barriers did Jesus break to get to you? How can knowing he was willing to do this help you embrace your enemies as neighbors?

_____
_____
_____
_____
_____
_____
_____

He was in the world, and though the world was made through him, the world did not recognize him (John 1:10).

The wall between heaven and earth? Shattered. The wall between God and humans? Demolished. The wall between holiness and sin? Destroyed. Jesus was in the business of destroying anything that stood in the way of unity. When we build walls of prejudice between one another, not only are we separating people from people, but we are also separating people from God's truth. Jesus prayed, "The glory which You have given Me I have given to them, that they may be one, just as We are one; I in them and You in Me, that they may be perfected in unity, so that the world may know that You sent Me, and loved them, even as You have loved Me" (John 17:22–23 NASB). Struggling with unity? Struggling with seeing someone as your neighbor? Then look back at Jesus' prayer. We are one with Jesus. He is in us. So we can ask him to pick up the mallet and break down any judgment in our hearts. It's demolition time!

Strive for full restoration, encourage one another, be of one mind, live in peace (2 Corinthians 13:11).

❧ POINTS TO REMEMBER ❧

❖ Jesus seeks to break down the cultural and spiritual walls that divide people.
❖ Neighborliness is not defined by where we live but how we love.
❖ Those who have experienced the love of Christ must show that same love to others—believers in Jesus have no excuse for prejudice.

❧ PRAYER FOR THE DAY ❧

Thank you, God, for loving us so much that you broke down the wall to find us in our lost state and redeem us through the sacrifice of your Son, Jesus. We pray that you will help us to break down any walls we have set up in our hearts that keep us from loving those you died to redeem. Help us to be your light in a dark world that needs you. In Jesus' name, amen.

Let your light shine before others (Matthew 5:16).

Day Four: A Life Forever Changed

THE MESSIAH REVEALED

"Woman," Jesus replied, "believe me, a time is coming when you will worship the Father neither on this mountain nor in Jerusalem. You Samaritans worship what you do not know; we worship what we do know, for salvation is from the Jews. Yet a time is coming and has now come when the true worshipers will worship the Father in the Spirit and in truth, for they are the kind of worshipers the Father seeks. God is spirit, and his worshipers must worship in the Spirit and in truth" (John 4:21–24).

"Where is God?" the Samaritan woman had asked. "I don't know where he is."

Jesus replied, "You Samaritans worship something you don't understand. . . . The time is coming when the true worshipers will worship the Father in spirit and truth, and that time is here already" (John 4:22–23 NCV)

"I know that the Messiah is coming," the woman replied. "When the Messiah comes, he will explain everything to us."

Jesus' response? "I am he—I, the one talking to you" (verses 25–26 NCV).

Just think about this for a moment. Of all the people God could have chosen to personally receive the secret of the ages, he chose to give it do a five-time divorcée Samaritan. An outcast among outcasts. The most "insignificant" person in the region.

Remarkable. Jesus didn't reveal the secret to King Herod. He didn't request an audience of the Sanhedrin and tell them the news. It wasn't within the colonnades of a Roman court that he announced his identity. No, it was in the shade of a well in a rejected land to an ostracized woman. His eyes must have danced as he whispered the secret.

"I am the Messiah."

The most important phrase in the chapter is one easily overlooked. "Then, leaving her water jar, the woman went back to the town and said to the people, 'Come, see a man who told me everything I ever did. Could this be the Messiah?'" (verses 28–29).

The woman said, "I know that Messiah . . . is coming. When he comes, he will explain everything to us" (verse 25).

1. Read John 4:25–29. What does the Samaritan woman say the Messiah will do (see verse 25)? How do you see Jesus already fulfilling this in her personal life?

   _____

   _____

   _____

2. What is the woman's reaction to Jesus telling her he is the Messiah?

   _____

   _____

   _____

3. How do you see the Samaritan woman transform from the beginning of the story to the end in verse 29? What does this say about the grace of Christ?

_____

_____

_____

"I will restore you to health and heal your wounds," declares the LORD, "because you are called an outcast" (Jeremiah 30:17).

4. How have you recently experienced the Messiah's transformation in your own life?

_____

_____

_____

INSIGNIFICANCE LEFT BEHIND

Don't miss the drama of the moment. Look at her eyes, wide with amazement. Listen to her as she struggles for words. "Y-y-y-you . . . a-a-a-are . . . the . . . M-m-m-messiah!" Watch as she scrambles to her feet, takes one last look at this grinning Nazarene, then turns and runs right into the burly chest of Peter. She almost falls, regains her balance, and hotfoots it toward her hometown.

Then Jesus declared, "I, the one speaking to you— I am he" (John 4:26).

Did you notice what she forgot? She forgot her water jar. She left behind the jug that had caused the sag in her shoulders. She left behind the burden she brought. Suddenly the shame of the tattered romances disappeared. Suddenly the insignificance of her life was swallowed by the significance of the moment.

Leaving her water jar, the woman went back to the town (verse 28).

"God is here! God has come! God cares . . . for me!" That is why she forgot her water jar. That is why she ran to the city. That is why she grabbed the first person she saw and announced her discovery: "I just talked to a man who knows everything I ever did . . . and he loves me anyway!"

Come, see a man who told me everything I ever did. Could this be the Messiah? (verse 29).

The disciples offered Jesus some food. He refused it—he was too excited! He had just done what he does best. He had taken a life that was drifting and given it direction. He was exuberant!

"My food," said Jesus, "is to do the will of him who sent me and to finish his work" (verse 34).

"Look!" he announced to the disciples, pointing at the woman who was running to the village. "Vast fields of human souls are ripening all around us, and are ready now for reaping" (verse 35 TLB).

Who could eat at a time like this?

5. Read John 4:30–34. The Samaritan woman had left behind the jug that had caused the "sag in her shoulders" and now ran with her head held high. She was a new woman! What "water jug" is God asking you to leave behind so that you can also embrace your new identity in Christ? How will you start to embrace that new identity?

_____

_____

_____

Whatever you do, work at it with all your heart, as working for the Lord, not for human masters, since you know that you will receive an inheritance from the Lord as a reward (Colossians 3:23–24).

6. The insignificance of the woman's life was swallowed by the significance of the moment. In Colossians 3:23 Paul writes, "Work willingly at whatever you do, as though you were working for the Lord rather than for people" (NLT). How does following Christ bring significance into every circumstance?

_____

_____

_____

_____

_____

7. The woman was so overcome by Jesus that she could not contain her excitement. She had to tell the whole town about the Messiah! When was the last time you were so excited about the grace of Jesus that you had to tell someone? What things tend to get in the way of basking in the wonder of his grace each day?

_____

_____

_____

_____

_____

He said to them, "I have food to eat that you know nothing about." Then his disciples said to each other, "Could someone have brought him food?" (John 4:32–33).

8. What was the disciples' question when they found Jesus at the well? What did Jesus mean when he said his food was "to do the will of him who sent me" (verse 34)?

_____

_____

_____

_____

_____

When the Messiah reveals himself to us, he also reveals who we really are. He tells us that because he is love, we are loved. He tells us that because he is merciful, we are forgiven. He tells us that because he is significant, our lives matter. The Samaritan woman had been hiding behind her shame, but now she boldly proclaimed, "Come, see a man who told me everything I ever did" (John 4:29). How could she share her shame with excitement? Because her shame didn't own her anymore. Jesus didn't condemn her, so she wasn't condemning herself. Instead, she was so focused on Jesus that her reputation no longer had any power over her. What a beautiful reminder that we, too, are not defined or owned by our sin. When we meet the Messiah, we meet our true selves—sons and daughters of God.

You have been born again, not of perishable seed, but of imperishable (1 Peter 1:23).

☙ POINTS TO REMEMBER ☙

❖ When we encounter Jesus, he lifts the burden of sin and shame from our lives.

❖ Knowing who Jesus is—our Messiah and Lord—transforms who we are.

❖ God rejoices when he sees a life transformed by his grace, and he asks us to reach out to others so they may experience that grace as well.

☙ PRAYER FOR THE DAY ☙

We praise you, Lord, for your power to transform our lives. Our sin and shame are washed away by your love and forgiveness! May we share the excitement of what you have done for us with others who need to meet the Messiah. In your name, amen.

Day Five: The Unlikely Messenger

WHEN GOD INTERVENES

When we think of the individuals God uses to bring his message to the world, we rarely think of people like the woman at the well. No, we think of men like William Carey, who founded a missionary society and worked to bring the gospel to India. Or we think of men like David Livingstone or Hudson Taylor, who spent their lives reaching the lost in Africa and China. Or even Mother Teresa, who tirelessly ministered to the poor in the slums of Calcutta, India.

No, people like the woman at the well do not rise to the top of the list. After all, she had some major strikes against her. Number one, discrimination. She was a Samaritan, hated by Jews. Number two, gender bias. She was a female, condescended to by the men. Third, she was a divorcée—not once, not twice. Let's see if we can count. Four? Five? Five marriages turned south, and now she was sharing a bed with a guy who wouldn't give her a ring.

When we add this up, we don't envision an evangelist as much as a happy-hour stool sitter who lives with her mad at half boil. Husky voice, cigarette breath, and a dress cut low at the top and high at the bottom. Certainly not Samaria's finest. Certainly not the woman you would put in charge of the Ladies' Bible Class.

Which makes the fact that Jesus did just that all the more surprising. Jesus didn't just put her in charge of the class—he put her in charge of

Anyone who believes in him will never be put to shame (Romans 10:11).

You did not choose me, but I chose you and appointed you so that you might go and bear fruit (John 15:16).

139

evangelizing *the whole town*. Before the day was over, the entire city had heard about a man who claimed to be God. "He told me everything I ever did" (John 4:39 NCV), she tells them.

She leaves unsaid the obvious: "And he loved me anyway."

I sent you to reap what you have not worked for. Others have done the hard work, and you have reaped the benefits of their labor (John 4:38).

1. Read John 4:35–42. The story of the Samaritan woman shows us that when God intervenes, he takes those the world might consider insignificant and gives them significant tasks. Look at Jesus' words in verse 38. What is the significant task that God calls each of us to do?

They came out of the town and made their way toward him (verse 30).

2. The Samaritan woman used just a few simple words to draw the townspeople to Jesus: "Come, see a Man who told me all things that I ever did. Could this be the Christ?" (verse 29 NKJV). What was the people's response to this simple testimony?

3. In what ways do you see yourself as a missionary for Christ? What does the story of the Samaritan woman tell us about the kinds of people God uses to spread the gospel?

Come and hear, all you who fear God; let me tell you what he has done for me (Psalm 66:16).

4. The Samaritan woman's approach to evangelism was simple. No frills, no memorized speeches, no deep-discussion theology—she just told people what Jesus did in her life. What is your story of God's grace that you can share with others? Write down your simple Samaritan woman-type testimony below.

No Lists

A little rain can straighten a flower stem. A little love can change a life. Who knew the last time this woman had been entrusted with anything, much less the biggest news in history! But this is exactly what Jesus does. And when we read John 4:39, we make this startling discovery: "Many of the Samaritans in that town believed in Jesus because of what the woman said" (NCV).

The people even begged Jesus to stay with them because they were so hungry to hear the message of God's love. So Jesus stayed with them two more days, and many Samaritans came to believe in him. Later, they would give this testimony to the woman at the well: "First we believed in Jesus because of what you said, but now we believe because we heard him ourselves. We know that this man really is the Savior of the world" (verses 42–43 NCV).

The woman at the well was Jesus' first missionary! She preceded the more noted names of gospel-spreaders like Peter, John, Stephen, Philip, Barnabas, Silas, and Paul that we read about in the Gospels and the book of Acts. The lineage of these early evangelists—and even later leaders like Patrick and Francis of Assisi—can all be traced back to this town trollop who was so overwhelmed by Christ that she had to speak.

The Samaritan woman's life was forever changed over this encounter with Christ. Why? Not just because of what Jesus did, though that was huge. Rather, it was because she let him do it. She let him see the rubbish in her life. She let him love her. She let him change her. She let him fill her with truth and grace. She and Zacchaeus and the apostle Paul and the woman in Capernaum and millions of others since have invited him into the hold of their hearts.

All of us can relate in some way to the Samaritan woman. Maybe, like her, we have a list of "strikes" against us and we can't see how God would ever use us. But the good news is that God doesn't keep a list of our wrongs. King David knew what he was saying when he wrote, "[God] has not punished us as our sins should be punished; he has not repaid us for the evil we have done" (Psalm 103:10 NCV). And he meant it when he prayed, "LORD, if you kept a record of our sins, who, O Lord, could ever survive?" (130:3 NLT).

You have not been sprinkled with forgiveness. You have not been spattered with grace. You have not been dusted with kindness. You have been *immersed* in it. You are submerged in mercy. You are a minnow in the ocean of his mercy. So let it change you! See if God's love doesn't do for you what it did for the woman in Samaria.

5. Why do you think Jesus chose the woman at the well to be his first missionary? What things in her made her a very unlikely candidate for this role?

_____
_____
_____
_____

Many of the Samaritans from that town believed in him because of the woman's testimony, "He told me everything I ever did." So when the Samaritans came to him, they urged him to stay with them, and he stayed two days. And because of his words many more became believers (John 4:39–41).

In the last days, God says, I will pour out my Spirit on all people (Acts 2:17).

You were once darkness, but now you are light in the Lord. Live as children of light (Ephesians 5:8).

6. The Samaritan woman allowed Jesus to see the rubbish in her life—and then allowed him to love her and change her. What keeps you from "allowing" Christ to change you?

_____

_____

_____

_____

7. The Father never keeps records of our wrongs, but we have a tendency to keep records of the wrongs of others. Do you struggle with keeping a list of wrongs? If so, why do you think you tend to hold on to those things?

_____

_____

_____

_____

Be kind and compassionate to one another, forgiving each other, just as in Christ God forgave you (4:32).

8. Read Ephesians 4:32 and 5:1–2. What does Paul call us to do in these verses? Who is someone you need to forgive as Christ has forgiven you? (Maybe that someone is you.) What steps will you take today to start ripping up any list of wrongs you've kept?

_____

_____

_____

_____

For some of us, the story of the Samaritan woman is touching but distant. We belong. We are needed, and we know it. We've got more friends than we can visit and more tasks than we can accomplish. Insignificance will not be chiseled on our tombstone like it was for Grace Llewellen Smith. Our epitaph will never read, *"Sleeps, but rests not. Loved, but was loved not. Tried to please, but pleased not. Died as she lived—alone."*

Be thankful.

But others among us are different. The story of the Samaritan woman resonates with us because it is our own. We see her face when we look into the mirror. We know why she was avoiding people . . . because we do the same thing. We know what it's like to have no one sit by us at the cafeteria. We've wondered what it would be like to have one good friend. We've been in love, and we wonder if it is worth the pain to do it again.

And like the Samaritan woman, we have also wondered where in the world God is.

God has said, "Never will I leave you; never will I forsake you" (Hebrews 13:5).

I had a friend named Joy who taught underprivileged children in an inner-city church. Her class was a lively group of nine-year-olds who loved life and weren't afraid of God. There was one exception, however——a timid girl by the name of Barbara.

Her difficult home life had left her afraid and insecure. For the weeks that my friend was teaching the class, Barbara never spoke. Never. While the other children talked, she sat. While the others sang, she was silent. While the others giggled, she was quiet. Always present. Always listening. Always speechless.

Until the day Joy gave a class on heaven. Joy talked about seeing God. She talked about tearless eyes and deathless lives. Barbara was fascinated. She wouldn't release Joy from her stare. She listened with hunger. Then she raised her hand. "Mrs. Joy?"

Joy was stunned. Barbara had never asked a question. "Yes, Barbara?"

"Is heaven for girls like me?"

Again, I would have given a thousand sunsets to have seen Jesus' face as this tiny prayer reached his throne. For indeed that is what it was—a prayer! An earnest prayer that a good God in heaven would remember a forgotten soul on earth. A prayer that God's grace would seep into the cracks and cover one whom the church had let slip through. A prayer to take a life that no one else could use and use it as no one else could.

The story of the Samaritan woman shows us how God answers these prayers. It shows us the lengths he will go to reach us where we are and remove the rubbish in our lives. It shows us that he can use us in spite of our past. For if he can take a rejected woman and make her into a missionary, he can do the same with us.

Then he said, "Jesus, remember me when you come into your kingdom." Jesus answered him, "Truly I tell you, today you will be with me in paradise" (Luke 23:42–43).

❧ POINTS TO REMEMBER ❧

❖ God takes those the world calls insignificant and gives them significant tasks.

❖ When we are immersed in God's love, it changes us and gives us a new identity that others will notice.

❖ Our mission is simple: to tell others what Jesus has done in our lives.

❧ PRAYER FOR THE DAY ❧

Jesus, thank you for the story of the Samaritan woman. Just as you gave her life significance, you give us significance. What a gift. Help us to share your truth with others so that they can also find purpose through you. Amen.

❧ WEEKLY MEMORY VERSE ❧

Whoever drinks of the water that I will give him will never be thirsty again. The water that I will give him will become in him a spring of water welling up to eternal life.
JOHN 4:14 (ESV)

For Further Reading

Selections throughout this lesson were taken from *No Wonder They Call Him Savior* (Nashville: Thomas Nelson, 1986); *And the Angels Were Silent* (Nashville: Thomas Nelson, 1987); *He Chose the Nails* (Nashville: Thomas Nelson, 2000); *A Love Worth Giving* (Nashville: Thomas Nelson, 2002); *Six Hours One Friday* (Nashville: Thomas Nelson, 2004); *Max on Life* (Nashville: Thomas Nelson, 2010); and *Outlive Your Life* (Nashville: Thomas Nelson, 2010).

THE CANAANITE WOMAN

WHEN GREAT FAITH MEETS GREAT ACTION

I HAVE A SKETCH OF JESUS LAUGHING. It hangs on the wall right across from my desk.

It's quite a drawing. His head is back. His mouth is open. His eyes are sparkling. He isn't just grinning. He isn't just chuckling. He's roaring. He hasn't heard or seen one like that in quite a while. He's having trouble catching his breath.

It was given to me by an Episcopal priest who carries cigars in his pocket and collects portraits of Jesus smiling. "I give them to anyone who might be inclined to take God too seriously," he explained as he handed me the gift.

He pegged me well.

I'm not one who easily envisions a smiling God. A weeping God, yes. An angry God, okay. A mighty God, you bet. But a chuckling God? It seems too . . . too . . . too unlike what God should do—and be. Which just shows how much I know—or don't know—about God.

What do I think he was doing when he stretched the neck of the giraffe? An exercise in engineering? What do I think he had in mind when he told the ostrich where to put his head? Spelunking? What do I think he was doing when he designed the mating call of an ape? Or the eight legs of the octopus? And what do I envision on his face when he saw Adam's first glance at Eve? A yawn?

As a bridegroom rejoices over his bride, so will your God rejoice over you (Isaiah 62:5).

The LORD God made a woman . . . and he brought her to the man (Genesis 2:22).

145

Hardly.

As my vision improves and I'm able to read without my stained glasses, I'm seeing that a sense of humor is perhaps the only way God has put up with us for so long.

Is that him with a smile as Moses does a double take at the burning bush that speaks?

Is he smiling again as Jonah lands on the beach, dripping gastric juices and smelling like whale breath?

Moses thought, "I will go over and see this strange sight—why the bush does not burn up" (Exodus 3:3).

Is that a twinkle in his eye as he watches the disciples feed thousands with one boy's lunch?

Do you think that his face is deadpan as he speaks about the man with a two-by-four in his eye who points out a speck in a friend's eye?

Can you honestly imagine Jesus bouncing children on his knee with a somber face?

Why do you look at the speck of sawdust in your brother's eye and pay no attention to the plank in your own eye? (Matthew 7:3).

No, I think that Jesus smiled. I think that he smiled a bit *at* people and a lot *with* people.

Let me explain with an example.

1. Are you ever inclined to take God "too seriously"? In what way?

_____

_____

_____

_____

2. How *do* you tend to imagine God? How does picturing him laughing and smiling bring you a lightheartedness when looking at your day?

_____

_____

_____

_____

Three times a year you are to celebrate a festival to me (Exodus 23:14).

God is not only the essence of love, power, and mercy . . . but also the essence of joy. We have a God who told his people to have fun. He set aside weeks for them to put down the plow and celebrate festivals with food and drink. He attended weddings and compared his relationship with us to a bridegroom and a bride . . . and one of the most joyful days in a woman's life is the day she sees her groom! Knowing this, how can we not believe in a God who delights in smiling and seeing his children smile? So today, take a moment to just delight in God and his works. Smile at him as he smiles at you. And the next time you find your faith becoming too rigid, remember the words of the man after God's own heart: "You will fill me with joy in your presence, with eternal pleasures at your right hand" (Psalm 16:11).

Take delight in the LORD, and he will give you the desires of your heart (Psalm 37:4).

Lord, sometimes life robs us of our joy in you. Sometimes our faith and our image of you become too serious. Today, we ask that you would restore in us the joy of our salvation. Thank you for delighting in us. Amen.

Day One: Spunky Faith

TWO STRIKES

We don't know a thing about her. We don't know her name . . . her background . . . her looks . . . her hometown. She came from nowhere and went nowhere. She disappeared the same way that she appeared, like a puff of smoke.

But what a delightful puff she was.

The disciples, during two years of training, hadn't done what she did in a few moments of conversing. She impressed God with her faith. The disciples' hearts may have been good. Their desire may have been sincere. But their faith didn't turn God's head.

Hers did. For all we don't know about her, we do know one remarkable truth: she impressed God with her faith. After that, anything else she ever did was insignificant.

"Woman, you have great faith!" Jesus stated (Matthew 15:28 NCV).

Some statement. Especially when you consider God said it. The God who can put a handful of galaxies into his palm. The One who creates Everests as a hobby. The One who paints rainbows without a canvas. The One who can measure the thickness of mosquito wings with one hand and level a mountain with the other.

One would think that the Creator would not be easily impressed. But something about this woman brought a sparkle to his eyes and . . . most likely . . . a smile to his face.

Matthew called her a "Canaanite woman," and, in doing so, called strikes one and two. Strike one? A Canaanite. An outsider. A foreigner. An apple in a family tree of oranges. Strike two? A woman. Might as well have been a junkyard dog. She lived in a culture that had little respect for women outside the bedroom and kitchen.

But she met the Teacher, who had plenty of respect for her.

Oh, it doesn't appear that way. In fact, the dialogue between the two seems harsh. It's not an easy passage to understand unless you're willing to concede that Jesus knew how to smile. If you have trouble with the

Leaving that place, Jesus withdrew to the region of Tyre and Sidon. A Canaanite woman from that vicinity came to him (Matthew 15:21).

In his hand are the depths of the earth, and the mountain peaks belong to him. The sea is his, for he made it, and his hands formed the dry land (Psalm 95:4–5).

sketch of the smiling Jesus hanging in my office, you'll have trouble with this story. But if you don't, if the thought of God smiling brings you a bit of relief, then you'll like what comes next.

[She] cried out to Him, saying, "Have mercy on me, O Lord, Son of David! My daughter is severely demon-possessed" (Matthew 15:22 NKJV).

1. Read Matthew 15:21–22. What are your initial observations about the Canaanite woman? What was her request?

_____

_____

_____

2. How would the fact she was a woman and a Canaanite represent two strikes against her in the culture of Jesus' day?

_____

_____

_____

Do not intermarry with them (Deuteronomy 7:3).

Love them as yourself, for you were foreigners (Leviticus 19:33)

3. Turn to Deuteronomy 7:3–4 and Leviticus 19:33–34. How did God tell his people to treat the Gentile nations? In what ways were the people to be cautious, yet compassionate, toward them?

_____

_____

_____

Woe to you, teachers of the law and Pharisees, you hypocrites! You shut the door of the kingdom of heaven in people's faces (Matthew 23:13).

4. Read Matthew 23:13–15. During Jesus' time, many of the Jewish religious leaders had twisted the heart behind God's law. Instead of being cautious yet welcoming to Gentiles, they self-righteously refused all interaction with them. What did Jesus say about the condition of the religious leaders' hearts? Why did he call the religious leaders hypocrites?

_____

_____

_____

_____

AN INTERPRETATION

Naked I came from my mother's womb, and naked I will depart. The LORD gave and the LORD has taken away; may the name of the LORD be praised (Job 1:21).

Here's my interpretation of the Jesus' interaction with the Canaanite woman. She is clearly desperate. Her daughter is demon possessed. She knows she has no right to ask anything of Jesus. She is not a Jew. She is not a disciple. She offers no money for the ministry. She makes no promises to devote herself to missionary service. You get the impression that she knows as well as anybody that Jesus doesn't owe her anything, and she is asking him for everything.

But that doesn't slow her down. She persists in her plea. "Lord, Son of David, have mercy on me!" (Matthew 15:22 NCV).

Jesus did not answer a word (Matthew 15:23).

Matthew notes that Jesus says nothing at first. *Nothing*. He doesn't open his mouth. Why? To test her? Most commentators suggest this. Maybe, they say, he is waiting to see how serious she is about her plea. My dad used to make me wait a week from the day I asked him for something to the day he gave me his answer. Most of the time, I forgot that I ever made the request. Time has a way of separating whims from needs. Is Jesus doing that?

I have another opinion. I think that he was admiring her. I think that it did his heart good to see some spunky faith for a change. I think that it refreshed him to see someone asking him to do the very thing he came to do—give great gifts to unworthy children.

How strange that we don't allow him to do it more often for us.

Perhaps the most amazing response to God's gift is our reluctance to accept it. We want it. But on our terms. For some odd reason, we feel better if we earn it. So we create religious hoops and hop through them—making God a trainer, us his pets, and religion a circus.

The Canaanite woman knew better. She had no résumé. She claimed no heritage. She had no earned degrees. She knew only two things: her daughter was weak, and Jesus was strong.

1. Read Matthew 15:1–9. In these verses leading up to this scene with the Canaanite woman, what was the Pharisees' issue with Jesus?

Then some Pharisees and teachers of the law came to Jesus from Jerusalem and asked, "Why do your disciples break the tradition of the elders?" (verses 1–2).

_____

_____

_____

2. How did Jesus describe the Pharisees? What did Jesus mean when he said they nullified the word of God for the sake of their tradition?

You hypocrites! Isaiah was right when he prophesied about you: "These people honor me with their lips, but their hearts are far from me. They worship me in vain; their teachings are merely human rules" (verses 7–9).

_____

_____

_____

_____

3. The Pharisees were the religious leaders of the people, yet Jesus said they were acting as "blind guides" (verse 14). Given this recent interaction, why do you think Jesus would have been impressed with the Canaanite woman's simple faith in him?

[Jesus] replied, "Leave them; they are blind guides. If the blind lead the blind, both will fall into a pit" (verses 13–14).

_____

_____

_____

_____

4. The Pharisees were creating religious hoops to hop through—"making God a trainer, us his pets, and religion a circus." In your relationship with God, how do you tend to create religious hoops in order to "earn" God's grace?

_____

_____

_____

_____

_____

_____

_____

_____

_____

God has always been, and will always be, a God of grace. From the beginning, he only asked that his people have faith in him. Even the laws he created for his children were so they could find grace. Sadly, people always look for a way to destroy that grace—much like the Pharisees did when they added to God's law and twisted his intent. But Jesus made it clear that all we need to do to receive God's grace is *believe*. This is what the Canaanite woman did. She knew she had nothing to offer. She didn't rely on her heritage, her race, her clout, her Torah skills—only on Christ. If only we could do the same! If only we could put down our knowledge, our good works, our religious "hoops." Christ was enough, and so our faith in him is enough.

If you declare with your mouth, "Jesus is Lord," and believe in your heart that God raised him from the dead, you will be saved (Romans 10:9).

❧ Points to Remember ❧

❖ Jesus is delighted when we ask him to do what he came to do: give great gifts to us, his unworthy children.
❖ When we know we are weak and Jesus is strong, we can see our needs and ask in faith for God to meet those needs.
❖ A simple faith is the object of God's grace.

❧ Prayer for the Day ❧

Lord, give us faith like the Canaanite woman. Help us to realize that because we have nothing to offer you—no rights before you—we must rely completely on you and not on ourselves. Help us to simply receive your free gift of grace today and believe that you will provide for us.
We love you, Lord. Amen.

The gift of God is eternal life in Christ Jesus our Lord (6:23).

Day Two: A Sincere Seeker

AN INTRIGUING DIALOGUE

It's clear from the text that the disciples are annoyed. As Jesus sits in silence, they grow more smug. "Tell the woman to go away," they demand (Matthew 15:23 NCV). The spotlight is put on Christ. He looks at the disciples, and then looks at the woman. What follows is one of the most intriguing dialogues in the New Testament.

"I was sent only to the lost sheep of Israel," Jesus says.

"Lord, help me!" the woman replies.

"It is not right to take the children's bread and toss it to the dogs," he answers. (verses 24–26)

"That's true, Lord," she responds, "but even dogs are allowed to eat the scraps that fall beneath their masters' table" (verse 27 NLT).

Is Jesus being rude? Is he worn-out? Is he frustrated? Is he calling this woman a dog? How do we explain this dialogue? Bible commentaries give us three options.

Some say that Jesus was trapped. He could not help the woman because he had been sent first to the lost sheep of Israel. Neat theory, but full of problems. One is the Samaritan woman. Another is the centurion. Jesus had already helped Gentiles and stayed faithful to the focus of his mission. So why couldn't he do it now?

Others think that Jesus was rude. Who can blame him? He was tired. It had been a long trip. The disciples were coming along pretty slowly. And this request was the straw that broke the camel's back. Like that explanation? I don't either. The one who had shown compassion on the 5,000 men . . . who had wept over the city of Jerusalem . . . who had come to seek and save ones like this one . . . would not snap so abruptly at such a needy woman.

The most popular theory is that he was testing her . . . again. Just to be sure that she was serious about her request. Just to make sure that her faith was real.

But by insinuating that she was a dog? I don't think Jesus would do that either. Let me suggest another alternative.

1. Look at Matthew 15:23–28. Why do you think Jesus was silent after the woman asked for his help? How did the disciples interpret his lack of response?

_____

_____

So his disciples came to him and urged him, "Send her away, for she keeps crying out after us" (Matthew 15:23).

The poor and needy search for water, but there is none. . . . But I the LORD will answer them; I, the God of Israel, will not forsake them (Isaiah 41:17).

*My people have been lost sheep;
their shepherds have led them astray*
(Jeremiah 50:6).

2. Who are the "lost sheep" and "children" in this passage?

_____

_____

_____

We all, like sheep, have gone astray
(Isaiah 53:6).

3. Jesus had previously instructed his disciples, "Do not go in the way of the Gentiles, and do not enter any city of the Samaritans; but rather go to the lost sheep of the house of Israel" (Matthew 10:5–6 NASB). How does this passage shed light on Jesus' words here?

_____

_____

_____

4. At first glance, Jesus' response to the woman seems to imply that he was being rude to her, or dismissing her, or is unwilling to help her. But what do the following passages of Scripture say about the heart of God?

Exodus 34:6–7: "The LORD is a God who shows mercy, who is kind, who doesn't become angry quickly, who has great love and faithfulness and is kind to thousands of people. The LORD forgives people for evil, for sin, and for turning against him, but he does not forget to punish guilty people" (NCV).

_____

_____

_____

Luke 6:35–36: "Love your enemies, and do good, and lend, expecting nothing in return; and your reward will be great, and you will be sons of the Most High; for He Himself is kind to ungrateful and evil men. Be merciful, just as your Father is merciful" (NASB).

_____

_____

_____

2 Peter 3:9: "The Lord isn't really being slow about his promise, as some people think. No, he is being patient for your sake. He does not want anyone to be destroyed, but wants everyone to repent" (NLT).

_____

_____

_____

1 John 4:16: "So we have known and believe the love that God has for us. God is love, and those who abide in love abide in God, and God abides in them" (NRSV).

_____

_____

_____

_____

A GOD WHO DELIGHTS

Could it be that Jesus' tongue is poking his cheek? Could it be that he and the woman are engaging in satirical banter? Is it a wry exchange in which God's unlimited grace is being highlighted? Could Jesus be so delighted to have found one who is not bartering with a religious system or proud of a heritage that he can't resist a bit of satire?

He knows he can heal her daughter. He knows he isn't bound by a plan. He knows her heart is good. So he decides to engage in a humorous moment with a faithful woman. In essence, here's what they said.

"Now, you know that God only cares about Jews," Jesus says, smiling.

When she catches on, she volleys back, "But your bread is so precious, I'll be happy to eat the crumbs."

In a spirit of exuberance, he bursts out, "Never have I seen such faith! Your daughter is healed."

This story does not portray a contemptuous God. It portrays a willing One who delights in a sincere seeker.

Aren't you glad he does?

5. What are your thoughts about this interpretation that Jesus and the woman were engaging in satirical banter? What clues in the text would support this idea?

_____

_____

_____

_____

6. The story of the Canaanite woman does not portray a contemptuous God but One who delights in a sincere seeker. What do the following passages of Scripture say about the way God delights in us?

Psalm 147:11: "The LORD is pleased with those who respect him, with those who trust his love" (NCV).

_____

_____

_____

_____

He answered, "I was sent only to the lost sheep of Israel. . . . It is not right to take the children's bread and toss it to the dogs" (Matthew 15:24, 26).

"Yes it is, Lord," she said. "Even the dogs eat the crumbs that fall from their master's table" (verse 27).

Psalm 149:4: "For the LORD takes pleasure in His people; He will beautify the humble with salvation" (NKJV).

_____

_____

_____

Zephaniah 3:17: "The LORD your God is with you; the mighty One will save you. He will rejoice over you. You will rest in his love; he will sing and be joyful about you" (NCV).

_____

_____

_____

Ephesians 2:4–5: "God is so rich in mercy, and he loved us so much, that even though we were dead because of our sins, he gave us life when he raised Christ from the dead" (NLT).

_____

_____

_____

7. Why do you think we often struggle believing that God could delight in us?

_____

_____

_____

_____

Why do your disciples break the tradition of the elders? (Matthew 15:2).

8. Look again at Matthew 15:2 and Matthew 15:22. Both the Canaanite woman and the Pharisees made a request of Jesus, but their approaches were very different. What differences do you find between them? To whom do you relate the most? Why?

Lord, Son of David, have mercy on me! (verse 22).

_____

_____

_____

[Jesus] replied, "Every plant that my heavenly Father has not planted will be pulled up by the roots" (verse 13).

Regardless of exactly why Jesus chose the words he did, it's obvious he chose to make an example out of the Canaanite woman. Jesus had just been with Pharisees, who would have called her a dog . . . and meant it. He had just been with religious rulers, who would never have shared their bread . . . much less the same room with a Gentile woman. He had just been with Jewish muckety-mucks who questioned his claims and doubted his authority. So can you imagine how sweet the woman's first word sounded to him: "Lord!" She had made him her Lord before even meeting him! No wonder Jesus delighted in her. No wonder with pure joy—and likely a wide smile—Jesus proclaimed, "Woman, you have great faith!" (Matthew 15:28). Today, do not doubt that Jesus smiles at you as well. If you've made him your Lord, you've made him a proud Papa.

Jesus said to her, "Woman, you have great faith! Your request is granted." And her daughter was healed at that moment (Matthew 15:28).

❧ POINTS TO REMEMBER ☙

❖ The Lord Jesus will patiently test the sincerity of our faith.
❖ God delights in building relationships with genuine seekers.
❖ Jesus loves to use our authentic expression of faith as an example to lead others to faith in him.

❧ PRAYER FOR THE DAY ☙

Lord, you are love. You are slow to anger. You are compassionate. Today, we ask that you take away any lie inside of us that says you are disappointed, angry, or condemning of us. We know we are hidden in Christ's righteousness and seen as yours. What a gift! Thank you. Amen.

Day Three: A Study in Faith

A BRUISED REED

In Mark's account of the story, we read that when the woman "had come to her house, she found the demon gone out, and her daughter lying on the bed" (Mark 7:30 NKJV). The Canaanite woman's faith in Christ and her actions in seeking him out had resulted in healing. It's a pattern we find repeated often throughout the Gospels.

He told her, "For such a reply, you may go; the demon has left your daughter" (Mark 7:29).

For instance, when the friends of a paralyzed man cut a hole in a roof so they can lower him to Jesus, Christ sees "the faith of these people" and responds to their need (Mark 2:5 NCV). When a blind man named Bartimaeus comes to Christ for healing, Jesus sees his faith and says, "Go, you are healed because you believed" (10:52 NCV). And when another woman simply reaches out in faith and touches Jesus' garment, she is also healed.

The prayer offered in faith will make the sick person well (James 5:15).

Like the Canaanite woman, we don't know her name or much of her past history. But we do know her situation. Her world was midnight black. Grope-in-the-dark-and-hope-for-help black. Read these three verses and see what I mean: "A large crowd followed Jesus and pushed very close around him. Among them was a woman who had been bleeding for twelve years. She had suffered very much from many doctors and had spent all the money she had, but instead of improving, she was getting worse" (Mark 5:24–26 NCV).

She was a bruised reed: "bleeding for twelve years," "suffered very much," "spent all the money she had," and "getting worse." A chronic menstrual disorder. A perpetual issue of blood. Such a condition would be difficult for any woman of any era. But for a Jewess, nothing could be worse. No part of her life was left unaffected.

Sexually . . . she could not touch her husband.

Maternally . . . she could not bear children.

Domestically . . . anything she touched was considered unclean. No washing dishes. No sweeping floors.

Spiritually . . . she was not allowed to enter the temple.

She was physically exhausted and socially ostracized.

She had sought help "under the care of many doctors" (verse 26). The Talmud gives no fewer than eleven cures for such a condition. No doubt she had tried them all. Some were legitimate treatments. Others, such as carrying the ashes of an ostrich egg in a linen cloth, were hollow superstitions.

She "had spent all she had" (verse 26). To dump financial strain on top of the physical strain is to add insult to injury. A friend who was battling cancer once told me that the hounding of the creditors who demanded payments for ongoing medical treatment was just as devastating as the pain.

In spite of all the woman's efforts, instead of getting better she had grown worse (see verse 26). She had awoken daily in a body that no one wanted. She was down to her last prayer. And on the day we encounter her, she is about to pray it.

By the time she gets to Jesus, he is surrounded by people. He is on his way to help the daughter of Jairus, the most important man in the community. What are the odds that Jesus will interrupt an urgent mission with a high official to help the likes of her? Very few. But what are the odds she will survive if she doesn't take a chance? Fewer still.

So she takes a chance.

1. Read Mark 5:24–28. How does this woman remind you of the Canaanite woman? How is she different?

_____

_____

_____

_____

_____

A woman was there who had been subject to bleeding for twelve years (Mark 5:25).

Then one of the synagoge leaders, a man named Jairus, came, and when he saw Jesus, he fell at his feet. . . . So Jesus went with him (verses 22, 24).

2. Turn to Leviticus 15:25–27. What were some of some of the regulations in the Jewish law that this woman would have faced each day?

_____

_____

_____

When a woman has a discharge of blood for many days at a time . . . she will be unclean (Leviticus 15:25).

3. The woman was considered ceremonially unclean and thus had a legal responsibility to avoid human touch. How would this have affected her emotionally and spiritually?

_____

_____

_____

Anything she sits on will be unclean. . . . Anyone who touches them will be unclean (verses 26–27).

4. When was a time in your life that you felt as if you "spent all you had," like the bleeding woman? How would you describe your faith during that time?

_____

_____

_____

_____

DEFINITION OF FAITH

"If I can just touch his clothes," she says to herself, "I will be healed" (Mark 5:28 NCV).

Risky decision. To touch Jesus, she will have to touch the people. If one of them recognizes her . . . hello rebuke, goodbye cure. But again, what choice does she have? She has no money, no clout, no friends, no solutions. All she has is a crazy hunch that Jesus can help and a high hope that he will.

Maybe that's all you have: a crazy hunch and a high hope. You have nothing to give. But you are hurting, and all you have to offer him is your hurt. Maybe that has kept you from coming to God. Oh, you've taken a step or two in his direction. But then you saw the other people around him. They seemed so clean, so neat, so trim and fit in their faith. And when you saw them, they blocked your view of him. So you stepped back.

If that describes you, note carefully that only one person was commended that day for having faith. It wasn't a wealthy giver. It wasn't a loyal follower. It wasn't an acclaimed teacher. It was a shame-struck outcast who—much like the Canaanite woman—clutched onto her hunch that Jesus could help her and her hope that he would.

Which, by the way, isn't a bad definition of faith: a conviction that Jesus *can* and a hope that he *will*. Sounds similar to the definition of

She came up behind him in the crowd and touched his cloak, because she thought, "If I just touch his clothes, I will be healed" (Mark 5:27–28).

Faith is confidence in what we hope for (Hebrews 11:1).

faith given by the author of Hebrews: "Without faith no one can please God. Anyone who comes to God must believe that he is real and that he rewards those who truly want to find him" (11:6 NCV).

Not too complicated, is it? Faith is the belief that God is real and that God is good. Faith is not a mystical experience or a midnight vision or a voice in the forest . . . it is a choice to believe that the One who made it all hasn't left it all and that he still sends light into shadows and responds to gestures of faith.

There was no guarantee, of course. The woman with the issue of blood hoped Jesus would respond . . . she longed for it . . . but she didn't know if he would. All she knew was that he was there and that he was good. That's faith. Faith is not the belief that God will do what you want. Faith is the belief that God will do what is right.

In this hope we were saved. But hope that is seen is no hope at all. Who hopes for what they already have? (Romans 8:24).

5. If the bleeding woman only focused on what she had to offer, she would have never touched Jesus. Do you ever focus more on what you have to offer God than on what God has to offer you? If so, how does that mindset keep you away from Jesus?

_____

_____

_____

_____

_____

The disciples came to Jesus . . . and asked, "Why couldn't we drive [the demon] out?" He replied, "Because you have so little faith" (Matthew 17:19–20).

6. In Matthew 17:20 Jesus said, "If you have faith as a mustard seed, you will say to this mountain, 'Move from here to there,' and it will move; and nothing will be impossible for you" (NKJV). What does this verse say about the power of God? What does it say about taking the focus and reliance off of ourselves?

_____

_____

_____

_____

7. Sometimes when we compare ourselves to others, we view them as being "clean, neat, trim and fit" in their faith, while we . . . are less so. But how can comparing our faith to others in this way "block our view" of truth?

_____

_____

_____

_____

8. A good definition of faith is that it is "the belief that God is good and will do what is right." Faith is making a choice to believe that the One who made it all hasn't left it all and that he still works in our midst today. In what ways might this idea of God doing "what is right" differ from what you want? Provide some examples.

_____

_____

_____

_____

_____

_____

_____

_____

_____

_____

How freeing it is to know that God acts based on the abundance of his power and not on the abundance of our faith! He only asks for a mustard-seed-sized faith. And how do we get this seed-sized faith? From God himself! The writer of Hebrews tells us that Jesus is "the author and perfecter of faith" (12:2 NASB). He does all the work! When we make God's response about our faith, our righteousness, our level of spiritual maturity, we lose sight of the gospel. We shift our eyes off Jesus and onto ourselves. We make healing about our good works. But the truth is that it is all about God's abundant grace. Our only job is to trust he is good and trust he is right.

> Let us run with perseverance the race marked out for us, fixing our eyes on Jesus, the pioneer and perfecter of faith. For the joy set before him he endured the cross, scorning its shame (Hebrews 12:1–2).

❧ POINTS TO REMEMBER ☙

❖ We have nothing to offer Jesus but our needs and our faith in him.
❖ Faith is not the belief that God will do what we want him to do but that he will do what is right.
❖ God acts through the abundance of his power, not the abundance of our faith.

❧ PRAYER FOR THE DAY ☙

Lord, no matter how tattered we are, how bruised we feel, or how small our faith is, help us to never fear approaching your throne. Your grace is bigger than our weakness. Your healing is about your goodness, not ours. Today, grow our reliance on you. Amen.

Day Four: God's Response to Faith

NEVER REJECTED

Blessed are the poor in spirit, for theirs is the kingdom of heaven. Blessed are those who mourn, for they will be comforted. Blessed are the meek, for they will inherit the earth. Blessed are those who hunger and thirst for righteousness, for they will be filled (Matthew 5:3–6).

"Blessed are the dirt-poor, nothing-to-give, trapped-in-a-corner, destitute, diseased," Jesus had said in the Sermon on the Mount, "for theirs is the kingdom of heaven" (Matthew 5:3–6, Lucado Paraphrase Version). Jesus revealed that God's economy is upside down—or right side up, and ours is upside down. God says the more hopeless our circumstances, the more likely our salvation. The greater our cares, the more genuine our prayers.

The Canaanite woman knew the desperate nature of her situation. Her daughter was suffering, and there was little hope for her to be well again. This is what drove her to follow after Christ in spite of the fact she was an outsider in his culture. It was what compelled her to call out to him. And when her dilemma met Jesus' dedication, a miracle occurred.

Notice that the Canaanite woman's part in the healing was actually quite small. All she did was follow after Jesus and cry for mercy. "If only I can speak with him." But what's important is not the form of the effort but the fact of the effort. The fact is, she *did* something. She refused to settle for her daughter's sickness another day and resolved to make a move.

Is anyone among you sick? Let them call the elders of the church to pray over them and anoint them with oil in the name of the Lord (James 5:14).

Healing begins when we *do something*. Healing begins when we reach out. Healing starts when we take a step. God's help is near and always available, but it is only given to those who seek it. Nothing results from apathy. The great work in this story is the mighty healing that occurred. But the great truth is that the healing began with the woman's faith—and with her action. And with that small, courageous gesture, she experienced Jesus' tender power.

Jesus never refused an intercessory request. Ever! Peter brought concerns for his sick mother-in-law. The centurion brought a request for his sick servant. Jairus had a sick daughter. The woman from Canaan had a demon-possessed daughter. From sunrise to sunset, Jesus heard one appeal after another: "My uncle cannot walk." "My son cannot see." "My wife is in pain." He heard so many requests that at times the disciples attempted to turn people away.

The disciples came to him and said . . . "Send the crowds away" (Matthew 14:15).

But Jesus would not let them. "Great crowds came to him, bringing the lame, the blind, the crippled, the mute and many others, and laid them at his feet; *and he healed them*" (Matthew 15:30, emphasis added). In each case, Jesus responded. His consistent kindness issues a welcome announcement: *God heeds the cries of those in need.*

Compared to God's part in the process, our part is minuscule . . . but necessary. We don't have to do much, but we do have to do *something*.

Write a letter.

Ask forgiveness.

Call a counselor.

Confess.

Call Mom.

Visit a doctor.

Be baptized.

Feed a hungry person.

Pray.

Teach.

Go.

We have to do something that demonstrates faith, for faith with no effort is no faith at all. And God will respond. He has never rejected a genuine gesture of faith. Never.

Faith by itself, if it is not accompanied by action, is dead (James 2:17).

1. Read James 2:18. How do you react to the statement that "we have to do something that demonstrates faith, for faith with no effort is no faith at all"? How does this verse in James describe genuine faith?

   _____

   _____

   _____

   _____

Someone will say, "You have faith; I have deeds." Show me your faith without deeds, and I will show you my faith by my deeds (verse 18).

2. Many people misinterpret James 2:18 and place too much focus on the work of people and not of God. However, the Scripture is clear that if no work is involved, our faith is dead. How do you walk the fine line of doing works for God out of a genuine faith and not out of legalism?

   _____

   _____

   _____

   _____

3. What causes apathy to develop in your faith walk? Is apathy getting in the way of an area in your life where God wants to bring healing? If so, what area?

   _____

   _____

   _____

4. When it comes to healing, we don't have to do much . . . but we do have to do something. Think about someone you know who needs healing, and then ask God if he is asking you to do something for

A person is considered righteous by what they do and not by faith alone (verse 24).

that person. In the space below, write down any ideas that God lays on your heart, and then spend some time talking with God about what steps he wants you to take to bring that about.

_____

_____

_____

_____

A WORD OF AFFECTION

All those the Father gives me will come to me, and whoever comes to me I will never drive away (John 6:37).

God honors radical, risk-taking faith. When arks are built, lives are saved. When soldiers march, Jerichos tumble. When staffs are raised, seas split open. When a lunch is shared, thousands are fed. When a man or woman calls out for mercy, Jesus stops. He stops and responds.

The Canaanite woman's willingness to take a risk led to her daughter being instantly healed. No neon lights or loud shouts. No razzle-dazzle. No fanfare. No hoopla. No splash. Just help. The same is true of the woman with the issue of blood. When she touched Christ, the power left him automatically and instantaneously. It's as if the Father short-circuited the system and the divinity of Christ went a step ahead of the humanity of Christ.

Immediately her bleeding stopped and she felt in her body that she was freed from her suffering (Mark 5:29).

Take note of how Jesus responds to these women. To the Canaanite woman, he says, "O woman, great is *your faith*!" (Matthew 15:28 NKJV, emphasis added). To the woman in Galilee, he says, "Daughter, *your faith* has made you well" (Mark 5:34 NKJV, emphasis added). In each case, Jesus comments on their faith. In each case, their action results in healing.

Notice also in the second story that Jesus calls the woman *daughter*. It's the only time recorded in the Bible that Jesus calls any woman anywhere *daughter*. Just imagine how that would have made her feel! Who could remember the last time she received a term of affection? Who knew the last time kind eyes had met hers?

Daughter, your faith has healed you. Go in peace and be freed from your suffering (verse 34).

Leo Tolstoy, the great Russian writer, told of a time he was walking down the street and passed a beggar. Tolstoy reached into his pocket to give the beggar some money, but his pocket was empty. He turned to the man and said, "I'm sorry, my brother, but I have nothing to give."

The beggar brightened and said, "You have given me more than I asked for—you have called me brother." To the loved, a word of affection is a morsel, but to the love-starved, a word of affection can be a feast. And Jesus gave these two women a banquet.

He turned around in the crowd and asked, "Who touched my clothes?" (verse 30).

5. Read Mark 5:29–34. What emotions do you think the bleeding woman was feeling when she saw Jesus looking around to see who had *touched* him? (Remember that she was considered "unclean"

according to Jewish law.) What emotions would she have felt when she heard Jesus call her "daughter"?

_____

_____

_____

_____

6. Turn to 1 John 3:1. When we reach out to Jesus in faith like the bleeding woman, in what way does God respond?

_____

_____

_____

_____

See what great love the Father has lavished on us, that we should be called children of God! (1 John 3:1).

7. Read Matthew 5:3. What does it mean to be "poor in spirit"? How were the Canaanite woman and bleeding woman poor in spirit? In what way did they receive the promise of the kingdom of heaven?

_____

_____

_____

_____

_____

8. What did Jesus say had brought healing to the woman? Describe a time in your life when God responded to *your* acts of genuine faith.

_____

_____

_____

_____

God honors radical, risk-taking faith. This can be a simple cry for mercy, like the Canaanite woman. Or a simple step of reaching toward Jesus and relying on his power, like the woman with the issue of blood. When we take such a step, he responds. He heals a body. Whispers affection into a downtrodden spirit. Provides a job. Produces perseverance. When we go to him in humility—poor in and of ourselves, completely reliant on his favor—he gives us the kingdom of heaven. Of course, this might not always look like the response we want. After all, the kingdom of heaven's economy looks very different from the economy of this world. But we can trust his response. Why? Because he is a good Father who claims us as his children. And he not only loves us, but he *lavishly* loves us.

This is the confidence we have in approaching God: that if we ask anything according to his will, he hears us (5:14).

❧ POINTS TO REMEMBER ❧

❖ The more hopeless our circumstances, the more likely our salvation.
❖ Healing begins when we reach out in faith toward Jesus and rely on his power.
❖ A word of affection to the love-starved person will fill his or her heart.

❧ PRAYER FOR THE DAY ❧

Lord, thank you for calling us your children and for claiming us as your own. Today, we pray that you would take away any apathy in our hearts and give us genuine faith—a faith that spurs us to love you not only with words or speech but also with action. In Jesus' name, amen.

$\mathscr{D}$ay Five: A New Mindset

OUR LOVE FOR PECKING ORDERS

When we look at the story of the Canaanite woman, we can't get away from the fact that people—both in Jesus' day and in our own—are prone to pecking orders. We love to sort people into categories. The affluent over the destitute. The educated over the dropout. The old-timer over the newcomer. The Jew over the Gentile.

The woman was a Greek, born in Syrian Phoenicia (Mark 7:26).

Mark's account of the story states that the woman was a Greek born in Syrian Phoenicia. Jesus met her when he traveled to the region of Tyre and Sidon, which were two of the main Phoenician cities on the coast located to the north of Mount Carmel. In Jesus' time, the people of this region tended to be of mixed nationalities, and there was what seemed to be an impassable gulf between the non-Jews (or Gentiles) and the Jews.

A reading of some of the regulations in Jesus' time shows us just how wide this gap had become. A Jew could not drink milk drawn by Gentiles or eat their food. Jews could not aid a Gentile mother in her hour of need. Jewish physicians could not attend to non-Jewish patients. No Jew would have anything to do with a Gentile. They were unclean.

There is neither Jew nor Gentile . . . for you are all one in Christ Jesus (Galatians 3:28).

Unless that Jew, of course, was Jesus. Jesus' curious conversation with the Canaanite woman brought suspicions to the disciples of a new coming order. When he healed the woman's daughter, he made his position clear. He was more concerned about bringing everyone *in* than shutting certain people *out*.

This tension between Jews and Gentiles would continue on after Jesus' death, resurrection, and ascension into heaven. Peter would feel it when he received a vision from God that led him to share a meal—and the message of Christ—with a Gentile named Cornelius (see Acts 10:9–33). His culture said, "Keep your distance from Gentiles." His Christ said, "Build bridges to Gentiles." Peter had to make a choice, and he had to defend that choice when other Jewish followers of Jesus criticized him and said, "You went into the house of uncircumcised men and ate with them" (Acts 11:3).

But Peter couldn't deny that God had sent him to share the gospel of Christ with these Gentiles. He couldn't deny the results he witnessed when the Holy Spirit came on them just as on the Jewish believers gathered in the upper room at Pentecost. In truth, all he could do was shake his head as all his old beliefs about the Gentiles faded to dust. "I really understand now that to God every person is the same," he said. "In every country God accepts anyone who worships him and does what is right" (Acts 10:34–35 NCV).

While Peter was wondering about the meaning of the vision, the men sent by Cornelius found out where Simon's house was and stopped at the gate. They called out, asking if Simon who was known as Peter was staying there. While Peter was still thinking about the vision, the Spirit said to him, "Simon, three men are looking for you. So get up and go downstairs. Do not hesitate to go with them, for I have sent them" (Acts 10:17–20).

1. Jesus' healing of the Canaanite woman is just one of many times in which he broke down social barriers. Based on what we see of the disciples' reactions to these episodes, it took a while for them to understand Jesus' acceptance of those outside their cultural identity. Read Peter's account of his struggle with this in Acts 10:1–34. What social barriers exist in this story?

He said to them: "You are well aware that it is against our law for a Jew to associate with or visit a Gentile (verse 28).

_____

_____

_____

_____

2. What did the vision that God gave to Peter symbolize? What was God saying to him through the words, "Rise, Peter; kill and eat" (verse 13 NKJV)?

The voice spoke to him a second time, "Do not call anything impure that God has made clean" (verse 15).

_____

_____

_____

3. How does Peter summarize the episode in verses 34–35? What indicates that he is finally beginning to see others the way Jesus saw the Canaanite woman?

_____

_____

_____

_____

4. In what ways do you take pride in your status or identity? What do the stories of Peter and the Canaanite woman tell you about the value we place on achievements and/or status?

_____

_____

_____

_____

A CLEAR MESSAGE

God has shown me that I should not call anyone impure or unclean. So when I was sent for, I came without raising any objection (Acts 10:28–29).

The story of the Canaanite woman leaves us pondering the same truth that Peter pondered when God led him to Cornelius's house: "God has shown me that he doesn't think anyone is unclean or unfit" (Acts 10:28 CEV). Life would be so much easier for us without this command. As long as we can call people *common* or *unfit*, we can plant them on some far-off place and go our separate ways. Labels relieve us of responsibility. Pigeonholing permits us to wash our hands and leave.

"Oh, I know John. He is an alcoholic." (Translation: "Why can't he control himself?")

"The new boss is a liberal Democrat." (Translation: "Can't he see how misguided he is?")

"Oh, I know her. She's divorced." (Translation: "She has a lot of baggage.")

Categorizing others creates distance and gives us a convenient exit strategy for avoiding involvement. But Jesus took an entirely different approach. He was all about including people, not excluding them. "The Word became flesh and blood, and moved into the neighborhood" (John 1:14 MSG). Jesus touched lepers and loved foreigners and spent so much time with partygoers that people called him a "lush, a friend of the riffraff" (Matthew 11:19 MSG).

I am convinced that neither death nor life . . . nor anything else in all creation, will be able to separate us from the love of God (Romans 8:38–39).

Racism couldn't keep him from helping the Canaanite woman. Demons couldn't keep him from freeing her daughter of demons. His Facebook page included the likes of Zacchaeus the Ponzi-meister, Matthew the IRS agent, and some floozy he met at Simon's house. Jesus spent thirty-three years walking in the mess of this world. As Paul would later remark, "He had equal status with God but didn't think so much of himself that he had to cling to the advantages of that status no matter what. Not at all. When the time came, he set aside the privileges of deity and took on the status of a slave, became *human*!" (Philippians 2:6–7 MSG).

When I was in elementary school, all the boys in my first-grade class bonded together to express our male superiority. We met daily at recess and, with arms interlocked, marched around the playground, shouting, "Boys are better than girls! Frankly, I didn't agree, but I enjoyed the fraternity. The girls, in response, formed their own club. They paraded around the school, announcing their disdain for boys.

Jesus' example sends this clear message: *no playground displays of superiority.* "Don't call any person common or unfit."

5. Where do you see "playground displays of superiority" in the world today?

_____

_____

_____

6. We all want to believe that categorizing people ends with high-school stereotypes. But the truth is that categorizing still continues as adults—even in the body of Christ. What categories of people have you consciously or subconsciously created in your mind?

_____

_____

_____

_____

Make my joy complete by being like-minded, having the same love, being one in spirit and of one mind (Philippians 2:2).

7. How has the statement "labels relieve us of responsibility" proven true in your life? How does putting a label on people allow us to dehumanize them?

_____

_____

_____

_____

8. Meditate on Philippians 2:5–8. What is a word or phrase in this passage that especially speaks to your heart today?

_____

_____

_____

He made himself nothing by taking the very nature of a servant, being made in human likeness (verse 7).

Peter's story of faith teaches us to see others the way Jesus sees them. The bleeding woman teaches us that it only takes a simple outstretched hand of faith. And through the Canaanite woman, we learn that the faith our God smiles on is one of total dependence on his power. She had no clout, no fancy heritage, or knowledge to offer. She simply relied on the work of the Savior and then received his gift of healing with humble gratitude. She didn't ask to repay his favor or ask what she could do to earn his act of kindness. No. She just received what Jesus had to give. When God smiles at our faith, when he gives us the gift of healed hearts, a new identity and heavenly home, may we do the same—just receive it.

Freely you have received (Matthew 10:8).

Jesus came to them and said, "All authority in heaven and on earth has been given to me" (Matthew 28:18).

It's like the story told about an alert private in Napoleon's army who went after his emperor's horse when it got away from him. When he finally caught up with the animal and returned it to Napoleon, the ruler took the reins, smiled at the willing private, and said, "Thank you, Captain." The soldier's eyes widened at what he had heard. He then straightened. Saluted. And snapped, "Thank you, sir!"

The soldier immediately went to the barracks. Got his bags. Moved into the officers' quarters. Took his old uniform to the quartermaster and exchanged it for that of a captain. By the emperor's word, he had become a private-turned-commissioned officer. He didn't argue. He didn't shrug. He didn't doubt. He knew that the one who had the power to do it had done it. And he accepted that.

We seldom accept it, though. We prefer to get salvation the old-fashioned way: *earn it*. We think that to accept grace is to admit failure . . . a step we are hesitant to take. So instead we opt to impress God with how good we are rather than confessing how great he is. We dizzy ourselves with doctrine. Burden ourselves with rules. Think that God will smile on our efforts.

He doesn't.

God's smile is not for the healthy hiker who boasts that he made the journey alone. It is, instead, for the crippled leper who begs God for a back on which to ride. Such were the Canaanite woman's words. She knew that her request was ludicrous. But she also knew that Jesus was Lord. The prophet Daniel's words could have been hers: "We do not make requests of you because we are righteous, but because of your great mercy."

The woman came and fell at Jesus' feet because she was banking on the hope that he would answer her prayer based on his goodness and not her worthiness. And he did. With a smile. And when I think about the prayers God has answered for me in spite of the life I've lived, I think he must be smiling still. So I think I'll keep his picture on the wall.

—❧ POINTS TO REMEMBER ❧—

- ❖ God is more concerned about bringing everyone in than in shutting certain people out.
- ❖ Jesus provides our example of how to love others without putting labels on them.
- ❖ Jesus takes joy in answering our prayers based on his goodness, not in our perceived sense of worthiness.

—❧ PRAYER FOR THE DAY ❧—

Lord, thank you for giving us a new name, a new status, and a new position in you. Help us not only to receive your grace each and every day but also to give it to others without bias or judgment. In Jesus' name we pray, amen.

⌐◦ WEEKLY MEMORY VERSE ◦⌐

Come near to God, and God will come near to you.
JAMES 4:8 (NCV)

For Further Reading

Selections throughout this lesson were taken from *He Still Moves Stones* (Nashville: Thomas Nelson, 1993); *In the Eye of the Storm* (Nashville: Thomas Nelson, 1991); *Fearless* (Nashville: Thomas Nelson, 2009); *Outlive Your Life* (Nashville: Thomas Nelson, 2010); and *Before Amen* (Nashville: Thomas Nelson, 2014).

LESSON 8

MARY OF BETHANY

RISKY ACTS OF LOVE

ARTFUL EDDIE LACKED NOTHING. He was the slickest of the slick lawyers. He was one of the roars of the Roaring Twenties. A crony of Al Capone, he ran the gangster's dog tracks. He mastered the simple technique of fixing the race by overfeeding seven dogs and betting on the eighth.

Wealth. Status. Style. Artful Eddie lacked nothing.

Then why did he turn himself in? Why did he offer to squeal on Capone? What was his motive? Didn't Eddie know the surefire consequences of ratting on the mob?

He knew, but he'd made up his mind.

What did he have to gain? What could society give him that he didn't have? He had money, power, prestige. What was the hitch?

Eddie revealed the hitch. His son. Eddie had spent his life with the despicable. He had smelled the stench of the underground long enough. For his son, he wanted more. He wanted to give his son a name. And to give his son a name, he would have to clear his own. Eddie was willing to take a risk so that his son could have a clean slate.

Artful Eddie never saw his dream come true. After Eddie squealed, the mob remembered. Two shotgun blasts silenced him forever. Was it worth it? For the son it was. Artful Eddie's boy lived up to the sacrifice. His is one of the best-known names in the world.

But before we talk about the son, let's talk about the principle: *risky love*. Love that takes a chance. Love that goes out on a limb. Love that makes a statement and leaves a legacy. Love that is unexpected, surprising, and stirring. Acts of love that steal the heart and leave impressions on the soul. Acts of love that are never forgotten.

A good name is more desirable than great riches; to be esteemed is better than silver or gold (Proverbs 22:1).

I have loved you with an everlasting love (Jeremiah 31:3).

Jesus came to Bethany, where Lazarus lived, whom Jesus had raised from the dead. Here a dinner was given in Jesus' honor (John 12:1–2).

Such an act of love was seen in the final days of Jesus' life. It took place in the town of Bethany during a dinner party that Jesus shared with his friend Lazarus and his two sisters, Martha and Mary. Within the week Jesus would feel the sting of the Roman whip, the point of the thorny crown, and the iron of the executioner's nail. But on this evening, he would only feel the love of these friends. And it was during this dinner party that Mary would provide a demonstration of devotion the world would never forget—an act of extravagant tenderness in which Jesus wasn't the giver but the receiver.

1. "Risky love" takes a chance, goes out on a limb, makes a statement, and leaves a legacy. How have you shown this kind of love to someone else?

   _____

   _____

   _____

   _____

2. Read Matthew 27:27–56. What is one verse in this passage that best embodies the idea of "risky love"? Why did you choose that verse?

   _____

   _____

   _____

   _____

They stripped him and put a scarlet robe on him, and then twisted together a crown of thorns and set it on his head. They put a staff in his right hand. Then they knelt in front of him and mocked him (Matthew 27:28–29).

Jesus not only set aside his reputation, his name, and his dignity to die on the cross, but he also set aside his power as God. We can only imagine the emotions he must have felt when he heard the people mock, "He saved others . . . but he can't save himself!" (Matthew 27:42). *Save yourself.* Isn't that what selfish love does? It saves our name, our reputation, our own physical bodies. Yet this is the very temptation that Jesus had prayed against in the Garden of Gethsemane, when he said to his disciples, "Watch and pray so that you will not fall into temptation. The Spirit is willing, but the flesh is weak" (26:41). He was focused on the "joy set before him" (Hebrews 12:2), focused on his Father, focused on the greater glory . . . focused on *us*. He knew dying would bring us to him. The riskiest act of love was done for you and me.

❦ PRAYER FOR THE WEEK ❦

Lord, we cannot thank you enough for risking everything on the cross so that we could be with you forever. Today, we ask that you would sink the truth of your love deeper into our hearts so it is the root of all that we are. We love you, Lord. Amen.

Day One: A Tale of Two Sisters

BOILING POINT

The dinner party, held in the home of a man named Simon a week before Jesus' crucifixion, isn't the only mention of Mary of Bethany that we find in the Bible. In fact, in an earlier account, related in Luke 10:38–42, we get an interesting picture of some of the family dynamics between her and her sister, Martha. The story takes place when Jesus takes a short break from his travels to rest in the home of his friends.

Martha is clearly a dear soul given to hospitality and organization. More frugal than frivolous, more practical than pensive, her household is a tight ship, and she is a stern captain. Ask her to choose between a book and a broom, and she'll take the broom. Her sister, Mary, on the other hand, will take the book. She has thoughts to think, and the dishes can wait. Let Martha go to the market—she will go to the library.

Two sisters. Two personalities. And as long as they understand each other, it's hand in glove. But when the one resents the other, it's flint and stone. Let's quietly step in the back door of Martha's kitchen and I'll show you what I mean.

Shhh. There she is. Over by the table. The one wearing the apron. My, look at her work! I told you this lady knows how to run a kitchen. How does she do that? Stirring with one hand, cracking eggs with the other, and nothing spills. She knows what she's doing. Must be a big crowd. That's them laughing in the next room. Sounds like they're having fun.

But Martha isn't. One look at the flour-covered scowl will tell you that. "Stupid sister."

What? Did you hear her mumble something?

"That Mary. Here I am alone in the kitchen while she's out there."

Hmm. Seems the oven isn't the only thing hot in here.

"Wouldn't have invited Jesus over if I'd known he was gonna bring the whole army. Those guys eat like horses, and that Peter always belches."

Oh boy. She's miffed. Look at her glaring over her shoulder through the doorway. That's Mary she's staring at. The one seated on the floor, listening to Jesus.

"Little sweet sister . . . always ready to listen and never ready to work. I wouldn't mind sitting down myself. But all I do is cook and sew, cook and sew. Well, enough is enough!"

Watch out! There she goes. Someone's about to get it.

As Jesus and his disciples were on their way, he came to a village where a woman named Martha opened her home to him (Luke 10:38).

She had a sister called Mary, who sat at the Lord's feet listening to what he said. But Martha was distracted by all the preparations that had to be made (verses 39–40).

Refrain from anger and turn from wrath; do not fret—it leads only to evil (Psalm 37:8).

1. Read Luke 10:38–42. What are some of your initial observations about each of the sisters? What are their actions, their words, their personality traits?

   _____

   _____

   _____

2. To which of the two sisters do you relate most? Why?

   _____

   _____

   _____

3. It is easy to paint Martha as the villain in this tale, but what verses in the story give us a glimpse of the kindness in her heart? What gifts had God given to her?

   _____

   _____

   _____

   _____

Do not judge, or you too will be judged (Matthew 7:1).

4. When we don't use our gifts to honor God, we may find ourselves using them as a means to judge others or compare ourselves to others—even to the point of resenting others, like Martha resented Mary. How have you recognized this danger in your life? What are you doing to ensure you are using your gifts to honor God?

   _____

   _____

   _____

   _____

SPOILED MILK

I have a confession to make: I am a milkaholic. One of the saddest days of my life was when I learned that whole milk was unhealthy. With great reluctance, I have since adapted to the watered-down version—but on occasion I still allow myself the hallowed ecstasy of a cold glass of whole milk and a hot, gooey, chocolate-chip cookie.

In my years of appreciating the fine fruit of the cow, I have come to learn that a high price is paid for leaving milk out of the refrigerator. (On one occasion I spewed the spoiled stuff all over the kitchen cabinet.) Sweet milk turns sour from being too warm too long. Sweet dispositions turn sour for the same reason. Let aggravation stew without a period of cooling down and the result is a bad, bitter, clabberish attitude.

The soothing tongue is a tree of life, but a perverse tongue crushes the spirit (Proverbs 15:4).

We see this spoiling process at work in the life of Martha. As she watches Mary sitting at the feet of Jesus like one of his own disciples, doing *nothing* while she is working away in the kitchen, a resentment builds within her and reaches a boiling point. Finally, when she can stand it no longer, her bitterness erupts like a volcano.

"Lord," she exclaims, "don't you care that my sister has left me alone to do all the work? Tell her to help me" (Luke 10:40 NCV).

My, my! Aren't we testy? All of a sudden Martha has gone from serving Jesus to making demands of Jesus. The room goes silent . . . deathly silent, except for the tap-tap-tapping of Martha's foot on the stone floor. She looms above the others, flour on her cheeks and fire in her eyes. We have to chuckle at the expression on the faces of the disciples. They stare wide-eyed at this fury that hell hath not known. And poor Mary, flushed red with embarrassment, sighs and sinks lower to the floor.

Only Jesus speaks. For only Jesus understands the problem. The problem is not the large crowd. The problem is not Mary's choice to listen. The problem is not Martha's choice to host. The problem is Martha's heart, a heart soured with anxiety. Bless her heart, Martha wanted to do right. But bless her heart, her heart was wrong. Her heart, Jesus said, was worried. As a result she turned from a happy servant into a beast of burden. She was worried: worried about cooking, worried about pleasing, worried about too much.

She came to him and asked, "Lord, don't you care that my sister has left me to do the work by myself?" (Luke 10:40).

5. Martha makes it clear that she is angry with Mary. But Martha's problem goes deeper than just Mary not helping. Why do you think Martha took out her frustrations on Mary? What compelled her to be concerned about what Mary was *not* doing?

_____

_____

_____

Cast your cares on the LORD and he will sustain you; he will never let the righteous be shaken (Psalm 55:22).

6. When worry sits too long in our hearts, it grows bigger and bigger. It can even turn into sins such as bitterness and resentment. When was a time in your life that you allowed worry to fester for too long? What happened as a result?

_____

_____

_____

Do not let the sun go down while you are still angry, and do not give the devil a foothold (Ephesians 4:26–27).

7. What do the following passages of Scripture advise you to do the next time you feel worry and stress stirring in your heart?

Isaiah 26:3: "You will keep in perfect peace all who trust in you, all whose thoughts are fixed on you!" (NLT).

_____

_____

Matthew 11:28–29: "Come to me, all who labor and are heavy laden, and I will give you rest. Take my yoke upon you, and learn from me, for I am gentle and lowly in heart, and you will find rest for your souls" (ESV).

Luke 12:29–31: "Don't always think about what you will eat or what you will drink, and don't keep worrying. All the people in the world are trying to get these things, and your Father knows you need them. But seek God's kingdom, and all your other needs will be met as well" (NCV).

Philippians 4:6–7: "Be anxious for nothing, but in everything by prayer and supplication with thanksgiving let your requests be made known to God. And the peace of God, which surpasses all comprehension, will guard your hearts and your minds in Christ Jesus" (NASB).

Your hope will not be cut off (Proverbs 23:18).

8. Although Martha could seem harsh at times, she wasn't afraid to be honest with Jesus. What "Martha worries" do you have today? Write them in the space below, and then spend some time in prayer taking them to Jesus.

Get rid of all bitterness, rage and anger, brawling and slander, along with every form of malice (Ephesians 4:31).

Worry can turn into resentment. Resentment can turn into bitterness. Bitterness can turn into harsh words. It's a vicious cycle. And the more worry sits in our lives, the more it spoils like milk left sitting out too long on the kitchen counter. The Bible is clear that when it comes to worries, we shouldn't let them sit in our hearts but submit them to Jesus. We need to follow Martha's model of authenticity and tell Christ all our fears, anxieties, stressors, and frustrations. Then, once we have handed them to Christ, we don't take them back but leave them with him.

❧ POINTS TO REMEMBER ☙

❖ Using our gifts to honor God, not ourselves, helps us to focus on him and not judge or resent others.

❖ When worry festers in our hearts, it can turn into sins such as bitterness and resentment.

❖ We can submit our worry to Jesus through prayer, binding it to him with a thankful heart.

Show proper respect to everyone, love the family of believers, fear God (1 Peter 2:17).

❧ PRAYER FOR THE DAY ☙

Lord, we do not want the worries of this world to distract us from the purposes and plans that you have for us. Today we ask that you teach us to trust you with all our worries. Help us to bring all our concerns to you, center our minds on you, and trust you with the results. Thank you, Lord, that you always care for us. Amen.

𝒟ay Two: Serving God Instead of Self

LONG ON ANXIETY AND SHORT ON MEMORY

What makes the story of these two sisters so interesting is that Martha was worried *about something good.* She was literally serving God, and her aim was to please Jesus. But she had made a common mistake: As she began to work for him, her work became more important than her Lord. What began as a way to serve Jesus became a way to serve herself.

Maybe the process went something like this. As she began to prepare the meal, she anticipated the compliments on the food. As she set the table, she imagined the approval. But things didn't turn out like she'd planned. No standing ovation. No compliments. No adulations. No one even noticed. And that irritated her. Martha was long on anxiety and short on memory. She forgot the invitation was her idea. She forgot that Mary had every right to be with Jesus. Most of all, she forgot the meal was to honor Jesus, not herself.

When you give to the needy, do not announce it with trumpets, as the hypocrites do in the synagogues and on the streets, to be honored by others. Truly I tell you, they have received their reward in full (Matthew 6:2).

I know exactly how Martha feels. I know what it's like to set out to serve God and end up serving self. I've labored long and hard over sermons only to have my feelings hurt if they aren't complimented. I've pushed myself deeply into a manuscript only to catch myself daydreaming about the post-publication compliments. I've spoken to conference audiences about the sufferings of Christ and then gotten frustrated that the hotel room wasn't ready.

It's easy to forget who is the servant and who is to be served.

We can only imagine how much Martha regretted this outburst. I bet that after she cooled down, she wished to have those words back. There is a principle here: to keep an attitude from souring, treat it like you would a cup of milk. Cool it off.

1. Martha quickly went from *welcoming* Jesus into her home to being *worried* about having Jesus in her home. What do you think shifted in Martha's heart to make her go from good to spoiled? Why did Jesus say Mary had chosen something better?

_____

_____

_____

_____

Love your enemies, do good to them, and lend to them without expecting to get anything back (Luke 6:35).

2. Remember a time in your life when you, like Martha, set out to serve God but only ended up serving self. What caused the shift of focus in your situation?

_____

_____

_____

_____

3. What do the following passages of Scripture say about serving? How can you apply these words to your attitude when you set out to serve others?

1 Samuel 12:24: "Only fear the LORD and serve Him in truth with all your heart; for consider what great things He has done for you" (NASB).

_____

_____

_____

_____

Matthew 20:27–28: "Whoever desires to be first among you, let him be your slave—just as the Son of Man did not come to be served, but to serve, and to give His life a ransom for many" (NKJV).

_____

_____

_____

_____

Romans 7:6: "In the past, the law held us like prisoners, but our old selves died, and we were made free from the law. So now we serve God in a new way with the Spirit, and not in the old way with written rules" (NCV).

1 Peter 4:10: "God has given each of you a gift from his great variety of spiritual gifts. Use them well to serve one another" (NLT).

4. Read Matthew 6:1–4. What does Jesus say your attitude and motives should be when it comes to serving God with the gifts he has given you? How can you go from a spoiled heart to a sincere heart in your service to others?

When you give to the needy, do not let your left hand know what your right hand is doing, so that your giving may be in secret. Then your Father, who sees what is done in secret, will reward you (Matthew 6:3–4).

The Heart Behind the Service

Martha's life was cluttered. She needed a break. "Martha, Martha, you are worried and upset about many things," the Master explained to her. "Only one thing is important. Mary has chosen the better thing" (Luke 10:41–42 NCV). What "better thing" had Mary chosen? She had chosen to sit at the feet of Christ. God is more pleased with the quiet attention of a sincere servant than the noisy service of a sour one.

People like Mary have one foot in heaven and the other on a cloud. It's not easy for them to come to earth, and sometimes they need to be reminded there are bills to be paid and classes to be taught. They need to be reminded that service is *also* worship. But don't remind them too harshly, for they are precious souls with tender hearts. If they have found a place at the foot of Jesus, don't ask them to leave. Much better to ask them to pray for you.

By the way, this story could easily have been reversed. Mary could have been the one to get angry. The sister on the floor could have resented the sister at the sink. Mary could have grabbed Jesus and dragged him into the kitchen and said, "Tell Martha to quit being so productive and to get reflective. Why do I have to do all the thinking and praying around here?" What matters more than the type of service is the heart behind the service. A bad attitude spoils the gift we leave on the altar for God.

"Martha, Martha," the Lord answered, "you are worried and upset about many things, but few things are needed—or indeed only one. Mary has chosen what is better, and it will not be taken away from her" (Luke 10:41–42).

Maybe you've heard the joke about the fellow who prayed with a bad attitude. "God," he asked, "why has my brother been blessed with wealth and I with nothing? All my life I have never missed a day without saying morning and evening prayers. My church attendance has been perfect. I have always loved my neighbor and given my money. Yet now, as I near the end of my life, I can hardly afford to pay my rent. My brother, on the other hand, drinks and gambles and plays all the time, yet he has more money than he can count! I don't ask you to punish him. But tell me, why has he been given so much and I have been given nothing?"

"Because," God replied, "you're such a self-righteous pain in the neck."

Do everything without grumbling or arguing (Philippians 2:14).

Guard your attitude. God has gifted you with talents. He has done the same to your neighbor. If you concern yourself with your neighbor's talents, you will neglect yours. But if you concern yourself with yours, you could inspire both.

5. "'Martha, Martha,' the Lord answered, 'you are worried and upset about many things'" (Luke 10:41). Jesus could have responded harshly to Martha's outburst, but he didn't. In fact, his saying Martha's name twice demonstrated his tenderness. What does this tell you about the heart of Jesus toward us when we make the same mistake as Martha?

_____

_____

_____

_____

I am saying this . . . that you may live in a right way in undivided devotion to the Lord (1 Corinthians 7:35).

6. Jesus said Mary had chosen the "better thing," which was sitting at his feet and listening to what he said. In your day-to-day life, how do you take time to do this "better thing"? What types of distractions tend to get in the way? How do you avoid those distractions?

_____

_____

_____

For I desire mercy, not sacrifice, and acknowledgment of God rather than burnt offerings (Hosea 6:6).

7. Mary shows us a picture of what true discipleship looks like in this story. Read Hosea 6:6. According to this verse, what does God desire from us? What does that look like in practical terms as we work and interact with others?

_____

_____

_____

8. Take a "Mary moment" today and just be still before the Lord and sit at his feet. In the space below, write what you sense the Lord is saying to you during your time together.

_____

_____

_____

_____

_____

_____

_____

_____

_____

_____

_____

_____

_____

Come, let us bow down in worship, let us kneel before the LORD our Maker (Psalm 95:6).

All too often, we set out to serve God with the best of intentions but soon find that our "good" service has morphed into something "bad." Our need for recognition creeps into the mix, and before long we are using our good deeds to compare ourselves to others and even "earn" God's favor. Mary and Martha's story serves as a reminder that when the "better thing" is forgotten—when Christ is not the center of what we do—our attempts to serve God will fail. So, how do we put him first? We do what Mary did. We take a disciple's stance. We sit at his feet, listen to him, and learn from him. In essence, we let him take over our lives. And as he takes over, he works in us and through us to do the good our sinful hearts fail to accomplish, "for it is God who works in you, both to will and to work for his good pleasure" (Philippians 2:13 ESV).

Whoever wants to be my disciple must deny themselves and take up their cross and follow me (Mark 8:34).

❧ POINTS TO REMEMBER ❧

❖ We may find at times that the good work we began to serve Jesus has become a way to serve ourselves.
❖ God is more pleased with the quiet attention of a sincere servant than the noisy service of a sour one.
❖ It is the heart behind the service that matters to God.

❧ PRAYER FOR THE DAY ❧

Jesus, today we lay all that we are before you—our attempts to do good, our spiritual gifts, our soured attitudes. We put our whole selves before you and ask you to take over. We are nothing without you. Forgive us when we think otherwise. Amen.

Day Three: The Funeral

BEWILDERED AMONG THE BEREAVED

Now a man named Lazarus was sick. He was from Bethany, the village of Mary and her sister Martha (John 11:1).

The next time we encounter Mary in the Gospels, the scene in Bethany has completely changed. In place of a festive dinner party, we find her and her sister, Martha, mourning over the death of a loved one. This loved one is none other than their own brother, Lazarus.

Imagine the scene for a moment as if it took place in modern times. The chapel is library quiet. People acknowledge each other with soft smiles and nods. The church is full, so you stand at the back. Stained glass prisms the afternoon sun, streaking faces with shafts of purple and gold. You recognize the two women on the front pew: Mary and Martha, the sisters of Lazarus. Quiet, pensive Mary. Bustling, busy Martha. Even now she can't sit still. She keeps looking over her shoulder. *Who for?* you wonder.

The sisters sent word to Jesus, "Lord, the one you love is sick" (verse 3).

In a matter of moments the answer enters. And when he does, Martha rushes up the aisle to meet him. Had you not known his name, the many whispers would have informed you. "It's Jesus." Every head turns. He's wearing a tie, though you get the impression he rarely does. His collar seems tight and his jacket dated. A dozen or so men follow him. Some stand in the aisle, others in the foyer. They have a well-traveled, wrinkled look, as if they rode all night.

Jesus embraces Martha, and she weeps. As she weeps, you wonder. *What is Jesus going to do? What is he going to say? He spoke to the winds and the demons. Remarkable. But death? Does he have anything to say about death?* Your thoughts are interrupted by Martha's accusation: "Lord, if you had been here, my brother would not have died" (John 11:21 NCV).

You can't fault her frustration. When Lazarus had become ill, she and Mary had blitzed a message to Jesus. If the Nazarene would heal anyone, it would be Lazarus. You'd expect the next part of the story to read: "Jesus loved Mary and her sister and Lazarus . . . so he made a fast dash to their house to heal Lazarus." But just the opposite occurred.

When he heard that Lazarus was sick, he stayed where he was two more days (verse 6).

Because Jesus loved the trio, he lingered until Lazarus died. And now that he has finally arrived, Martha is so broken up she hardly knows what to say. She is like so many we find at the funeral—the bewildered among the bereaved. "Help me understand this one, Jesus."

"I am the resurrection and the life," you hear Jesus say to her. "Those who believe in me will have life even if they die. And everyone who lives and believes in me will never die. Martha, do you believe this?" You see Martha slowly nod. "Yes, Lord. I believe that you are the Christ, the Son of God, the One coming to the world" (John 11:25–27 NCV).

1. Read John 11:1–27. Notice in verse 6 that when Jesus "heard that Lazarus was sick, he stayed where he was for two more days" (NCV). Why do you think Jesus remained where he was instead of rushing to Lazarus's bedside?

   _____

   _____

   _____

   He went on to tell them, "Our friend Lazarus has fallen asleep; but I am going there to wake him up." His disciples replied, "Lord, if he sleeps, he will get better." . . . So then he told them plainly, "Lazarus is dead, and for your sake I am glad I was not there, so that you may believe. But let us go to him" (John 11:11–12, 14).

2. Martha was bewildered at Jesus' delay, and no doubt Mary was as well. When in your life were you confused by God's seemingly delayed response to a problem? What was your prayer to God during that time?

   _____

   _____

   _____

3. Look at verses 20–21. What are the differences in the way Mary and Martha act when Jesus finally arrives? What does this tell us about the way they deal with the confusion they are feeling at Jesus' delay?

   _____

   _____

   _____

   When Martha heard that Jesus was coming, she went out to meet him, but Mary stayed at home (verse 20).

4. In spite of Lazarus's death, Martha tells Jesus that she believes he can still work a miracle. What can we take away from her example of faith? How can we model this kind of faith when we don't understand God's plan?

   _____

   _____

   _____

   I know that even now God will give you whatever you ask (verse 22).

LORD OF THE LIVING AND THE DEAD

You watch from your seat in the back to see what Jesus will do next. But what really *can* he do? After all, Lazarus has been in the tomb for four days now, and his body has begun to decompose. Any hope for Lazarus, however small, has long since passed.

What you see next surprises you. Jesus sits on the pew next to Mary, puts an arm around her and her sister . . . and *sobs*. Among the three, a monsoon of tears is released. Tears that reduce to streaks your water-color conceptions of a cavalier Christ. Jesus weeps.

When Jesus saw her weeping, and the Jews who had come along with her also weeping, he was deeply moved in spirit and troubled. "Where have you laid him?" he asked (verses 32–33).

"Take away the stone," he said
(John 11:39).

After some time, Jesus gives Mary a hug, stands, and turns to face the corpse. The casket lid is closed. He tells Martha to have it opened. She shakes her head and starts to refuse, but then pauses. Turning to the funeral home director, she says, "Open it."

You can see the face of Lazarus as the lid is removed. It's waxy and white. You think Jesus is going to weep again. You never expect him to speak to his friend. But he does. A few feet from the casket Jesus yells, "Lazarus, come out!" (John 11:43 NCV). Preachers always address the living. But the dead? One thing is sure. There better be a rumble in that casket or this preacher is going to therapy. You and everyone else hear the rumble.

There is movement in the coffin. Lazarus jolts up, blinks, and looks around the room as if someone carted him there during a nap. A woman screams. Another faints. Everyone shouts. And you? You stare in wonder. *Dead men don't come out of the grave . . . do they?* Dead men don't wake up. Dead hearts don't beat. Dried blood doesn't rush. Empty lungs don't inhale. No, dead men don't come out—unless they hear the voice of the Lord of life.

The dead man came out,
his hands and feet wrapped with
strips of linen (verse 44).

Christ is, after all, "Lord of both the dead and the living" (Romans 14:9). When he speaks to the dead, the dead listen. Indeed, had Jesus not addressed Lazarus by name, the tenant of every tomb on earth would have stepped forth.

You never know what to say at funerals. But on this day, you learn something: *there is a time to say nothing.* Your words can't dispel a fog, but your presence can warm it. Your words can't give a Lazarus back to his sisters, but God's can. And it's just a matter of time before he speaks. "The Lord himself will come down from heaven with a commanding shout. . . . First, the believers who have died will rise from their graves" (1 Thessalonians 4:16 NLT).

Until then, like Mary, you will grieve. But not like those who have no hope. And you will listen for the voice of the Master. For you now know that he has the final say about death.

Lord, if you had been here,
my brother would not have died
(verse 32).

5. Read the rest of the story in John 11:28–44. Martha and Mary reacted differently when Jesus arrived in Bethany. But what are the similarities in their first words to Jesus (see verses 21, 32)? What emotions do you sense are behind these words?

   _____

   _____

   _____

Jesus wept (verse 35).

6. Notice in verse 35 that even though Jesus knew he was about to raise Lazarus from the dead, he still wept with Mary. Why do you think he did this? What moved him to tears in this particular moment?

   _____

   _____

   _____

7. What does Jesus' weeping with Mary say about the kind of God we serve? What comfort do you gain from knowing that Christ mourned with those who mourned? Why do you think Paul instructs us to "weep with those who weep" (Romans 12:15 NLT)?

_____

_____

_____

_____

_____

Rejoice with those who rejoice; mourn with those who mourn (Romans 12:15).

8. After empathizing with Mary, Jesus displayed his lordship over death and commanded Lazarus to rise. What do the following verses say about the resurrections that all believers in Christ will one day experience?

Psalm 17:15: "As for me, I will see Your face in righteousness; I shall be satisfied when I awake in Your likeness" (NKJV).

_____

_____

_____

_____

Romans 8:11: "If the Spirit of him who raised Jesus from the dead dwells in you, he who raised Christ Jesus from the dead will also give life to your mortal bodies through his Spirit who dwells in you" (ESV).

_____

_____

_____

_____

1 Corinthians 15:51–52: "We're not all going to die—*but* we are all going to be changed. You hear a blast to end all blasts from a trumpet, and in the time that you look up and blink your eyes— it's over. On signal from that trumpet from heaven, the dead will be up and out of their graves, beyond the reach of death, never to die again. At the same moment and in the same way, we'll all be changed" (MSG).

_____

_____

_____

_____

Revelation 22:3–5: No longer will there be a curse upon anything. For the throne of God and of the Lamb will be there, and his servants will worship him. And they will see his face, and his name will be written on their foreheads. And there will be no night there—no need for lamps or sun—for the Lord God will shine on them. And they will reign forever and ever" (NLT).

_____

Therefore, since we have a great high priest who has ascended into heaven, Jesus the Son of God, let us hold firmly to the faith we profess. For we do not have a high priest who is unable to empathize with our weaknesses, but we have one who has been tempted in every way, just as we are—yet he did not sin (Hebrews 4:14–15).

The story of Mary, Martha, and Lazarus shows us that when we are in pain, we not only have a God who walks with us but also a God who holds us and weeps with us. As the writer of Hebrews states, "We do not have a high priest who is unable to empathize" (4:15). In Scripture we see that one of the most beautiful characteristics of God is his ability to so closely relate to his children yet so sovereignly remain in control. On one hand he is intimately close to us, while on the other he is supremely in charge. He is One who can meet us where we are yet assure us of the hopeful ending to come. And isn't that the kind of comforter our souls need?

❧ POINTS TO REMEMBER ❧

❖ Jesus is the resurrection and the life, and he has won the victory over death.
❖ Jesus empathizes with us in our grief, but he brings hope to us through his lordship over death.
❖ If Jesus' Spirit dwells within us, we will experience eternal life.

❧ PRAYER FOR THE DAY ❧

Lord, thank you for being a God who can empathize with our suffering. Because you came to this earth in bodily form and lived among us, we know that we serve a Savior who can relate to all of our emotions, needs, and desires. As we walk through suffering, may we hold your hand while holding on to the hope of eternity you provide. Amen.

Comfort, comfort my people, says your God (Isaiah 40:1).

Day Four: The Dinner Party

AN ACT OF LOVE REMEMBERED

The Mary of Bethany we have seen has been more of a background character. She listened at the feet of Jesus and drew the ire of her more overbearing sister, but we don't have a record of her response. When her brother died and she heard Jesus was finally coming, she stayed home while Martha went out to meet Christ. Only when Martha told her Jesus was asking for her did she venture out. When she met Jesus, her statement expressed the same astonished disbelief as her sister's: "Lord, if you had been here, my brother would not have died" (John 11:32 NCV).

But the next time we meet Mary, shortly after the resurrection of Lazarus, she takes center stage by demonstrating an act of risky love the world would remember forever after. The scene takes place six days before the Passover feast, again in the city of Bethany, when Jesus is in town for a dinner party. This time, the setting for the party is in the home of a man named Simon, who we read "had a skin disease" (Matthew 26:6 NCV).

He had once been known as Simon the leper, but no longer. Now he is just Simon. We don't know when Jesus healed him, but we do know what he was like before Jesus healed him. Stooped shoulders. Fingerless hand. Scabbed arm and infected back draped in rags. A tattered wrap that hides all of the face except for two screaming white eyes.

But that was before Jesus' touch. Now, he is having Jesus and his disciples over for dinner. A simple act, but a significant one. After all, the Pharisees are already clearing a cell for Jesus. Won't be long until they finger Lazarus as an accomplice—and they could all be on wanted posters by the end of the week. It takes nerve to have a wanted man in your home.

But it takes more nerve to put your hand on a leper's sore. Simon hadn't forgotten what Jesus had done. He couldn't forget. Where there had been a nub, there was now a finger for his daughter to hold. Where there had been ulcerous sores, there was now skin for his wife to stroke. And where there had been lonely hours in quarantine, there were now happy hours such as this—a house full of friends, a table full of food.

1. Read Matthew 26:1–5. What had happened just before Jesus had this dinner party at Simon's house? What was the plot against Christ?

_____

_____

_____

When Martha heard that Jesus was coming, she went out to meet him, but Mary stayed at home (John 11:20).

Jesus was in Bethany in the home of Simon the Leper (Matthew 26:6).

Some of them went to the Pharisees and told them what Jesus had done (John 11:46).

The chief priests and the elders of the people assembled in the palace of the high priest . . . and they schemed to arrest Jesus secretly (Matthew 26:3–4).

Meanwhile a large crowd of Jews found out that Jesus was there and came, not only because of him but also to see Lazarus, whom he had raised from the dead (John 12:9).

2. The Jewish leaders were plotting Jesus' death, and his followers were in danger (see John 12:9–10). For this reason, it was quite risky for Jesus and the disciples to attend Simon's dinner. Describe a situation in your life when you encountered people hostile to Christ. Were you bold like Simon or more timid about your faith? Explain.

_____

_____

_____

3. What does it say about Simon that he was willing to host this party even though the priests and elders were conspiring to kill Jesus?

_____

_____

_____

Give thanks for everything to God the Father in the name of our Lord Jesus Christ (Ephesians 5:20 NLT).

4. Although we can't invite Jesus over to our house for a physical meal, we, like Simon, can take time to thank him. What has Jesus healed you from? What are you thankful for? Write the words of a prayer below expressing your gratitude to God.

_____

_____

_____

_____

No Doubts

When looking at the events of the crucifixion that follow, we can't help but wonder, *What if?* What if Pilate had come to the defense of the innocent? What if Herod had asked Jesus for help and not entertainment? What if the high priest had been as concerned with truth as he was his position? What if one of them had turned his back on the crowd and his face toward the Christ and made a stand?

But no one did. The mountain of prestige was too high. The fall would have been too great. But Simon did. Simon took a chance. He gave Jesus a good meal. Not much, but more than most. And when the priests accused and the soldiers slapped, perhaps Jesus remembered what Simon did and was strengthened. And when he remembered Simon's meal, perhaps he remembered Mary's gesture that took place there as well.

[Jesus] was in Bethany, reclining at the table in the home of Simon (Mark 14:3).

At that dinner party given in Jesus' honor, we read that Martha served while Lazarus was among those reclining at the table. But for Mary, simply giving the dinner was not enough. "Mary came in with a jar of very expensive aromatic oils, anointed and massaged Jesus' feet, and then wiped them with her hair. The fragrance of the oils filled the house" (John 12:3 MSG).

Martha served, while Lazarus was among those reclining at the table with him (John 12:2).

This time, we don't read that Martha objected. She had evidently learned there is a place for praise and worship, and that is what her sister, Mary, was doing. Mary was worshiping, for that is what she loved to do. The smell of the perfume filled the house, just like the sound of praise can fill a church. Jesus received the gesture as an extravagant demonstration of love—as a friend surrendering her most treasured gift.

As Jesus hung on the cross, we have to wonder if he detected the fragrance on his skin. It's not unlikely that he could. After all, it was twelve ounces' worth. Imported. Concentrated. Sweet. Strong enough to scent a man's clothes for days.

Between the lashings, we have to wonder if he relived the moment. As he hugged the Roman post and braced himself for the next ripping of his back, did he remember the oil that soothed his skin? Could he, in the faces of the women who stared, see the small, soft face of Mary, who cared?

She was the only one who believed him. Whenever he spoke of his death, the others shrugged, the others doubted, but Mary believed. Mary believed because he spoke with a firmness she'd heard before. "Lazarus, come out!" he'd demanded, and her brother came out. After four days in a stone-sealed grave, he walked out. As she had kissed the now-warm hands of her just-dead brother, she had turned to see Jesus. His tear streaks were dry now and his teeth shone. He was smiling.

In her heart, at that moment, she knew she would never doubt his words.

We are to God the pleasing aroma of Christ among those who are being saved (2 Corinthians 2:15).

5. Read John 12:1–3. When did this dinner take place? How did Mary anoint Jesus?

_____

_____

_____

_____

_____

_____

6. John says the perfume Mary used was expensive. Judas said it was worth 300 denarii. It is believed one denarius was a laborer's wage for one day, so the cost of the oil would be approximately a year's wages.[1] What does this reveal about Mary's gesture?

_____

_____

_____

_____

_____

_____

Let us go to his dwelling place, let us worship at his footstool (Psalm 132:7).

7. How was pouring out this expensive perfume on Jesus an act of worship on Mary's part?

_____

_____

_____

_____

_____

8. What can you pour out before Jesus as an act of worship at this very moment?

_____

_____

_____

_____

_____

He did not enter by means of the blood of goats and calves; but he entered the Most Holy Place once for all by his own blood, thus obtaining eternal redemption (Hebrews 9:12).

In the Old Testament, the law of God commanded the people to make offerings to the Lord at the temple. A ram on the day of atonement, a farmer's first crop, a peasant's pigeon . . . all of these were sacrificed on the altar of the temple. The sacrifices were a way for the people to express their worship to God and their gratitude for his forgiveness of sins. But most of all, the sacrifices pointed to the greatest sacrifice to come: the death of Christ. Mary's loving worship of Christ thus involved pouring an offering over the greatest offering ever given. She gave Jesus her most expensive earthly possession to anoint him for the death and burial he would endure to pay the price for our sins. May we all worship like Mary. May we love him so much that we put everything we own, every person we love, everything we are at his feet.

❧ POINTS TO REMEMBER ☙

❖ Jesus deserves our honor and worship for the healing work that he has done in our lives.
❖ Worship allows us to lay our lives down at Jesus' feet.
❖ Our sacrifice of worship is a sweet-smelling offering that points to Jesus, the greatest sacrifice ever given.

❧ PRAYER FOR THE DAY ☙

When we were still powerless, Christ died for the ungodly (Romans 5:6).

Jesus, today we thank you for the sacrifice you made for us at the cross. We thank you for pouring out your body before the Father so that we could stand before you in eternity. You are worthy of all our glory and praise. We love you. Amen.

Day Five: A Chance-Taking Love

THE FRAGRANCE OF FAITH

So it was that when Jesus spoke of his death, Mary believed. And when she saw Simon, Jesus, and Lazarus together, she couldn't resist. Simon, the healed leper, head thrown back in laughter. Lazarus, the resurrected corpse, leaning in to see what Jesus has said. And Jesus, the source of life for both, beginning his joke a second time.

Now is the right time, she had told herself. It wasn't an act of impulse. She had carried the large vial of perfume from her house to Simon's. It wasn't a spontaneous gesture. But it was an extravagant one. The perfume was worth a year's wages. Maybe the only thing of value she had. It wasn't a logical thing to do, but since when has love been led by logic?

Logic hadn't touched Simon. Common sense hadn't wept at Lazarus's tomb. Practicality hadn't fed the crowds or loved the children. Love did. Extravagant, risky, chance-taking love. And now someone needed to show the same to the giver of such love.

So Mary did. She stepped up behind him and stood with the jar in her hand. Within a couple of moments every mouth was silent and every eye wide as they watched her nervous fingers remove the ornate cover. Only Jesus was unaware of her presence. Just as he noticed everyone looking behind him, she began to pour. Over his head. Over his shoulders. Down his back. She would have poured herself out for him if she could.

The fragrance rushed through the room. Smells of cooked lamb and herbs were lost in the aroma of the sweet ointment. "Wherever you go," the gesture of Mary spoke, "breathe the aroma and remember one who cares." On his skin the fragrance of faith. In his clothing the balm of belief. Even as the Roman soldiers later divided his garments, her gesture brought a bouquet into a cemetery.

She broke the jar and poured the perfume on his head (Mark 14:3).

1. Read John 12:4–11. Why did Judas object to this act of worship on Mary's part? What does John reveal was the true motive behind his complaint?

He did not say this because he cared about the poor but because he was a thief (John 12:6).

_____

_____

_____

2. How did Jesus reply to Judas's objection? What did he mean when he said, "She did this in preparation for my burial" (verse 7 NLT)?

It was intended that she should save this perfume for the day of my burial (verse 7).

_____

_____

_____

She poured it on Jesus' feet (John 12:3).

3. Look at Matthew 26:7 and John 12:3. The custom of the time was to anoint the heads of guests, but Mary takes it a step further by anointing Jesus' feet. What does it say about Mary that she was willing to sit at the feet of Jesus? What does it say about her relationship with Christ?

_____

_____

_____

If you remain in me and I in you, you will bear much fruit (15:5).

4. Mary's love for Jesus ran deep. Maybe you easily love Jesus like Mary, but maybe you struggle. Regardless of where your love is today, how can you love Jesus more (see John 15:5–7 and 1 John 4:19)?

_____

_____

_____

_____

AN ACT REMEMBERED

When the disciples saw this, they were indignant (Matthew 26:8).

The other disciples mocked her extravagance. They thought it foolish. Ironic. Jesus had saved them from a sinking boat in a stormy sea. He had enabled them to heal and preach. He had brought focus into their fuzzy lives. Yet now, these disciples—the recipients of Christ's exorbitant love—chastised her generosity.

"Why waste that perfume? It could have been sold for a great deal of money and the money given to the poor," they smirk. Don't miss Jesus' prompt defense of Mary. "Why are you troubling this woman? She did an excellent thing for me" (Matthew 26:10 NCV). Jesus' message is just as powerful today as it was then. Don't miss it: "There is a time for risky love. There is a time for extravagant gestures. There is a time to pour out your affections on one you love. And when the time comes—seize it, don't miss it."

The poor you will always have with you, and you can help them any time you want. But you will not always have me (Mark 14:7).

The young husband is packing his wife's belongings. His task solemn. His heart heavy. He never dreamed she would die so young. But the cancer came so sure, so quickly. At the bottom of the drawer he finds a box, a negligee. Unworn. Still wrapped in paper. "She was always waiting for a special occasion," he says to himself, "always waiting . . ."

As the boy on the bicycle watches the students taunt, he churns inside. That's his little brother they are laughing at. He knows he should step in and stand up for his brother, but . . . those are his friends doing the teasing. What will they think? And because it matters what they think, he turns and pedals away.

As the husband looks in the jewelry case, he rationalizes, "Sure she would want the watch, but it's too expensive. She's a practical woman. I'll just get the bracelet today. I'll buy the watch . . . someday."

Someday. The enemy of risky love is a snake whose tongue has mastered the talk of deception. "Someday," he hisses.

"Someday, I can take her on the cruise."

"Someday, I will have time to call and chat."

"Someday, the children will understand why I was so busy."

But you know the truth, don't you? You know even before I write it. You could say it better than I. *Somedays never come.* The price of practicality is sometimes higher than extravagance. But the rewards of risky love are always greater than its cost. Go to the effort. Invest the time. Write the letter. Make the apology. Purchase the gift. Do it. The seized opportunity renders joy. The neglected opportunity brings regret.

You do not even know what will happen tomorrow. . . . You are a mist that appears for a little while and then vanishes (James 4:14).

5. We all, like the disciples, have judged someone else's extravagant act of worship out of jealousy, misunderstanding, or self-righteousness. But what does this story reveal to us about the kind of worship that God desires from us?

_____

_____

_____

_____

6. In what ways have you worshiped God with risky love? What were the results of worshiping God in that way for both yourself and for others?

_____

_____

_____

_____

_____

7. As the name implies, risky love involves *risk*. What do we read happened at the end of this story (see John 12:9–11)? What were the consequences to Mary and her family for her act of risky love? Do you think this was worth the price for her?

_____

_____

_____

A large crowd of Jews found out that Jesus was there and came, not only because of him but also to see Lazarus, whom he had raised from the dead. So the chief priests made plans to kill Lazarus as well (John 12:9–10).

8. Our acts of risky love for Christ should be given to others. What is at least one way you can show someone a generous act of love like Mary showed Jesus? How will you put this risky act of love into practice so you don't just rely on doing it "someday"?

_____

_____

_____

Truly I tell you, wherever the gospel is preached throughout the world, what she has done will also be told, in memory of her (Mark 14:9).

At the end of the story, Jesus said, "[Mary] did an excellent thing for me. . . . This woman poured perfume on my body to prepare me for burial. I tell you the truth, wherever the Good News is preached in all the world, what this woman has done will be told, and people will remember her" (Matthew 26:10, 12–13). Mary's gesture of worship to her Lord would never be forgotten. Her act of risky love in anointing Christ for his burial was a risky gift given at just the right time.

Which brings us back to the story of Artful Eddie, the Chicago mobster we discussed at the beginning of this lesson. As you will recall, Eddie squealed on Al Capone so his son could have a fair chance—and paid the price when the mob silenced him forever. Was it worth it? I believe Eddie would have said so had he lived to see his son, Butch, grow up.

I think he would have been proud of Butch's appointment to Annapolis. I think he would have been proud of the young man's commissioning as a World War II Navy pilot. I think he would have been proud as he read of his son downing five bombers in the Pacific night and saving the lives of hundreds of crewmen on the carrier *Lexington*. He would have been proud that his son cleared the family name. The Congressional Medal of Honor that Butch received was proof.

When people say the name O'Hare in Chicago, they no longer think *gangsters*—they think *aviation heroism*. And now when you say his name, you have something else to think about: the undying dividends of risky love. Think about it the next time you hear it. Think about it the next time you fly into the airport named after the son of a gangster gone good.

The son of Eddie O'Hare.

Gracious words are a honeycomb, sweet to the soul and healing to the bones (Proverbs 16:24).

Today, you can follow the example of risky love that Mary modeled for Christ. There is an elderly man in your community who just lost his wife. An hour of your time would mean the world to him. Some kids in your city have no dad. No father takes them to movies or baseball games. Maybe you can. They can't pay you back. They can't even afford the popcorn or sodas. But they'll smile like a cantaloupe slice at your kindness.

Or how about this one? Down the hall from your bedroom is a person who shares your last name. Shock that person with kindness. Something outlandish. Your homework done with no complaints. Coffee served before he awakens. A love letter written to her for no special reason. Alabaster poured . . . *just because.*

Want to snatch a day from the manacles of boredom? Do over-generous deeds, acts beyond reimbursement. Kindness without compensation. Do a deed for which you cannot be repaid. Be risky with your acts of love, just as Mary was risky with hers.

POINTS TO REMEMBER

❖ Jesus is the author of risky, chance-taking love, and he desires for us to extend that same type of love to others.

❖ There is a time for us to do acts of extravagant love—and the reward for those acts is always greater than the cost.

❖ We need to engage in overgenerous deeds, kindness without compensation, and service beyond reimbursement—for this is the love God shows to us.

PRAYER FOR THE DAY

Lord Jesus, you are our example of risky, chance-taking love, for you gave us the extravagant gift of yourself through your death on the cross. Today we are humbled and overflowing with gratitude for your sacrifice on our behalf. May we generously spread your amazing love to others. In your name we pray, amen.

WEEKLY MEMORY VERSE

This is My commandment, that you love one another, just as I have loved you. Greater love has no one than this, that one lay down his life for his friends.
JOHN 15:12–13 (NASB)

For Further Reading

Selections throughout this lesson were taken from *And the Angels Were Silent* (Nashville: Thomas Nelson, 1987); *He Still Moves Stones* (Nashville: Thomas Nelson, 1993); *A Gentle Thunder* (Nashville: Thomas Nelson, 1995); *Next Door Savior* (Nashville: Thomas Nelson, 2003); and *It's Not About Me* (Nashville: Thomas Nelson, 2004).

Note
1. Earl Radmacher, Ronald B. Allen, H. Wayne House, eds., *Nelson's New Illustrated Bible Commentary* (Nashville: Thomas Nelson, 1999), p. 1343.

MARY MAGDALENE

ENCOUNTERING THE GOD OF SURPRISES

Y OU KNOW HOW YOU CAN READ A STORY YOU THINK YOU KNOW, and then you read it again and see something you've never seen? You know how you can read about the same event 100 times and then on the one hundred and first hear something so striking and new that it makes you wonder if you slept through the other times?

Maybe it's because you started in the middle of the story instead of at the beginning. Or perhaps it's because someone else reads it aloud and pauses at a place where you normally wouldn't and POW! It hits you. You grab the book and look at it, knowing that someone copied or read something wrong. But then you read it and well-how-do-you-do. Look at that!

Well, it happened to me. Today. Only God knows how many times I've read the resurrection story. At least a couple of dozen Easters and a couple of hundred times in between. I've taught it. I've written about it. I've meditated on it. I've underlined it. But what I saw today I'd never seen before.

What did I see? Before I tell you, let me recount the story.

It's early dawn on Sunday morning and the sky is dark. Those, in fact, are John's words. "It was still dark . . ." (John 20:1). It's a dark Sunday morning. It had been dark since Friday. Dark with Peter's denial. Dark with the disciples' betrayal. Dark with Pilate's cowardice. Dark with Christ's anguish. Dark with Satan's glee. The only ember of light is the small band of women standing at a distance from the cross—"watching from a distance" (Matthew 27:55).

Among them are two Marys. One the mother of James and Joseph, and the other is Mary Magdalene. Why are they there? They are there

Early on the first day of the week, while it was still dark, Mary Magdalene went to the tomb (John 20:1).

Many women were there, watching from a distance (Matthew 27:55).

197

They had followed Jesus from Galilee to care for his needs (Matthew 27:55).

Joseph took the body . . . and placed it in his own new tomb. . . . Mary Magdalene and the other Mary were sitting there opposite the tomb (verses 59–61).

to call Jesus' name. To be the final voices he hears before his death. To prepare his body for burial. They are there to clean the blood from his beard. To wipe the crimson from his legs. To close his eyes. To touch his face. They are there. The last to leave Calvary and the first to arrive at the grave.

So, early on that Sunday morning, they leave their pallets and walk out onto the tree-shadowed path. Theirs is a somber task. The morning promises only one encounter: an encounter with a corpse. Remember, Mary Magdalene and the other Mary don't know this is the first Easter. They are not hoping the tomb will be vacant. They aren't discussing what their response will be when they see Jesus. Their dreams have been dashed.

They have absolutely no idea that the grave has been vacated.

Blessed are those who find wisdom, those who gain understanding (Proverbs 3:13).

1. In James 1:5, we read, "If any of you lacks wisdom, let him ask of God, who gives to all liberally and without reproach, and it will be given to him" (NKJV). What fresh insights do you need from God today for a problem you are facing?

_____

_____

_____

_____

2. In what ways are you feeling stuck or stagnant in your walk with God? In what areas of your life do you need to encounter "the God of surprises"?

_____

_____

_____

_____

Jesus . . . endured the cross, scorning its shame (Hebrews 12:22).

Mary Magdalene's tears show us that she didn't wake up that Sunday morning expecting Jesus to be alive. Her Lord was dead, and she was devastated. Yet, even though he was executed on a cross—a shameful way to die—she wasn't ashamed of him. She wasn't angry with him. She didn't betray him. She was the last at the cross and the first at the grave. Mary Magdalene embodies loyalty. No matter what other people said about him, what she understood of him, or what hopelessness she felt, she chose to stand by Jesus. She served him till the end . . . or what she thought was the end. This lesson, as we look at her faith, let's ask God to give us Mary Magdalene devotion. Let's ask God to help us stand by him and serve him no matter what life brings or how hopeless we feel. Let's ask him to allow the resurrection story to stir fresh excitement in our hearts and remind us of the devotion our risen Savior deserves.

Day One: The Woman with Seven Demons

OPPRESSED BY DEMONS

The woman we know as Mary Magdalene is one of the more intriguing characters we find in the New Testament. She is named at least twelve times in the four Gospels, more than most of the other apostles, yet we know little about her life before she met Jesus. One thing we do know is her place of birth, for her name is derived from her hometown of Magdala, a town that in Jesus' day was located on the western shore of the Sea of Galilee.

A brief note in two of the Gospels reveals another fascinating detail about Mary's early life: she had been possessed by seven demons before Jesus cast them out (see Luke 8:2). We have no idea exactly when or how this occurred, but another story told in the Gospels of Matthew, Mark, and Luke gives us a picture of what such demon possession looked like and how Jesus went about casting them out.

The person whom Jesus healed in this instance was afflicted not with seven demons but perhaps with *thousands*. Jesus met him shortly after performing a miracle of calming the wind and waves that had threatened to overturn the disciples' boat on the Sea of Galilee. After that harrowing ordeal for the disciples, they stepped off the boat and onto the shore in a region known as the Gadarenes. There they were met by another terrifying sight.

When He got out of the boat, immediately a man from the tombs with an unclean spirit met Him, and he had his dwelling among the tombs. And no one was able to bind him anymore, even with a chain; because he had often been bound with shackles and chains, and the chains had been torn apart by him and the shackles broken in pieces, and no one was strong enough to subdue him. Constantly, night and day, he was screaming among the

The Twelve were with him, and also some women who had been cured of evil spirits and diseases: Mary (called Magdalene) (Luke 8:1–2).

Mary . . . from whom seven demons had come out (verse 2).

They sailed to the region of the Gerasenes, which is across the lake from Galilee. When Jesus stepped ashore, he was met by a demon-possessed man from the town (Luke 8:26-27).

tombs and in the mountains, and gashing himself with stones (Mark 5:2–5 NASB).

For a long time this man had not worn clothes or lived in a house, but had lived in the tombs (Luke 8:27).

Just picture this man the disciples saw on that day. Wiry, clumpy hair. A beard to the chest, ribboned with blood. Furtive eyes, darting in all directions, refusing to fix. Naked. No sandals to protect feet from the rocks of the ground or clothing to protect skin from the rocks of his hand. He beats himself with stones. Bruises blotch his skin like ink stains. Open sores and gashes attract flies.

His home is a limestone mausoleum, a graveyard of Galilean shoreline caves cut out of the cliffs. Apparently he feels more secure among the dead than the living. Which pleases the living. He baffles them. See the cracked shackles on his legs and broken chains on his wrists? They can't control the guy. Nothing holds him. How do you manage chaos?

Travelers skirt the area out of fear, for the demons in the man are "so violent that no one could pass that way" (Matthew 8:28). The villagers were left with a problem, and we are left with a picture—a picture of the work of Satan.

1. The Bible tells us little about Mary Magdalene's past and how she came to follow Jesus. Read Luke's short account in Luke 8:1–3. From these few verses, what do you initially observe about Mary? What she did do after Christ healed her?

   _____

   _____

   _____

   _____

Night and day among the tombs and in the hills he would cry out and cut himself with stones (Mark 5:5).

2. Read Mark 5:1–5. Just as Jesus freed Mary of the demons that possessed her, so he freed a man living along the Galilean seashore from the demons that possessed him. What were the demons causing this man to do? What was life like for him?

   _____

   _____

   _____

   _____

You believe that there is one God. Good! Even the demons believe that—and shudder (James 2:19).

3. "When Jesus had stepped out of the boat, *immediately* there met him out of the tombs a man with an unclean spirit" (Mark 5:2 ESV, emphasis added). Not all translations include the word *immediately*, but in the original Greek, Mark includes this adverb. Why is this word significant? What does it say about Jesus and the demonic world?

   _____

   _____

   _____

   _____

4. What happened when the people of the region tried to subdue the man with chains? What does this say about the power of the flesh against the spiritual world?

_____

_____

_____

_____

SATAN'S GOALS

Satan does not sit still in this world, and a glimpse of this wild man reveals his goals for you and me. *Self-imposed pain.* The demoniac used rocks. We are more sophisticated—we use drugs, sex, work, violence, and food. Hell makes us hurt ourselves.

Obsession with death and darkness. Even unchained, the wild man loitered among the dead. Evil feels at home there. Communing with the deceased, sacrificing the living, a morbid fascination with death and dying—this is not the work of God.

Endless restlessness. The man on the eastern shore screamed day and night (see Mark 5:5). Satan begets raging frenzy. "When an impure spirit comes out of a person," Jesus says, "it goes through arid places seeking rest" (Matthew 12:43).

Isolation. The man is all alone in his suffering. Such is Satan's plan. "The devil prowls around like a roaring lion looking for *someone* to devour" (1 Peter 5:8, emphasis added). Fellowship foils his work.

And Jesus? Jesus wrecks his work. Christ steps out of the boat with both pistols blasting. "Come out of the man, unclean spirit!" (Mark 5:8 NKJV). No chitchat. No niceties. No salutations. Demons deserve no tolerance. They throw themselves at the feet and mercy of Christ. The leader of the horde begs for the others: "What have you to do with me, Jesus, Son of the Most High God? I adjure you by God, do not torment me" (verse 6 NRSV).

When Jesus commands the demons to identify themselves, they reply, "My name is Legion; for we are many" (verse 9 NRSV). *Legion* is a Roman military term. A Roman legion involved 6,000 soldiers. To envision that many demons inhabiting this man is frightening but not unrealistic. What bats are to a cave, demons are to hell—too many to number.

5. Read Mark 5:6–9. What did Jesus do when he saw the man? How did the demons within the man respond to Christ?

_____

_____

_____

_____

We know that we are children of God, and that the whole world is under the control of the evil one (1 John 5:19).

The reason the Son of God appeared was to destroy the devil's work (1 John 3:8).

Jesus asked him, "What is your name?" "Legion," he replied, because many demons had gone into him (Luke 8:30).

Jesus had commanded the impure spirit to come out of the man (verse 29).

[He] had been driven by the demon into solitary places (Mark 5:29).

6. Satan imprisoned this man through self-imposed pain, obsession with death and darkness, endless restlessness, and isolation. In what ways has the enemy used these weapons against you or someone you love? How did you combat these attacks?

_____

_____

_____

_____

_____

Be sober-minded; be watchful. Resist [the devil], firm in your faith (1 Peter 5:8–9 ESV).

7. Read 1 Peter 5:8–9. What does Peter warn us, as Christians, to do in these verses? What does it mean to be "sober-minded"? How can we "resist" the devil?

_____

_____

_____

_____

_____

8. C. S. Lewis wrote, "There are two equal and opposite errors into which our race can fall about the devils. One is to disbelieve in their existence. The other is to believe, and to feel an excessive and unhealthy interest in them."[1] Which of these "errors" do you tend to commit? What is the downside of each of these errors?

_____

_____

_____

_____

_____

We do not belong to the night or to the darkness. So then . . . let us be awake and sober (1 Thessalonians 5:5–6).

The enemy of our souls is on the prowl. He loves it when we forget he exists, because this causes us to let down our defenses. He also loves it when we obsess over his existence, because this causes us to focus less on the existence and power of God. There is a fine spiritual line for us to walk. For while it is true that the devil is just as real today as he was during the time of Mary Magdalene—and that he seeks to imprison people today just as he imprisoned the man on the Galilean seashore—God doesn't want us to be filled with worry or angst over him. As Peter says, we are to "keep a cool head. Stay alert." We are to be alert, but alert with a cool head. We should be peacefully aware of the enemy. We should be aware of his strategies so we are ready to fight, but at peace because we know the Victor is on our side.

POINTS TO REMEMBER

❖ Satan uses self-imposed pain, darkness, and isolation to try to keep us distant from God and God's plans for us.
❖ Jesus reaches out to us when we are held in bondage by the enemy, frees us from Satan's power, and brings us healing and restoration.
❖ We need to recognize evil in the world and confidently fight it through the power of Jesus Christ within us.

To him who loves us and has freed us from our sins by his blood (Revelation 1:5).

PRAYER FOR THE DAY

Lord, help us to resist the devil and his schemes. Help us to be aware of the devil so that we do not fall into his traps but be at peace because we know that you are the Lord over all, including our enemy. We know that in you we have nothing to fear. Amen.

Day Two: The Authority of Christ

INTO THE SWINE

The demons in this man are numerous, just as they were in Mary Magdalene, and they are also equipped. A legion is a battalion in arms. Satan and his friends come to fight. Hence, we are urged to "take up the full armor of God, so that you will be able to resist in the evil day, and having done everything, to stand firm" (Ephesians 6:13 NASB).

Let us put aside the deeds of darkness and put on the armor of light (Romans 13:12).

Well we should, for they are organized. "We are fighting against forces and authorities and against rulers of darkness and powers in the spiritual world" (verse 12 CEV). Jesus spoke of the "gates of hell" (Matthew 16:18 KJV), a phrase that suggests the "council of hell." Our enemy has a complex and conniving spiritual army. Dismiss any image of a red-suited Satan with pitchfork and pointy tail. The devil is a strong devil.

But—and this is the point of the passage—in God's presence, the devil is a wimp. Satan is to God what a mosquito is to an atomic bomb. Just as Jesus cast the seven demons out of Mary Magdalene, so he would cast out the legion of demons in this man. The number didn't matter to Jesus, for he had authority over *all* demons.

Take heart! I have overcome the world (John 16:33).

Mark tells us that a large herd of pigs was feeding nearby. So all the demons begged Jesus to send them "to the swine, that we may enter them" (Mark 5:12 NKJV). How hell's court cowers in Christ's presence!

Demons bow before him, solicit him, and obey him. They can't even lease a pig without his permission. "Then the unclean spirits went out and entered the swine . . . and the herd ran violently down the steep place into the sea, and drowned in the sea" (verse 13 NKJV).

He begged Jesus again and again not to send them out of the area (Mark 5:10).

1. Read Mark 5:10–14. What did Legion, or the group of demons within the man, request of Jesus? What happened as a result?

_____

_____

_____

Put on the full armor of God, so that you can take your stand against the devil's schemes (Ephesians 6:11).

2. Turn to Ephesians 6:10–20. What is the "armor of God"? Why does Paul say we need to equip this armor? How often are we to equip it?

_____

_____

_____

Our struggle is not against flesh and blood, but against . . . the spiritual forces of evil in the heavenly realms (verse 12).

3. According to verse 12, against whom do we battle? How can remembering this verse give you a better perspective the next time conflict arises?

_____

_____

_____

Take up the shield of faith, with which you can extinguish all the flaming arrows of the evil one (verse 16).

4. Paul's "above all" piece of armor which he urges us to take is the shield of faith (verse 16 KJV). A Roman soldier's shield typically measured two and a half feet by four feet, which means it protected the whole body. How does faith protect your whole being from Satan's attacks? How does faith extinguish the arrows of the enemy?

_____

_____

_____

THE SERPENT IS CRUSHED

Mary Magdalene was delivered from seven demons. This man from the Gadarenes was delivered from thousands. These stories remind us that while Satan can disturb us, he cannot defeat us. The head of the serpent is crushed (see Genesis 3:15).

He will crush your head, and you will strike his heel (Genesis 3:15).

I saw a literal picture of this in a prairie ditch. A petroleum company was hiring strong backs and weak minds to lay a pipeline. Because I qualified, much of a high-school summer was spent shoveling in a shoulder-high, multi-mile West Texas trough. A large digging machine trenched ahead of us. We followed, scooping out the excess dirt and rocks.

One afternoon the machine dislodged more than dirt. "Snake!" shouted the foreman. We popped out of that hole faster than a jack-in-the-box and looked down at the rattlesnake nest. Big momma hissed, and her little kids squirmed. Reentering the trench was not an option. One worker launched his shovel and beheaded the rattler. We stood on the higher ground and watched as she—now headless—writhed and twisted in the soft dirt below. Though defanged, the snake still spooked us.

Gee, Max, thanks for the inspirational image. Inspirational? Maybe not. But hopeful? I think so. That scene in the West Texas summer is a parable of where we are in life. Is the devil not a snake? John calls him "that old snake who is the devil" (Revelation 20:2 NCV). Has he not been decapitated? Not with a shovel, but with a cross. "[God] disarmed the spiritual rulers and authorities. He shamed them publicly by his victory over them on the cross" (Colossians 2:15 NLT).

So how does that leave us? *Confident.* The punch line of the passage is Jesus' power over Satan. One word from Christ, and the demons are swimming with the swine, and the wild man is "clothed, and in his right mind" (Mark 5:15 NCV). Just one command! No séance needed. No hocus-pocus. No chants were heard or candles lit. Hell is an anthill against heaven's steamroller. Jesus "commands . . . evil spirits, and they obey him" (Mark 1:27 NCV). The snake in the ditch and Lucifer in the pit—both have met their match.

> *The great dragon was hurled down—that ancient serpent called the devil, or Satan, who leads the whole world astray* (Revelation 12:9).

> *They found the man from whom the demons had gone out, sitting at Jesus' feet, dressed and in his right mind* (Luke 8:35).

5. Read Mark 5:15–20. Why do you think the people were afraid when they saw the Galilean man in his right mind? Why did they plead with Jesus to leave the region?

> *Those who had seen it told the people what had happened to the demon-possessed man—and told about the pigs as well. Then the people began to plead with Jesus to leave their region* (Mark 5:16–17).

_____

_____

_____

_____

_____

6. What request did the former demon-possessed man make of Jesus? Why do you think Jesus refused? How did you think the man served as a witness to Christ back in his hometown—where the people had previously feared him?

> *The man . . . begged to go with [Jesus]* (verse 18).

_____

_____

_____

_____

_____

_____

The woman said, "The serpent deceived me, and I ate" (Genesis 3:13).

Her Seed . . . shall bruise your head (Genesis 3:15 NKJV).

7. Turn to Genesis 3:9–15. After Adam and Eve sinned, God issued a curse against both them and the serpent (Satan). What did God promise would happen between them? What did God mean when he said the woman's "Seed" would bruise Satan's head?

_____

_____

_____

When you are tempted, he will also provide a way out (1 Corinthians 10:13).

Everyone born of God overcomes the world (1 John 5:4).

8. Christ destroyed the power of Satan at the cross, yet the enemy still slithers around, tempting us with forbidden fruit. Read 1 Corinthians 10:13 and 1 John 5:4. What promise are we given in these verses when we resist the devil's schemes? In what ways are you living by the victorious truth of this promise?

_____

_____

_____

Not only did Christ declare victory over evil when he rose from the grave, but he also gave us victory over evil in this fallen world. If we find ourselves beaten down by Satan's lies or mired in his temptations, it means we are doing one of two things: (1) not *believing* in the power of the cross, or (2) not *standing* in the power of the cross. Both are important, for the first requires us to have faith in Jesus, while the other requires us to have a relationship with Jesus. Only as we believe in Jesus and stand in the power of his might can we fight the enemy (see Ephesians 6:10). Only when we rely on the power of our Lord and Savior can we—like Mary Magdalene and the demon-possessed man in Galilee—be free of the darkness in our lives. As John wrote, "You are of God, little children, and have overcome [evil spirits], because He who is in you is greater than he who is in the world" (1 John 4:4 NKJV).

Do not be overcome by evil, but overcome evil with good (Romans 12:21).

Finally, be strong in the Lord and in his mighty power (Ephesians 6:10).

⟶ POINTS TO REMEMBER ⟵

❖ We should not underestimate the strength of the devil—for he is a powerful foe—but we must remember he is no match for the power of the cross!
❖ When we equip the full armor of God, it enables us to resist the devil and stand firm in the face of his attacks.
❖ Although Satan can *challenge* those of us who are followers of Christ, we can be confident that he cannot *defeat* us.

⟶ PRAYER FOR THE DAY ⟵

Jesus, you are alive! You are victorious! And through you we have been given the ultimate power over the enemy today and forever. Thank you for the cross. Thank you that the battle belongs to you. And thank you for your promises that we can always trust in your might. In your name, Lord, we pray. Amen.

Day Three: Mary at the Cross

THE WOMAN WHO REMAINED

As I've said, we don't know if Jesus' deliverance of Mary Magdalene happened in this same way. But we do know the *effects* of the healing were the same. After Jesus healed the man from Gadarenes, he became his follower. After Jesus healed Mary, she also became his devoted follower. Hippolytus of Rome, a third-century theologian, would later go as far as to call her "the Apostle to the Apostles."[2]

Mary's devotion led her to stay in Jerusalem while Jesus was being put to death. The religious leaders had been concerned about Jesus' disciples. They had gone to Pilate and said, "Give the order for the tomb to be guarded closely till the third day. Otherwise, his followers might come and steal the body and tell people that he has risen from the dead" (Matthew 27:64 NCV). But no such concern was really necessary. The disciples were at meltdown.

When Jesus was arrested, "All the disciples forsook Him and fled" (Matthew 26:56 NKJV). Peter followed from a distance but caved in and cursed Christ. John watched Jesus die, but we have no record that John gave any thought to ever seeing him again. The other followers didn't even linger. They cowered in Jerusalem's cupboards and corners for fear of the cross that bore their names. But not Mary. She had heard the leaders clamor for Jesus' blood. She had witnessed the Roman whip rip the skin off his back. She had winced as the thorns sliced his brow and had wept at the weight of the cross.

In the Louvre hangs a painting of the scene at the cross. In the painting the stars are dead and the world is wrapped in darkness. In the shadows there is a kneeling form. It is Mary. She is holding her hands and lips against the bleeding feet of the Christ. We don't know if Mary did that, but we know she could have. She was there. She was there to hold her arm around the shoulder of Mary, the mother of Jesus. She was there to close his eyes. She was there.

1. Read Matthew 26:31–35. What did Jesus predict would happen that night? Notice that Jesus quoted prophecy here (see Zechariah 13:7). In spite of this, what bold claims did Peter and the other disciples make?

_____

_____

_____

_____

Mary (called Magdalene) . . . Joanna the wife of Chuza, the manager of Herod's household; Susanna; and many others . . . women were helping to support them out of their own means (Luke 8:2–3).

"Take a guard," Pilate answered. "Go, make the tomb as secure as you know how" (Matthew 27:65).

Peter remembered the word the Lord had spoken to him: "Before the rooster crows today, you will disown me three times." And he went outside and wept bitterly (Luke 22:61–62).

Many other women who had come up with him to Jerusalem were also there (Mark 15:41).

Strike the shepherd, and the sheep will be scattered (Zechariah 13:7).

How then would the Scriptures be fulfilled that say it must happen in this way? (Matthew 26:54).

2. Read verses 47–56. How did Jesus' words come true? Why did Jesus say these events had to come to pass?

_____

_____

_____

Near the cross of Jesus stood his mother, his mother's sister, Mary the wife of Clopas, and Mary Magdalene (John 19:25).

3. Turn to John 19:23–26. Where is Mary Magdalene when Jesus dies? How, in the face of the angry crowd, does Mary's presence at the cross show her devotion to Christ?

_____

_____

_____

_____

If we are faithless, he remains faithful, for he cannot disown himself (2 Timothy 2:13).

4. When was a time that you acted like the disciples who betrayed Jesus? When was a time you displayed your devotion to him like Mary? What words of comfort does Paul provide in 2 Timothy 2:13 for those times when we are either faithful or faithless?

_____

_____

_____

_____

TOO LATE FOR THE INCREDIBLE

Given Mary's devotion to Jesus, it's not surprising that she wants to be at his tomb the next day. But once again, as we read the account, it's clear no one is dreaming of a Sunday-morning miracle. Mary doesn't ponder, *How will he appear?* She and the other disciples are not encouraging one another with quotes of his promised return. They could have. At least four times Jesus had said words like these: "The Son of Man is being betrayed into the hands of men, and they will kill Him. And after He is killed, He will rise the third day" (Mark 9:31 NKJV).

You'd think someone would mention this prophecy and do the math. "Hmm, he died yesterday. Today is the second day. He promised to rise on the third day. Tomorrow is the third day . . . Friends, I think we'd better wake up early tomorrow." But Saturday saw no such plans. So, in the early morning mist, the two Marys arise, take their spices and aloes, and leave the house, past the Gate of Gennath and up to the hillside. They anticipate a somber task. By now the body will be swollen. Jesus' face will be white. Death's odor will be pungent.

But [the disciples] did not understand what he meant and were afraid to ask him about it (Mark 8:32).

For Mary, it's too late for the incredible. The feet that walked on water had been pierced. The hands that healed lepers had been stilled. Noble aspirations had been spiked into Friday's cross. Mary had only come to place warm oils on a cold body and bid farewell to the one man who gave reason to their hopes.

Mary Magdalene, Mary the mother of James, and Salome bought spices so that they might go to anoint Jesus' body (Mark 16:1).

5. The Gospels include multiple accounts of Jesus predicting his death and resurrection. What details does Jesus provide to his disciples in the following passages? How do the disciples respond to his words each time?

Mark 8:31–32: "He began to teach them that the Son of Man must suffer many things and be rejected by the elders and the chief priests and the scribes, and be killed, and after three days rise again. And He was stating the matter plainly. And Peter took Him aside and began to rebuke Him" (NASB).

He was oppressed and afflicted, yet he did not open his mouth; he was led like a lamb to the slaughter (Isaiah 53:7).

_____

_____

_____

_____

Matthew 17:22–23: "Now while they were staying in Galilee, Jesus said to them, 'The Son of Man is about to be betrayed into the hands of men, and they will kill Him, and the third day He will be raised up.' And they were exceedingly sorrowful" (NKJV).

_____

_____

_____

_____

Matthew 20:17–19: "As Jesus was going up to Jerusalem, he took the twelve disciples aside, and on the way he said to them, 'See, we are going up to Jerusalem. And the Son of Man will be delivered over to the chief priests and scribes, and they will condemn him to death and deliver him over to the Gentiles to be mocked and flogged and crucified, and he will be raised on the third day'" (ESV).

_____

_____

_____

_____

6. Given the number of times Jesus made these predictions, why do you think the disciples did not rush to the tomb Sunday morning alongside Mary expecting to see him alive? What do you think prevented them from seeing that Jesus would rise from the dead?

As Jonah was three days and three nights in the belly of a huge fish, so the Son of Man will be three days and three nights in the heart of the earth (Matthew 12:40).

_____

_____

_____

_____

_____

_____

Very early on the first day of the week, just after sunrise, they were on their way to the tomb and they asked each other, "Who will roll the stone away from the entrance of the tomb?" (Mark 16:2–3).

7. Read Mark 16:1–3. What are the women's concerns as they approach Jesus' tomb? How does this reveal that Mary Magdalene was not expecting to find a risen Christ?

_____

_____

_____

_____

_____

8. For Mary, all looked hopeless after the crucifixion, and yet she still woke early to be the first to see him in the grave Sunday morning. What does this tell us about her love for Jesus? What acts of service are you doing to demonstrate your love for Christ?

_____

_____

_____

_____

_____

No matter how many times we hear a passage of Scripture, it is easy for us to forget God's promises to us when we are in the heat of the moment. A friend hurts us with cutting words. A loved one dies. We don't get the job we wanted. In these moments, we lose sight of God's promises—his promise to never leave us, his promise to be strong in our weakness, his promise to produce perseverance in our suffering. Like the disciples, we forget the words Jesus has spoken to us and give in to worry, fear, sorrow, anguish, and doubt. In such times, we need to remember the example of Mary. Even though she was confused and uncertain of where life would lead next, she chose to wake up Sunday morning and go to Jesus. In the same way, no matter how devastated we may feel, or how far we feel we have gone from God's promises, we can choose to wake up in the morning and turn to Jesus.

If we died with him, we will also live with him; if we endure, we will also reign with him (2 Timothy 2:11–12).

❥ POINTS TO REMEMBER ❧

❖ The promise of God is that even when we are faithless toward him, he is always loving and faithful toward us.
❖ Remembering the promises that God has provided to us in his Word can keep us from giving in to fear, worry, doubt, and the deceptions of the enemy.
❖ When life is uncertain and we are unsure of where to turn next, we should always go to Jesus and find our security in him.

∽ PRAYER FOR THE DAY ∼

Lord, thank you for being faithful to us even when we are forgetful of your promises. Thank you for being faithful even when we betray our faith. Although we will not always understand why things have turned out the way they have, let us find our strength in you and seek you out in our hour of need. Give us a deeper devotion to you. Amen.

Great is your faithfulness (Lamentations 3:23).

Day Four: A Surprise at the Tomb

STAYING THE COURSE

No, it isn't hope that leads the two Marys up the mountain to the tomb. It is *duty*. Naked devotion. They expect nothing in return, for what can a dead man offer? The two Marys are not climbing the mountain to receive but are going to the tomb to give. Period.

After the Sabbath, at dawn on the first day of the week, Mary Magdalene and the other Mary went to look at the tomb (Matthew 28:1).

There is no motivation more noble. There are times when we, too, are called to love, expecting nothing in return. Times when we are called to give money to people who will never say thanks, to forgive those who won't forgive us, to come early and stay late when no one else notices. Service prompted by duty. This is the call of discipleship.

Mary and Mary knew a task had to be done: Jesus' body had to be prepared for burial. Peter didn't offer to do it. Andrew didn't volunteer. The forgiven adulteress or healed lepers are nowhere to be seen. So the two Marys decide to do it.

I wonder if halfway to the tomb they had sat down and reconsidered. What if they had looked at each other and shrugged. "What's the use?" What if they had given up? What if one had thrown up her arms in frustration and bemoaned, "I'm tired of being the only one who cares. Let Andrew do something for a change. Let Nathaniel show some leadership."

Whether or not they were tempted to quit, I'm glad they stayed the course. For if they hadn't, it would have been tragic. You see, we know something they didn't. We know the Father was watching. Mary and Mary thought they were alone. They weren't. They thought their journey was unnoticed. They were wrong. God knew. He was watching them walk up the mountain. He was measuring their steps. He was smiling at their hearts and thrilled at their devotion. And he had a surprise waiting for them.

Let us not become weary in doing good (Galatians 6:9).

211

1. Mary chose to serve Christ even though there was nothing promised to her in return. In what way are your motives the same as or different from Mary's when it comes to serving God? What obstacles tend to get in the way of selflessly serving Christ?

_____

_____

_____

_____

2. Jesus is the ultimate example of giving with no expectation of receiving anything in return. What do the following passages say about what he gave for us?

Luke 24:46–47: "Thus it is written, that the Christ should suffer and on the third day rise from the dead, and that repentance and forgiveness of sins should be proclaimed in his name to all nations" (ESV).

_____

_____

_____

_____

2 Corinthians 8:9: "You know the generous grace of our Lord Jesus Christ. Though he was rich, yet for your sakes he became poor, so that by his poverty he could make you rich" (NLT).

_____

_____

_____

_____

Philippians 2:5–7: "Let this mind be in you which was also in Christ Jesus, who, being in the form of God, did not consider it robbery to be equal with God, but made Himself of no reputation, taking the form of a bondservant, and coming in the likeness of men" (NKJV).

_____

_____

_____

Hebrews 12:2: "Let us look only to Jesus, the One who began our faith and who makes it perfect. He suffered death on the cross. But he accepted the shame as if it were nothing because of the joy that God put before him. And now he is sitting at the right side of God's throne" (NCV).

_____

_____

_____

3. In Job 34:21 we read, "God watches where people go; he sees every step they take" (NCV). God is always watching over us, just as he was watching over Mary as she made her way to Jesus' tomb. What feelings does this evoke in you to know that God is watching over everything you do? Explain.

_____

_____

_____

_____

I lay down and slept, yet I woke up in safety, for the LORD was watching over me (Psalm 3:5 NLT).

4. Like Mary, the way we love and serve God should be the way we serve others—with no expectation of anything in return. Take a moment to think about some of the people you consistently serve in your home, your workplace, or at your church. What can you do this week to show your love for them with no expectation of anything in return?

_____

_____

_____

_____

THE STONE IS ROLLED AWAY

Now, read the next part of the story carefully, because this is what I noticed for the first time today. "At that time there was a strong earthquake. An angel of the Lord came down from heaven, went to the tomb, and rolled the stone away from the entrance. Then he sat on the stone. He was shining as bright as lightning, and his clothes were white as snow. The soldiers guarding the tomb shook with fear because of the angel" (Matthew 28:2–4 NCV).

Why did the angel move the stone? For whom did he roll away the rock? For Jesus? That's what I always thought. I assumed that the angel moved the stone so Jesus could come out. But think about it. Did the stone have to be removed in order for Jesus to exit? Did God have to have help? Was the death conqueror so weak that he couldn't push away a rock? ("Hey, could somebody out there move this rock so I can get out?")

I don't think so. The text gives the impression that Jesus was already out when the stone was moved! Nowhere do the Gospels say that the angel moved the stone for Jesus. For whom, then, was the stone moved? Listen to what the angel says: "Come and see the place where his body was" (verse 6). The stone was moved not for Jesus but for the women. God didn't move the rock so Jesus could come out but so the women could see inside!

When Mary enters the tomb, she finds that the angel's words are true: *the body of Jesus is not there.* The thoughts race through her mind. She runs to awaken Peter and John. They rush to see for themselves. She tries to keep up with them, but she can't. Peter comes out of the tomb

When they looked up, they saw that the stone, which was very large, had been rolled away (Mark 16:4).

As they entered the tomb, they saw a young man dressed in a white robe sitting on the right side (verse 5).

He has risen! He is not here. See the place where they laid him (verse 6).

Trembling and bewildered, the women went out and fled from the tomb (verse 8).

She came running to Simon Peter and the other disciple (John 20:2).

bewildered and John comes out believing, but Mary just sits in front of it weeping. The two men go home and leave her alone.

But one surprise still awaits her. For as Mary sits there, something tells her she is not alone. Maybe she hears a noise. Maybe she hears a whisper. Or maybe she just hears her own heart tell her to take a look for herself. Whatever the reason, she does. She stoops down, sticks her head into the hewn entrance, and waits for her eyes to adjust to the dark.

1. Read Matthew 28:1–10. What is your first reaction to the idea that the stone was not moved for Jesus but for the women who came to the tomb? Why do you think God wanted Mary to see the empty tomb?

_____

_____

_____

_____

"Don't be alarmed," he said. "You are looking for Jesus the Nazarene, who was crucified" (Mark 16:6).

2. Read Mark 16:4–7. What did the angel say to Mary in this passage? What instruction did he give to her after she saw that Jesus' body was not in the tomb?

_____

_____

_____

_____

The cloth was still lying in its place, separate from the linen (John 20:7).

3. Now turn to John 20:1–11. What details does John provide about what Peter and John discovered in the tomb? Why are these details significant?

_____

_____

_____

_____

4. What "rocks" has God moved in your life so you could better see his glory? How is he teaching you more about his miraculous power through the trials, victories, and even monotonous routines you go through in your everyday life?

_____

_____

_____

_____

I have fought the good fight, I have finished the race, I have kept the faith (2 Timothy 4:7).

Mary Magdalene stayed the course. She loved Jesus, served him thanklessly, and devoted her life to him—even when she believed he was dead. How could she do this? Perhaps the answer can be found in the handful of words Luke wrote about her: "The Twelve were *with* him, and also . . . Mary (called Magdalene)" (Luke 8:1–2, emphasis added). Mary was with Jesus. She watched him, talked to him, and let him influence her life. Her love for Christ did not come from herself but from being with him, for he is the very essence of love (see 1 John 4:8). So, if we want to love Jesus like Mary did, we have spend time with Love himself. We have to ask him for more of his love, not our own. As we do, we will find that everything we do—late-night laundry sessions, listening to a friend in need, making dinner for a neighbor—will lead to thankless acts of services with no strings attached . . . only joy.

Whoever does not love does not know God, because God is love (1 John 4:8).

❧ POINTS TO REMEMBER ☙

❖ Jesus sees the acts of faithful service we perform in his name and will reward us for staying the course and following him.
❖ We should love and serve others in the same way we love and serve God.
❖ Our love for Christ does not come from ourselves but from being with him.

❧ PRAYER FOR THE DAY ☙

Lord, we tend to love you and others with wrong motives. Our human nature drives us to want to see what is in it for us when we do acts of service and how we will benefit. Today, we ask that you would change our hearts and help us to give our lives the way that you gave yours. Thank you for loving us and for your example to us. Amen.

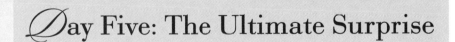

Day Five: The Ultimate Surprise

THE MYSTERY MAN

As Mary's eyes adjust to the dark, she hears a voice say, "Why are you crying?" Mary sees what looks to be a man, but he's white—radiantly white. He is one of two lights on either end of the vacant slab. Two candles blazing on an altar. *Why are you crying?* An uncommon question to be asked in a cemetery. In fact, the question is rude. That is, unless the questioner knows something the questionee doesn't.

"They have taken my Lord away, and I don't know where they have put him" (John 20:13). Mary still calls him "my Lord." As far as she knows, his lips were silent. As far as she knows, his corpse had been carted off by grave robbers. But in spite of it all, he is still her Lord.

They asked her, "Woman, why are you crying?" (John 20:13).

Such devotion moves Jesus. It moves him closer to her. So close she hears him breathing. She turns, and there he stands. But she thinks he is the gardener. Now, Jesus could have revealed himself at this point. He could have called for an angel to present him or a band to announce his presence. But he didn't.

"Why are you crying? Whom are you looking for?" he asks. Mary still thinks he's the gardener. "Did you take him away, sir?" she asks. "Tell me where you put him, and I will get him" (verse 15 NCV). Jesus doesn't leave her wondering long, just long enough to remind us that he loves to surprise us. He waits for us to despair of human strength and then intervenes with heavenly. God waits for us to give up and then—surprise!

"Mary," he says softly.

Surprise! God has appeared in the strangest of places. Doing the strangest of things. Stretching smiles where there had hung only frowns. Placing twinkles where there were only tears. Hanging a bright star in a dark sky. Arching rainbows in the midst of thunderclouds. Calling names in a cemetery.

Mary is shocked. After all, it's not often you hear your name spoken by an eternal tongue. But when she did, she recognized it. And when she did, she responded correctly. She worshiped him.

He asked her, "Woman, why are you crying? Who is it you are looking for?" Thinking he was the gardener, she said, "Sir, if you have carried him away, tell me where you have put him, and I will get him" (John 20:15).

She turned toward him and cried out in Aramaic, "Rabboni!" (which means "Teacher") (verse 16).

"They have taken my Lord away," she said (verse 13).

1. Read John 20:12–18. Mary still calls Jesus "my Lord." What does this say about her heart toward Christ even though she believes he is dead? What does this say about the impact that Jesus made on her life?

   _____

   _____

   _____

   _____

2. Why do you think Jesus chose to ask Mary questions before revealing himself to her? Why did he want to know why she was weeping?

   _____

   _____

   _____

   _____

   _____

When they came back from the tomb, they told all these things to the Eleven and to all the others (Luke 24:9).

3. Mary left the tomb declaring, "I have seen the Lord" (verse 18). When is a time that God revealed his lordship to you? What did that look like in your life?

   _____

   _____

   _____

   _____

4. All the Gospel accounts agree that Mary Magdalene was one of the first people to witness the risen Christ. At first glance this is an odd choice, for the testimony of women in first-century Jewish culture was considered inferior to that of men. What does this teach you about the way God operates in this world? How does he surprise us each day?

_____

_____

_____

_____

GET READY FOR A SURPRISE

The God of surprises had struck again. It's as if he had said, "I can't wait any longer. Mary came this far to see me. I'm going to drop in on her." God does that for the faithful. Just when the womb gets too old for babies, Sarah gets pregnant. Just when the failure is too great for grace, David is pardoned. And just when the road is too dark for Mary, the angel glows, and the Savior shows, and Mary will never be the same again.

Has it been a while since you let God surprise you? It's easy to reach the point where we have God figured out. We know exactly what God does. We break the code. We chart his tendencies. God is a computer. If we push all the right buttons and insert the right data, God is exactly who we thought he was. No variations. No alterations. God is a jukebox. Insert a tithe. Punch in the right numbers and—bam—the divine music we want fills the room.

I look across my desk and see a box of tissues. Ten minutes ago that box sat in the lap of a young woman—mid-thirties, mother of three. She told me of the telephone call she received from her husband this morning. He wants a divorce. She had to leave work and weep. She wanted a word of hope. I reminded her that God is at his best when our life is at its worst. God has been known to plan a celebration in a cemetery.

I told her, "Get ready; you may be in for a surprise."

Have you got God figured out? Have you got God captured on a flowchart and frozen on a flannel board? If so, then listen. Listen to God's surprises.

Hear the rocks meant for the body of the adulterous woman drop to the ground. Listen as Jesus invites a death-row convict to ride with him to the kingdom in the front seat of the limo. Listen as the Messiah whispers to the Samaritan woman, "I who speak to you am he." Listen to the conversation as the widow from Nain eats dinner with her son who is supposed to be dead. And listen to the surprise as Mary's name is spoken by a man she loved—a man she had buried.

The lesson? Three words. *Don't give up.* Is the trail dark? Don't sit. Is the road long? Don't stop. Is the night black? Don't quit. God is

217

watching. For all you know, right at this moment he may be telling the angel to move the stone.

5. God waits for us to despair of our own human strength and then intervenes with his heavenly strength. When have you been surprised by the strength of God during a point of despair? How did God lift you up and bring peace?

_____

_____

_____

_____

6. In what ways have you been guilty of believing that you had God "figured out"? What lessons do you learn from Mary's story about the way God likes to shake up our world, get us out of our comfort zones, and surprise us?

_____

_____

_____

_____

7. Read 1 Corinthians 2:9. What is the hope that Paul offers to all believers in this verse? What does it say to those of us who want to put God in a box?

_____

_____

_____

_____

8. The author of Hebrews writes, "Without faith no one can please God" (11:6 NCV). Think of a situation in your life in which you have given up hope. In the space below, write out a prayer to God asking him to intervene in this seemingly impossible situation. Ask God to give you devotion to him like Mary had for Christ and to surprise you with the outcome.

_____

_____

_____

_____

The scene between Mary Magdalene and Jesus outside the tomb has all the elements of a surprise party—secrecy, wide eyes, amazement, gratitude. But this celebration is timid in comparison with the one that is being planned for the future. It will be similar to Mary's, but a lot bigger. Many more graves will open. Many more names will be called. Many more knees will bow. Many more seekers will celebrate. And we will all be given new resurrected bodies.

Let us rejoice and be glad and give him glory! For the wedding of the Lamb has come (Revelation 19:7).

If you want a sneak preview of what that new body will be like, just look at the resurrected body of our Lord. When Jesus appeared to Mary, it wasn't as a mist or a wind or a ghostly specter. He came in a body. A body that maintained a substantial connection with the body he originally had. A body that had flesh and bones. For did he not tell his followers, "A spirit has not flesh and bones as you see that I have" (Luke 24:39 RSV)?

Look at my hands and my feet. It is I myself! (Luke 24:39).

Jesus' resurrected body was a *real* body. Real enough to appear in the form of a gardener. Real enough to later walk along the road to Emmaus with two other disciples (see Luke 24:13–35). Real enough to eat breakfast with the rest of the disciples at Galilee (see John 21). Real enough for Thomas to touch his nail marks and believe (see John 20:24–29).

He said to Thomas, "Put your finger here; see my hands. Reach out your hand and put it into my side" (John 20:27).

At the same time, this body was not a *clone* of his earthly body. Mark tells us that Jesus "appeared in another form" (Mark 16:12 NRSV). While he was the same, he was different. So different that Mary Magdalene, his disciples on the path to Emmaus, and his disciples on the sea did not recognize him. Although Jesus invited Thomas to touch his body, he passed through a closed door to be in Thomas's presence.

Though the doors were locked, Jesus came and stood among them (verse 26).

So what do we know about the resurrected body of Jesus? It was unlike any the world had ever seen. What do we know about our resurrected bodies? They will be unlike any we have ever imagined. It will take only a second—as quickly as an eye blinks—when the last trumpet sounds. "The trumpet will sound, and those who have died will be raised to live forever, and we will all be changed" (1 Corinthians 15:52).

The Lord himself will come down from heaven . . . with the trumpet call of God, and the dead in Christ will rise first (1 Thessalonians 4:16).

A party was the last thing Mary Magdalene expected as she approached the tomb on that Sunday morning. But the God of surprises met her, shook up her life (literally), and led her to understand what Paul would later write for us: "No eye has seen, no ear has heard, and no mind has imagined what God has prepared for those who love him" (1 Corinthians 2:9 NLT).

The God of surprises had a great party planned for Mary at the tomb. He has a great party planned for us as well at the end of our lives. And I, for one, plan to make sure my name is on the guest list. How about you?

Blessed are those who are invited to the wedding supper of the Lamb (Revelation 19:9).

❧ POINTS TO REMEMBER ❧

❖ Jesus waits for us to quit relying on our own human strength and then intervenes with his own heavenly strength.
❖ We must never lose hope, for the Lord is always at work in our world and is at his best when life is at its worst.
❖ The God of surprises has great things planned for those who love him.

⤙ PRAYER FOR THE DAY ⤚

Thank you, God, that we can rest in your strength. Help us to persevere faithfully each day as we serve you with our lives. We wait in joyful expectation for your surprises and that ultimate party on the day we see you face to face! Amen.

⤙ WEEKLY MEMORY VERSE ⤚

Have you never heard? Have you never understood? The Lord is the everlasting God, the Creator of all the earth. He never grows weak or weary. No one can measure the depths of his understanding. He gives power to the weak and strength to the powerless.
ISAIAH 40:28–29 (NLT)

For Further Reading

Selections throughout this lesson were taken from *He Still Moves Stones* (Nashville: Thomas Nelson, 1993); *When Christ Comes* (Nashville: Thomas Nelson, 1998); *He Chose the Nails* (Nashville: Thomas Nelson, 2000); *Six Hours One Friday* (Nashville: Thomas Nelson, 2004); and *More to Your Story* (Nashville: Thomas Nelson, 2016).

Notes
1. C. S. Lewis, *The Screwtape Letters* (San Francisco: HarperOne, 2015).
2. Hippolytus, *Commentary on the Canticle of Canticles*, 8.2; 24.60.

SAPPHIRA

DO GOOD . . . *QUIETLY*

SAPPHIRA AND HER HUSBAND SAT AT THE KITCHEN TABLE. They stared at the check for $15,000. The silence was a respite. The last half hour had been twelve rounds of verbal jabs and uppercuts. She blamed him for the idea. "You just had to give the money away."

"You didn't complain when everyone clapped for you at church," he snapped back.

"Who would have thought that piece of dirt would bring this kind of price?"

Ananias hadn't expected to get $15,000. Ten thousand at best. Eight thousand at least. But $15,000 for an undeveloped acre off a one-lane road south of Jerusalem? He had inherited the property from his Uncle Ernie, who had left this note with the will: "Hang on to the land, Andy. You never know. If the road expands from one lane to four, you've got a nest egg."

Ananias had taken the advice, locked the deed in a safe, and never thought about it until Sapphira, his wife, got wind of a generous deed done by Barnabas.

"He sold his beachfront condo and gave the money to the church."

"You're kidding. The condo in Jaffa?"

"That's what I heard."

"Whoa, that's prime real estate."

Ananias knew Barnabas from Rotary. Of course, everyone knew Barnabas. The guy had more friends than the temple had priests. Ananias couldn't help but notice the tone people used when discussing Barnabas's gift. Respect. Appreciation. It would be nice to be thought of that way. So he mentioned the acre to Sapphira.

"We're never going to build on it. I'm sure we can get $8,000. Let's give the money to the church."

"All of it?"

"Why not?"

Now a man named Ananias, together with his wife Sapphira, also sold a piece of property (Acts 5:1).

From time to time those who owned land or houses sold them, brought the money from the sales and put it at the apostles' feet (4:34–35).

1. *Giving for glory*. Ananias and Sapphira aren't the only ones who have struggled with this desire. How can you relate to the scene you just read?

_____

_____

_____

_____

_____

_____

_____

_____

_____

2. Why do you think it's such a temptation for us to want others to see our good deeds? Why is it often so difficult for us to give without expecting to receive anything back?

_____

_____

_____

_____

_____

_____

_____

_____

Do your best to present yourself to God as one approved, a worker who does not need to be ashamed and who correctly handles the word of truth (2 Timothy 2:15).

We want to be applauded by others. We want to be noticed by others. We want to be respected by others. This hunger for other people's approval can be ravenous. But what if our desire to be seen by others is rooted in a deeper desire? What if we long for the approval of others because, deep down, we want the approval of our Creator? Our souls want to be seen, noticed, and loved by God, and this deep longing overflows into our relationships. The more we believe in and receive the love of God, the less we live for the love of others. But the more we distance ourselves from God's love, the hungrier we become for the approval of others. So hungry, in fact, that like Sapphira we might find ourselves compromising our integrity.

⟿ PRAYER FOR THE WEEK ⟾

Lord, we know that all of our longings for approval, for recognition, and for affirmation can be found in you. Help us to sense your love today and to turn to you to meet these so we are not tempted to seek the approval of others. Forgive us when we do good deeds for the approval of others instead of your glory. In Jesus' name we pray, amen.

*D*ay One: Good Deed Gone Bad

MOUTH MANAGEMENT

Ananias and Sapphira would have been better off just keeping their mouths shut and giving the gift. They didn't need to tell a soul. But Ananias never excelled at mouth management. During the next Sunday's worship service, the apostle Peter opened the floor for testimonials and prayer requests. Ananias popped up and took his place at the front.

"Sapphira and I've been blessed beyond words since coming here to the Jerusalem church. We want to say thank you. We are selling an acre, and we pledge to give every mite to the Widows' Fund."

The congregation, several thousand members strong, broke into applause. Ananias gestured for Sapphira to wave . . . she did. She stood and turned a full circle and blew a kiss toward Ananias. He returned the gesture and saluted Peter. But Peter was not smiling. Ananias chose not to think much of it and stepped back to his seat.

Later that night, Ananias called a real-estate agent and listed the property. He fell asleep with the thought of a foyer named after him.

Uncle Ernie's hunch was spot-on. Two land developers wanted the property. Neither winced at the $10,000 price tag. By the time the bidding was finished, the couple had a check for $15,000.

With his wife's full knowledge he kept back part of the money for himself, but brought the rest and put it at the apostles' feet (Acts 5:2).

1. Read Acts 4:32–37. How would you describe the attitude of the believers in the early church? In what ways did they love and care for one another?

   _____

   _____

   _____

All the believers were one in heart and mind. No one claimed that any of their possessions was their own, but they shared everything they had (4:32).

2. What did Joseph—better known to us as Barnabas—do for the community? Why do you think this deed of service stood out to Luke, the author of the book of Acts?

   _____

   _____

   _____

Barnabas . . . sold a field he owned and brought the money and put it at the apostles' feet (4:36–37).

3. Luke tells us that Barnabas's name means "son of encouragement" (verse 36). Turn to Acts 11:19–29. How do you see Barnabas living up to his name? What does Luke say about his character (see verse 24)?

   _____

   _____

   _____

He was a good man, full of the Holy Spirit and faith (11:24).

For a whole year Barnabas and Saul met with the church and taught great numbers of people (Acts 11:26).

4. In what ways are you like Barnabas when it comes to encouraging others, sharing your gifts and talents, and serving God's people in love? How could you better model Barnabas's example?

_____

_____

_____

_____

THE PLAN

The couple sat at their kitchen table in silence. Sapphira stirred her coffee. Ananias stared at the check. It was Sapphira who first suggested the plan.

"What if we tell them we sold the property for just $10,000?"

"What?"

"Who has to know?"

The LORD does not look at the things people look at. People look at the outward appearance, but the LORD looks at the heart (1 Samuel 16:7).

Ananias thought for a moment. "Yeah, we'll just let everyone think we closed at $10,000. That way we get credit for the gift and a little cash for something special."

Sapphira smiled. "Like a $5,000 down payment on a Jaffa condo?"

"No harm in that."

"No harm at all."

And so, on the following Sunday, Ananias stood in front of the church again. He waved a check and announced, "We sold the property for $10,000!" and he placed the check in the offering basket. He basked in the applause and signaled for Sapphira to stand.

She did.

They thought their cover-up was a success.

He who loves money will not be satisfied with money, nor he who loves wealth with his income (Ecclesiastes 5:10).

On Sunday afternoon the apostles called Ananias to a meeting. "They surely want to thank us," he told Sapphira as he tightened his necktie. "Probably wondering if we'd be self-conscious at a recognition banquet."

"I'd be okay with one," she assured him.

He smiled and walked out the door, never thinking he wouldn't return.

5. Read Acts 5:1–2. Why do you think Ananias and Sapphira chose to keep back some of the money? Were they wrong in doing so?

_____

_____

_____

_____

6. Turn to Matthew 6:1–4. How did Jesus instruct his followers when it came to giving money to the needy? What do you think he meant when he said the Pharisees—who liked to be seen giving—had received their reward in full?

_____

_____

_____

_____

Be careful not to practice your righteousness in front of others to be seen by them. If you do, you will have no reward from your Father in heaven. So when you give to the needy, do not announce it with trumpets, as the hypocrites do in the synagogues and on the streets, to be honored by others (Matthew 6:1–2).

7. How does living in our culture today make it all the more tempting to flaunt our good deeds?

_____

_____

_____

_____

_____

_____

_____

8. Think about a time in your life when you performed an act of service that no one noticed. In what ways was it difficult for you to not share your good deed and seek the praise of others? What rewards and good fruit have you seen God provide in your life because of selfless acts of service you have done for others?

What good will it be for someone to gain the whole world, yet forfeit their soul? (16:26).

_____

_____

_____

_____

_____

_____

Ananias and Sapphira had wanted to be like Barnabas, who had given the proceeds of a field he sold to the church . . . or at least they wanted the *recognition* Barnabas had received when he made the generous gift. The problem was their selfish motives. They didn't just hold back their money from God—they held back their hearts from him as well. In the same way, when we give with our hands but our hearts are not in it, our gift loses value. Maybe not monetarily, but certainly spiritually. However, when we give with a sincere heart—holding nothing back and trusting in the Lord to provide for our needs—we receive spiritual blessings. As we read in Proverbs, "The one who blesses others is abundantly blessed" (11:25 MSG), but "the stingy . . . are unaware that poverty awaits them" (Proverbs 28:22).

When you ask, you do not receive, because you ask with wrong motives (James 4:3).

God's grace was so powerfully at work in them all that there were no needy persons among them (Acts 4:33–34).

∽ POINTS TO REMEMBER ∾

❖ The body of Christ is encouraged when we lovingly share our gifts and talents with God's people.
❖ God rewards selfless acts of service—when we give, holding nothing back and trusting the Lord's provision, we receive spiritual blessings.
❖ When we give our service but not our hearts to God, our gift loses its value; God does not need our gifts, but he wants our hearts.

∽ PRAYER FOR THE DAY ∾

Lord, we confess that giving is hard. We want others to notice our acts, and we struggle with holding on to our earthly treasures for ourselves. Today, we pray that you would change our hearts and help us to give the way you gave—with a joyful and generous heart. Thank you, Lord. Amen.

*D*ay Two: The Verdict

PETER'S FOUR QUESTIONS

Peter said, "Ananias, how is it that Satan has so filled your heart that you have lied to the Holy Spirit and have kept for yourself some of the money you received for the land? Didn't it belong to you before it was sold? And after it was sold, wasn't the money at your disposal? What made you think of doing such a thing? You have not lied just to human beings but to God" (5:3–4).

According to the book of Acts, the meeting lasted only long enough for Peter to ask four questions and render a single verdict. Peter's first question was, "Ananias, why has Satan filled your heart to lie to the Holy Spirit and keep back *part* of the price of the land for yourself?"(Acts 5:3 NKJV). So much for the cover-up. Luke's phrase for *keep back* means "misappropriate." The apostles sniffed out the couple's scheme for what it was: financial fraud.

Peter's second question was, "While it remained unsold, did it not remain your own?" (verse 4 ESV). No one forced Ananias and Sapphira to sell the property. They had acted of their own accord and their own free will.

Peter's third question was, "After it was sold, was it not under your control?" (verse 4 NASB). At any point the couple could have changed their minds or altered their contribution. Their sin was not in keeping a portion of the proceeds but in pretending they gave it all. They wanted the appearance of sacrifice without the sacrifice.

Peter's fourth and final question was, "Why is it that you have conceived this deed in your heart?" (verse 4 NASB). This deceitful act on the part of Ananias and Sapphira was not an impulsive stumble but a calculated, premeditated swindle. The couple had every intention of misleading the church. Did they not realize they were lying to God?

Peter made it clear with this verdict: "You have not lied just to human beings but to God" (verse 4). Luke tells us what happens next: "When Ananias heard this, he fell down and died. And great fear seized all who heard what had happened" (verse 5).

1. Read Acts 5:3–6. What did Peter mean when he said that Ananias had "lied to the Holy Spirit" (verse 3)?

_____

_____

_____

_____

2. Peter told Ananias that Satan had filled his heart and led him to lie to the church. What do the following passages of Scripture say about the sin of lying?

Proverbs 12:22: "Lying lips are an abomination to the LORD, but those who act faithfully are his delight" (ESV).

_____

_____

_____

Proverbs 19:9: "A false witness will not go unpunished, and he who speaks lies shall perish" (NKJV).

_____

_____

_____

Psalm 101:7: "No one who is dishonest will live in my house; no liars will stay around me" (NCV).

_____

_____

_____

Luke 8:17: "All that is secret will eventually be brought into the open, and everything that is concealed will be brought to light and made known to all" (NLT).

_____

_____

_____

Do not grieve the Holy Spirit of God, with whom you were sealed for the day of redemption (Ephesians 4:30).

227

Colossians 3:9–10: "Do not lie to one another, seeing that you have stripped off the old self with its practices and have clothed yourselves with the new self, which is being renewed in knowledge according to the image of its creator" (NRSV).

_____

_____

_____

_____

James 1:26: "Anyone who sets himself up as 'religious' by talking a good game is self-deceived. This kind of religion is hot air and only hot air" (MSG).

_____

_____

_____

_____

You belong to your father, the devil, and you want to carry out your father's desires. He was a murderer from the beginning, not holding to the truth, for there is no truth in him. When he lies, he speaks his native language, for he is a liar and the father of lies (John 8:44).

3. Peter says Satan filled Ananias's heart. Read John 8:44. What does Jesus call Satan in this verse? Explain a time when the "father of lies" planted deceit in your heart that you believed and acted upon?

_____

_____

_____

_____

4. When we lie or deceive people, it's easy for us to overlook the fact that our sin is not just against that person but also against God. How does lying affect our relationships with others and with God? Is it possible for us to separate our relationship with God from our relationships with other? Explain your thoughts.

_____

_____

_____

_____

SAPPHIRA'S LAST CHANCE

When Ananias heard this, he fell down and died. And great fear seized all who heard what had happened. Then some young men came forward, wrapped up his body, and carried him out and buried him (Acts 5:5–6).

The young men in the community rose and carried the body of Ananias outside the gathering. His body was wrapped and buried before Sapphira had any clue what had happened. When she came to meet with Peter, she expected a word of appreciation.

Peter gave her a chance to come clean. "Tell me whether you sold the land for so much," he said (Acts 5:8 ESV).

Come on, Sapphira, tell the truth. You're in over your head. Just shoot straight and you may live to tell about it. She doesn't.

"Yes, for so much," she replied (verse 8 ESV).

Peter shakes his head. "How is it that you have agreed together to test the Spirit of the Lord? Behold, the feet of those who have buried your husband are at the door, and they will carry you out" (verse 9 ESV).

As they carry Sapphira to join her husband in the cemetery, we also shake our heads. Dare we wonder out loud what we're wondering inside? Dare we ask the question that we all are thinking? Well, since no one else will ask it, I will.

Was this really necessary? I mean, Ananias and Sapphira deserved punishment, for sure. They deserved a stiff sentence. But the *death* sentence? Does the punishment fit the crime? What they did was bad. But was it *that* bad?

5. Read the rest of Sapphira's story in Acts 5:7–11. How did Peter give her a chance to come clean and tell the truth? Why do you think Sapphira persisted in the lie?

_____

_____

_____

6. Peter told Ananias that he had lied to the Holy Spirit. What did he say Sapphira had done? What do you think he meant by this?

_____

_____

_____

7. Based on what you read about the early church in Acts 4:32–37, why do you think Satan made it a point to try to tempt some of the members to sin against other members? Why was it important for Peter to quickly deal with the situation?

_____

_____

_____

_____

8. Does the punishment fit the crime in your mind? Why do you think God chose to punish Ananias and Sapphira with death?

_____

_____

_____

_____

The believers in the early church "were one in heart and mind" because God's grace was "powerfully at work in them all" (Acts 4:32–33). More and more people each day were coming into the body of Christ

At that moment she fell down at his feet and died. Then the young men came in and, finding her dead, carried her out and buried her beside her husband. Great fear seized the whole church and all who heard about these events (Acts 5:10–11).

How could you conspire to test the Spirit of the Lord? (verse 9).

The apostles were teaching the people, proclaiming in Jesus the resurrection of the dead (4:2).

They devoted themselves to the apostles' teaching and to fellowship, to the breaking of bread and to prayer. Everyone was filled with awe at the many wonders and signs performed by the apostles. All the believers were together and had everything in common (Acts 2:42–44).

and experiencing the transformational power of God in new and profound ways (see Acts 2:41–47). The lost were being saved, the needy were being cared for, and there was great unity of purpose among the early believers. Given this, it is no wonder that Satan tried to break up the unity among the fellowship. In Ananias and Sapphira, he found two individuals in whom God's grace was not powerfully at work. This was not because that grace wasn't available to them, but because they would not receive it. The lesson of their lives reveals to us that to *give* generously, we first and foremost have to *receive* generously—we must receive from the grace of God.

⤚✜ POINTS TO REMEMBER ✜⤙

❖ When we lie to others, we have to remember that we are also lying to God and to the Holy Spirit.

❖ Dealing with our wrongdoings quickly and not overlooking them protects the body of Christ from becoming complacent about sin and shows that God does not tolerate hypocrisy and deceit.

❖ The gift of grace we receive through faith in Jesus allows us to be rid of the guilt of sin, live generously, and be united in service to God.

⤚✜ PRAYER FOR THE DAY ✜⤙

Satan himself masquerades as an angel of light (2 Corinthians 11:14).

Lord, forgive us when we pull away from your heart and mind and believe the lies of the enemy. Forgive us when we sin against other members of your family and bring division to the church instead of unity. We want to live from the grace you have given that is powerfully at work within us so we can give to others generously. Amen.

$\mathcal{D}$ay Three: Deadly Deception

PUTTING ON A MASK

If anyone loves the world, love for the Father is not in them (1 John 2:15).

Let's think about the story of Ananias and Sapphira for a moment. Exactly what did they do? Well, for starters they used the church for self-promotion. They leveraged God's family for personal gain. They attempted to turn a congregation into a personal stage across which they could strut.

God has a strong word for such behavior: *hypocrisy*. When Jesus used it, people ducked for cover. He once lambasted the Pharisees with this blowtorch: "All their works they do to be seen by men. . . . They love the best places at feasts, the best seats in the synagogues, greetings in the marketplaces, and to be called by men, 'Rabbi, Rabbi'" (Matthew 23:5–7 NKJV).

Jesus went on to proclaim, "Woe to you, scribes and Pharisees, hypocrites! For you shut up the kingdom of heaven against men. . . . You devour widows' houses, and for a pretense make long prayers. . . . You cleanse the outside of the cup and dish, but inside they are full of extortion and self-indulgence" (verses 13–14, 25 NKJV).

Jesus never spoke to anyone else with such intensity. But when he saw the religious hypocrite, he flipped on the spotlight and exposed every self-righteous mole and pimple. "When you pray, you shall not be like the hypocrites. For they love to pray standing in the synagogues and on the corners of the streets, that they may be seen by men. Assuredly, I say to you, they have their reward" (6:5 NKJV).

The working definition of *hypocrisy* is "to be seen by men." The Greek word for hypocrite, *hupokrites*, originally meant "actor." (An early use is seen in the writings of Demosthenes, a fourth-century BC Greek orator who used the term to ridicule one of his rivals who had been a successful actor.) First-century actors wore masks.

A hypocrite, then, is one who puts on a mask—a false face. God says of them, "These people draw near to Me with their mouth, and honor Me with their lips, but their heart is far from Me. And in vain they worship Me, teaching as doctrines the commandments of men" (15:8–9 NKJV).

1. Look at Jesus' words in Matthew 23:1–12. How were Ananias and Sapphira like the Pharisees and religious leaders that Jesus describes in these verses? What did Jesus say that they sought when it came to doing good works?

   _____

   _____

   _____

   _____

   _____

2. In what way did Jesus say the Pharisees and religious leaders did not practice what they preached? Based on what we know of the first church, how was this also true of Sapphira and Ananias?

   _____

   _____

   _____

   _____

Then Jesus said to the crowds and to his disciples: "The teachers of the law and the Pharisees sit in Moses' seat. So you must be careful to do everything they tell you. But do not do what they do, for they do not practice what they preach" (Matthew 23:1–3).

They claim to know God, but by their actions they deny him (Titus 1:16).

Those who exalt themselves will be humbled, and those who humble themselves will be exalted (Matthew 23:12).

231

Everything exposed by the light becomes visible—and everything that is illuminated becomes a light (Ephesians 5:13).

3. When Jesus saw a religious hypocrite, he flipped on the spotlight and exposed every self-righteous mole and pimple. Why do you think this was? How was Jesus actually showing love to them by exposing what they were doing to God's people?

_____

_____

_____

_____

First take the plank out of your own eye, and then you will see clearly (Matthew 7:5).

4. Read Matthew 7:3–5. In what situations are you most likely to put on a "false face" to keep up appearances like Sapphira and Ananias? Write out a prayer, asking God to deliver you from any hypocritical tendency.

_____

_____

_____

_____

The Allure of Falsehood

Those who know your name trust in you, for you, LORD, have never forsaken those who seek you (Psalm 9:10).

Ananias and Sapphira's sin was not in holding back some of the money for themselves but in misrepresenting the truth. Most of us can understand their temptation, for we do not trust the truth. We can sympathize with the fellow who received a call from his wife just as she was about to fly home from Europe.

"How's my cat?" she asked.

"Dead," he replied.

"Oh, honey, don't be so honest. Why didn't you break the news to me slowly? You've ruined my trip."

"What do you mean?"

"Well, you could have told me that he was on the roof. Then, when I called you from Paris, you could have told me he was acting sluggish. Then, when I called from London, you could have said he was sick, and when I called you from New York, you could have said he was at the vet. Then, when I arrived home, you could have said he was dead."

The husband had never been exposed to such protocol, but he was willing to learn. "Okay," he said. "I'll do better next time."

"By the way," his wife asked, "how's Mom?"

There was a long silence. "Uh . . ." he said, "she's on the roof."

Light has come into the world, but people loved darkness instead of light (John 3:19).

The plain fact is that our credo is often, *You shall know the truth, and the truth shall make you squirm.* Our dislike for the truth began early on when Mom walked into our room and asked, "Did you hit your little brother?"

We knew then and there that honesty had its consequences. So we learned to, uhhh, well, it's not really lying . . . we learned to cover things up. "Did I hit baby brother? Well, that all depends on how you interpret the word *hit*. I mean, sure I made contact with him, but would a jury consider it a hit? Everything is relative, you know."

The truth, we learn early, is not fun. So we avoid it. We want our bosses to like us, so we flatter. We call it polishing the apple. God calls it a lie. We want people to admire us, so we exaggerate. We call it stretching the truth. God calls it a lie. We want people to respect us, so we live in houses we can't afford and charge bills we can't pay. We call it the American way. God calls it living a lie.

Never was Jeremiah more the prophet than when he announced, "The heart is deceitful above all things" (Jeremiah 17:9). And that deceit, as the story of Ananias and Sapphira shows, always leads to unfortunate consequences.

5. Read John 8:31–32. Who was Jesus addressing in these verses? What did he mean when he said the "the truth" would set them free?

_____

_____

_____

To the Jews who had believed him, Jesus said, "If you hold to my teaching, you are really my disciples. Then you will know the truth, and the truth will set you free" (John 8:31–32).

6. Why is it often so difficult for us as believers to tell the truth? What fears do we have when it comes to admitting that we don't have it all together or that we are not as holy as we would like others to believe?

_____

_____

_____

_____

7. Read God's words in Jeremiah 17:9–10. What does the Lord say is the natural state of our hearts? What does God do to reveal what is in our hearts?

_____

_____

_____

_____

I the LORD search the heart and examine the mind, to reward each person according to their conduct (Jeremiah 17:10).

8. Turn to Ezekiel 36:26. What hope does this verse give us when it comes to the deceitful state of our hearts? How have you seen God fulfill these words in your life?

_____

_____

_____

_____

I will give you a new heart and put a new spirit in you; I will remove from you your heart of stone and give you a heart of flesh (Ezekiel 36:26).

We don't have to attend the Juilliard School to become expert actors, for acting is just part of our fallen nature. Each of us is guilty at times

There is no difference between Jew and Gentile, for all have sinned and fall short of the glory of God, and all are justified freely by his grace through the redemption that came by Christ Jesus (Romans 3:22–24).

of putting on the innocent mask, saying the right lines, and wearing the religious costume. We gasp when we hear that yet another pastor has been caught in an affair. We sneer at the television evangelist caught embezzling money. We shake our heads when we hear someone else has been caught in a lie. "I'm so glad I'm not like *that*," we tell ourselves. But the truth is we are *all* hypocrites. We have all deceived others by hiding our sin. We have all worshiped God with the same mouth that judges others. Until we acknowledge who we really are—sinners in need of grace—we will always struggle with deception. Until we adopt the mindset of the tax collector in Jesus' parable who said, "God have mercy on me, a sinner" (Luke 18:13), we will never experience the humility that God desires us to have. So today, let's leave the acting for Hollywood and humbly accept our brokenness. For when we do, we will have hearts that bring honor to God.

❧ POINTS TO REMEMBER ☙

❖ A hypocrite is interested in looking good in the eyes of others and will use deception to keep up appearances.
❖ We can be tempted to misrepresent the truth because it makes us uncomfortable—honesty can have consequences we are unwilling to invite.
❖ If we acknowledge our need of grace and honestly accept that we are sinners, we can honor God in our hearts.

❧ PRAYER FOR THE DAY ☙

Lord, thank you for loving us just as we are. Thank you that we do not have to hide our true selves from you—and that we couldn't even if we tried! Forgive us for those times when we worship you with the same mouth that curses others. Give us honest and transparent hearts and let everything we do be pleasing to you. In Jesus' name, amen.

Out of the same mouth come praise and cursing. My brothers and sisters, this should not be (James 3:10).

ⅅay Four: Deceit Leads to Death

FAITHFUL IN THE SMALL THINGS

More than once I've heard people refer to the story of Sapphira and her husband, Ananias, with a nervous chuckle. "I'm glad God doesn't still strike people dead for lying," they say. I'm not so sure he doesn't. It seems to me that the wages of deceit is still death.

When you offer yourselves to someone as obedient slaves, you are slaves of the one you obey (Romans 3:16).

Perhaps this is not the death of the body. But it could lead to the death of a marriage, for falsehoods are termites in the trunk of the family tree. Or the death of a conscience, for the tragedy of the second lie is that it is always easier to tell than the first. Or the death of a career. Just ask the student who got booted out for cheating or the employee who got fired for embezzlement. Or the death of one's faith. The language of faith and the language of falsehood have two different vocabularies. Those fluent in the language of falsehood find terms like *confession* and *repentance* hard to pronounce.

We could also list the deaths of intimacy, trust, peace, credibility, and self-respect. But perhaps the most tragic death that occurs from deceit is our witness. The court won't listen to the testimony of a perjured witness. Neither will the world. Do we think our coworkers will believe our words about Jesus when they can't even believe our words about how we handled our expense account? Even more significantly, do we think God will use us as witnesses if we won't tell the truth?

Every high school football team has a player whose assignment is to carry the play from the coach to the huddle. What if the player doesn't tell the truth? What if the coach calls for a pass but the courier says the coach called for a run? One thing is certain: the coach won't call on that player very long. God says if we are faithful with the small things, he'll trust us with greater things (see Matthew 25:21). Can he trust you with the small things?

Wide is the gate and broad is the road that leads to destruction, and many enter through it (Matthew 7:13).

You have been faithful with a few things; I will put you in charge of many things (Matthew 25:21).

1. Read the parable of the talents in Matthew 25:14–30. What does the money that the master gives to each of his servants represent? What was the master's expectation that the servants would do with the money?

   _____

   _____

   _____

   _____

To one he gave five bags of gold, to another two bags, and to another one bag, each according to his ability (verse 15).

2. Notice the master gave the first servant more than he did the second servant. What did the master say to each of the servants? What does this tell us about what God expects in how we use whatever gifts and abilities he has given to us?

   _____

   _____

   _____

   _____

His master replied, "Well done, good and faithful servant!" (verses 21, 23).

3. Why did the master call the third servant lazy and wicked? Why wasn't he happy that the third servant had just kept the money he had been given safe and secure?

   _____

   _____

You should have put my money on deposit with the bankers, so that when I returned I would have received it back with interest (verse 27).

235

4. The master told the first and second servant, "You have been faithful with a few things; I will put you in charge of many things" (verses 21, 23). What does this tell us that God expects when it comes to telling the truth? Why is there no such thing as a "small" lie?

_____

_____

_____

Facing the Music

Many years ago, a man conned his way into the orchestra of the emperor of China even though he could not play a note. Whenever the group practiced or performed, the man would hold his flute against his lips, pretending to play but not making a sound. He received a modest salary and enjoyed a comfortable living.

Then one day, the emperor requested a solo from each musician. The flutist got nervous. There wasn't enough time to learn the instrument. He pretended to be sick, but the royal physician wasn't fooled. On the day of his solo performance, the impostor took poison and killed himself. The explanation of his suicide led to a phrase that found its way into the English language: "He refused to face the music."

The cure for deceit is simply this: *face the music.* Tell the truth. Some of us are living in deceit. Some of us are walking in the shadows. The lies of Ananias and Sapphira resulted in death . . . and so have ours. Some of us have buried a marriage, parts of a conscience, and even parts of our faith—all because we won't tell the truth.

Are you in a dilemma, wondering if you should tell the truth or not? The questions to ask in such moments are, *Will God bless my deceit? Will he, who hates lies, bless a strategy built on lies? Will the Lord, who loves the truth, bless the business of falsehoods? Will God honor the career of the manipulator? Will God come to the aid of the cheater? Will God bless my dishonesty?* I don't think so either.

So examine your heart. Ask yourself some tough questions. *Am I being completely honest with my spouse and children? Are my relationships marked by candor? What about my work or school environment? Am I honest in my dealings? Am I a trustworthy student? An honest taxpayer? A reliable witness at work?*

Do you tell the truth . . . always?

If not, start today. Don't wait until tomorrow. The ripple of today's lie is tomorrow's wave and next year's flood. Start today. Be just like Jesus. Tell the truth, the whole truth, and nothing but the truth.

5. In the parable of the talents, what were the consequences of the third servant's unfaithfulness? How have you seen God bless you when you have been faithful with the little things?

_____

_____

6. Perhaps the most tragic death that occurs from deceit is the death of our witness. In what ways have you seen hypocrisy and deception in the church turn away unbelievers? What kind of damage does this cause when it comes to attracting people to Jesus?

_____

_____

_____

_____

Always be prepared to give an answer to everyone who asks you to give the reason for the hope that you have (1 Peter 3:15).

7. Jesus often spoke about the power of the truth. What does he say in the following verses about what the truth is and how it should guide our lives?

John 8:32: "You will know the truth, and the truth will make you free" (NASB).

_____

_____

_____

_____

John 14:6: "I am the way, the truth, and the life. No one comes to the Father except through Me" (NKJV).

_____

_____

_____

_____

John 16:13: "When the Spirit of truth comes, he will guide you into all truth. He will not speak on his own but will tell you what he has heard. He will tell you about the future" (NLT).

_____

_____

_____

_____

John 17:17: "Make them ready for your service through your truth; your teaching is truth" (NCV).

_____

_____

_____

_____

John 18:37–38: "You say that I am a king. For this purpose I was born and for this purpose I have come into the world—to bear witness to the truth. Everyone who is of the truth listens to my voice" (ESV).

_____

_____

_____

_____

You were taught, with regard to your former way of life, to put off your old self, which is being corrupted by its deceitful desires (Ephesians 4:22).

8. Read Ephesians 4:20–24. How do we rid ourselves of deceit? How do we put off our old self and put on the new self, as Paul instructs us in this passage?

_____

_____

_____

_____

The Spirit clearly says that in later times some will abandon the faith and follow deceiving spirits and things taught by demons. Such teachings come through hypocritical liars, whose consciences have been seared as with a hot iron (1 Timothy 4:1–2).

We live in a world so twisted by the enemy that we may find ourselves numb to the sting of deceit and lies. We may even find ourselves carelessly telling small lies, our consciences unfazed, "for the tragedy of the second lie is that it is always easier to tell than the first." Scripture warns us of false teachers who are full of hypocrisy and have consciences "seared as with a hot iron" (1 Timothy 4:2). The farther we step away from truth, the more comfortable we become with lies, the more our eyes adjust to the darkness, and the more our consciences are seared. So let's flee from the father of lies and run toward the Father of truth. Let's "stand firm then, with the belt of truth buckled" around our waist (Ephesians 6:14). And as we fill our minds and hearts with the truth of God, it will overflow onto our lips and into our actions. "For the mouth speaks what the heart is full of" (Luke 6:45).

⤚ POINTS TO REMEMBER ⤙

❖ Deceit leads to death in one form or another and ultimately destroys our witness for Jesus.
❖ Telling the truth is part of being faithful in the small things God asks of us—and that leads to him entrusting us with greater things.
❖ The cure for deceit is to tell the truth, knowing that God hates lies but honors those whose hearts are honest.

⤚ PRAYER FOR THE DAY ⤙

Lord, examine our hearts today and reveal any area in our lives where we are not being completely honest in our dealings. Help us to always tell the truth, no matter how difficult it may seem at the time. We know that only through you can our hearts become clean and centered on your truth. Amen.

Day Five: A Solemn Warning to Us

A JEALOUS GOD

God's judgment has never been a problem for me. In fact, it's always seemed right. Burning sulfur on Sodom and Gomorrah. Good job, God. Egyptians swallowed in the Red Sea. They had it coming. Forty years of wandering to loosen the stiff necks of the Israelites? Would've done it myself. Ananias and Sapphira? *You bet.*

The couple's story is a solemn warning to us. Up to this point in the early church's history, it had all been glory days. Miracles, sermons, baptisms, and growth. The book of Acts is all good fruit and fanfare . . . until Ananias and Sapphira. When this couple decided to steal what belonged to God, the age-old problem of sin entered the equation.

God is jealous for our trust. He doesn't request it, suggest it, or recommend it—he *demands* it. His unvarnished message is clear: "Trust me and me alone." On this topic of faith, God is serious. Dead serious.

The Israelites had discovered this truth centuries before when God led them into the Promised Land. The first stop was Jericho, and the Lord had miraculously thrown down the city walls. But he had also given the people a command: "Do not take any of the things set apart for destruction, or you yourselves will be completely destroyed, and you will bring trouble on the camp of Israel. Everything made from silver, gold, bronze, or iron is sacred to the LORD and must be brought into his treasury" (Joshua 6:18–19 NLT).

The instructions were clear. Don't touch the stuff. Don't make necklaces out of the gold. Don't make medals out of the bronze. No souvenirs. No trinkets. No Jericho jewelry. No kidding. But a man named Achan saw the bling and forgot his King. He took some of the treasure of Jericho in violation of God's direct command and then hid the loot under his tent.

God's discipline was immediate and severe. Joshua, flush with the Jericho victory, assumed the next small town of Ai would be easy pickings. But the people of Ai bit back, and Joshua's division raced home discouraged, disheveled, and licking their wounds. It's not that the people of Ai were formidable. It's more that the Hebrew camp was poisoned. God told Joshua, in so many words, to find the rotten apple before it ruined the whole bushel.

The judgment was swift and the punishment stiff. Achan and his family were publicly executed, their possessions burned. A monument was built as a warning to the people. It was a solemn day in Gilgal.

They serve as an example of those who suffer the punishment of eternal fire (Jude 1:7).

You shall have no other gods before me (Exodus 20:3).

The Israelites were unfaithful in regard to the devoted things. Achan . . . took some of them (Joshua 7:1).

The men of Ai . . . chased the Israelites from the city gate as far as the stone quarries and struck them down on the slopes (verses 4–5).

All Israel stoned him, and . . . stoned the rest (verse 25).

Achan replied . . . "When I saw in the plunder . . . I coveted them and took them" (Joshua 7:20–21).

1. Read Joshua 7:1–26. How was Achan's sin similar to the sin committed by Ananias and Sapphira? How was his confession different?

_____

_____

_____

_____

2. Ananias and Sapphira were part of the first-generation church. Achan was a part of the new generation of Israel. How were these two groups similar?

_____

_____

_____

_____

3. What was the result of Achan's sin? Who did it affect? How did Sapphira and Ananias's sins likewise affect more than just themselves?

_____

_____

_____

_____

_____

Joshua said, "Why have you brought this trouble on us? The LORD will bring trouble on you today" (verse 25).

4. The new church and the new Israel were fresh in their infancy and passionate about following God, but they were also susceptible to deception, division, and sin. Knowing this, why do you think God punished Ananias, Sapphira, and Achan so severely and so publicly?

_____

_____

_____

_____

_____

RICH IN ETERNITY

Be careful to do what the LORD your God has commanded you; do not turn aside (Deuteronomy 5:32).

Achan in Gilgal. Ananias and Sapphira in Jerusalem. Their graves remind us: _be careful._ For our own sakes, we can't put our trust in stuff. As Paul told Timothy, "Command those who are rich in this present world not to be arrogant nor to put their hope in wealth, which is so uncertain, but to put their hope in God, who richly provides us with everything for our enjoyment" (1 Timothy 6:17).

Humility is the fear of the LORD; its wages are riches and honor and life (Proverbs 22:4).

The "rich in this present world." That is you. That is me. If you have enough education to read this page, enough resources to own this book, you likely qualify as a prosperous person. And that is okay. Prosperity is a common consequence of faithfulness (see Proverbs 22:4). Paul didn't tell the rich to feel guilty about being rich. He just urged caution.

Why? The story of Sapphira and Ananias points us to the reason: *nothing breeds failure like success.* Money is just a short-term condition. The abundance or lack of money will only be felt for one life. So we can't get tangled up in it.

Imagine you were living in the South during the Civil War and had accumulated large amounts of Confederate currency. Through a series of events, you became convinced that the South was going to lose and your money would soon be worthless. What would you do? If you had any common sense, you would get rid of your Southern cents. You'd put every penny you could into the currency that is to come and prepare yourself for the end of the war.

Are you investing in the currency of heaven? The world economy is going down. Your wallet is full of soon-to-be-useless paper. The currency of this world will be worth nothing when you die or when Christ returns—both of which could happen at any moment. If you stockpile earthly treasures, what does that say about where you put your trust?

Today, honestly ask yourself, *Whom do I trust? God or King More?* King More is a rotten ruler. He never satisfies. He rusts. He rots. He loses his value. He goes out of style. For all the promises he makes, he cannot keep a single one. King More will break your heart.

But the King of Kings? He will catch you every single time.

5. Read 1 Timothy 6:17–19. What are God's commands to those who are rich in this world? What will they be doing if they follow these commands according to verse 19?

_____

_____

_____

_____

6. Paul writes that those who are rich in good deeds will "build a treasury that will last, gaining life that is truly life" (verse 19 MSG). What is the difference between life on this earth and "life that is truly life"? What kind of life did Sapphira and Ananias pursue?

_____

_____

_____

_____

7. What do the following passages of Scripture say we must do to store up riches in heaven? How are you applying these truths to your life?

Matthew 6:19-21: "Don't store up treasures here on earth, where moths eat them and rust destroys them, and where thieves break in and steal. Store your treasures in heaven, where moths and rust

*Pride goes before destruction,
a haughty spirit before a fall*
(Proverbs 16:18).

*The world and its desires pass away,
but whoever does the will of God
lives forever* (1 John 2:17).

*Command them to do good,
to be rich in good deeds, and to
be generous and willing to share.
In this way they will lay up treasure
for themselves as a firm foundation
for the coming age*
(1 Timothy 6:18–19).

cannot destroy, and thieves do not break in and steal. Wherever your treasure is, there the desires of your heart will also be" (NLT).

_____

_____

_____

_____

Matthew 19:21: "If you want to be perfect, go, sell what you have and give to the poor, and you will have treasure in heaven; and come, follow Me" (NKJV).

_____

_____

_____

_____

Acts 20:35: "In all things I have shown you that by working hard in this way we must help the weak and remember the words of the Lord Jesus, how he himself said, 'It is more blessed to give than to receive'" (ESV).

_____

_____

_____

_____

Colossians 3:1–2: "Since you were raised from the dead with Christ, aim at what is in heaven, where Christ is sitting at the right hand of God. Think only about the things in heaven, not the things on earth" (NCV).

_____

_____

_____

_____

8. Is it possible to give of our earthly possessions with completely pure motives and without any trace of Sapphira hypocrisy? If so, how? Explain your thoughts.

_____

_____

_____

_____

As the body without the spirit is dead, so faith without deeds is dead (James 2:26).

In the end, what are we to make of the story of Ananias and Sapphira? Certainly, the point is not to avoid the problem of hypocrisy altogether by not doing good works. As James points out, we must do good works, for "faith without works is dead" (James 2:20 NKJV). And some works—such as benevolence or teaching—must be seen by others in order to have an impact. So let's be clear: To do a good thing is a good thing. To do good to be seen is not. In fact, to do good to be seen is a serious offense. Here's why.

Hypocrisy turns people away from God. When God-hungry souls walk into a congregation of wannabe superstars, what happens? When God-seekers see singers strut like Las Vegas entertainers . . . when they hear the preacher—a man of slick words, dress, and hair—play to the crowd and exclude God . . . when other attendees dress to be seen and make much to-do over their gifts and offerings . . . when people enter a church to see God yet can't see God because of the church, don't think for a second that God doesn't react.

You are the salt of the earth. But if the salt loses its saltiness, how can it be made salty again? It is no longer good for anything, except to be thrown out (Matthew 5:13).

"Be especially careful when you are trying to be good so that you don't make a performance out of it. It might be good theater, but the God who made you won't be applauding" (Matthew 6:1 MSG). Hypocrisy turns people against God. So God has a no-tolerance policy. Let the cold, lifeless bodies of Sapphira and her husband issue their intended warning. Let's take hypocrisy as seriously as God does.

How do you do this? First, by *not expecting credit for good deeds*. This means that if no one notices your good deed, you aren't disappointed. If someone does, you give the credit to God. You can test your motives by asking yourself this question: *If no one knew of the good I do, would I still do it?* If the answer is no, you know that you're doing it to be seen by people.

A second way to avoid hypocrisy is to *give financial gifts in secret*. Money will stir the phony within you. We all like to be seen earning it, and we all like to be seen giving it. So, as Jesus says, "When you give to someone in need, don't let your left hand know what your right hand is doing" (Matthew 6:3 NLT).

A third way to avoid hypocrisy is to *not fake spirituality*. When you go to church, don't select a seat just to be seen or sing just to be heard. If you raise your hands in worship, raise holy ones, not showy ones. When you talk, don't doctor your vocabulary with trendy religious terms. Nothing nauseates more than a fake "praise the Lord" or a shallow "Hallelujah" or an insincere "glory be to God."

When you pray, do not keep on babbling like pagans, for they think they will be heard because of their many words (6:7).

The bottom line is this: don't make a theater production out of your faith. "Watch me! Watch me!" is a call used on the playground, not in God's kingdom. So silence the trumpets. Cancel the parade. Enough with the name-dropping. If accolades come, politely deflect them before you believe them. Slay the desire to be noticed. Stir the desire to serve God.

Heed the counsel of Christ: "First wash the inside of the cup and the dish, and then the outside will become clean, too" (Matthew 23:26 NLT). Focus on the inside, and the outside will take care of itself. Lay your motives before God daily, hourly. As the psalmist wrote, "Search me, O God, and know my heart; test me and know my anxious thoughts. Point out anything in me that offends you, and lead me along the path of everlasting life" (Psalm 139:23–24 NLT).

Though outwardly we are wasting away, yet inwardly we are being renewed day by day (2 Corinthians 4:16).

Do good things . . . but do them *quietly*. Don't do them just to be noticed. After all, as the story of Sapphira and Ananias shows, we can be too good for our own good.

～ POINTS TO REMEMBER ～

❖ Because hypocrisy turns people away from God, the Lord is uncompromising in his demand for our trust and obedience.
❖ Our sin not only has consequences for us, but it also impacts the lives and faith of our family members at home, at church, and in the community.
❖ We can invest our trust in the temporary riches of this world and lose it all, or we can invest it in the faithfulness of the God of eternity and live forever.

～ PRAYER FOR THE DAY ～

Lord, forgive us when we put our hope in anything other than you. Living for the pleasures and attention of this world do not bring us true life. You are real life. You are the real treasure. We love you, Lord. Amen.

～ WEEKLY MEMORY VERSE ～

Humble yourselves in the presence of the Lord, and He will exalt you.
JAMES 4:10 (NASB)

For Further Reading

Selections throughout this lesson were taken from *Just Like Jesus* (Nashville: Thomas Nelson, 1998); *When God Whispers Your Name* (Nashville: Thomas Nelson, 1999); *Outlive Your Life* (Nashville: Thomas Nelson, 2010); and *Glory Days* (Nashville: Thomas Nelson, 2015).

Ten Women of The Bible

. . . .

LEADER'S GUIDE

. . . .

Thank you for your willingness to lead a group through *Ten Women of the Bible*. The rewards of being a leader are different from those of participating, and we hope you find your own walk with Jesus deepened by this experience. During the ten lessons in this study, you'll be helping your group explore the lives of ten fascinating characters in the Bible through inspirational readings by Max Lucado, thought-provoking group discussion questions, and practical takeaway exercises. There are several elements in this leader's guide that will help you as you structure your study and reflection time, so follow along and take advantage of each one.

ℬefore You Begin

Before your first meeting, have the group participants get a copy of *Ten Women of the Bible* so they can follow along in the study guide and have their answers written out ahead of time. Alternately, you can hand out the study guides at your first meeting and give the group members some time to look over the material and ask any preliminary questions. During your first meeting, be sure to send a sheet around the room and have the members write down their name, phone number, and email address so you can keep in touch with them during the week.

Generally, the ideal size for a group is between eight to ten people, which ensures everyone will have enough time to participate in discussions. If you have more people, you might want to break up the main group into smaller subgroups. Encourage those who show up at the first meeting to commit to attending the duration of the study, as this will help the group members get to know each other, create stability for the group, and help you know how to prepare each week.

Note that each of the sessions begins with an opening story from Max Lucado that focuses on that week's Bible character. The two questions that follow serve as an icebreaker to get the group members thinking about the person and the topic at hand. Some people may want to tell a long story in response to one of these questions, but the goal is to keep the answers brief. Ideally, you want everyone in the group to get a chance to answer at least one of these opening questions, so try to keep the responses to a minute or less. If you have talkative group members, say up front that everyone needs to limit his or her answer to one minute.

Give the group members a chance to answer, but tell them to feel free to pass if they wish. With the rest of the study, it's generally not a good idea to have everyone answer every question—a free-flowing discussion is more desirable. But with the opening icebreaker questions, you can go around the circle. Encourage shy people to share, but don't force them.

Before your first meeting, let the group members know the lessons are broken down into five days' worth of reading material. The goal of structuring the material in this format is to encourage group members to spend time each day in God's Word. During your group discussion time the participants will be drawing on the answers they wrote down during the week, so encourage them to always complete these ahead of time. Also invite them to bring any questions and insights they uncovered while reading to your next meeting, especially if they had a breakthrough moment or if they didn't understand something.

*W*eekly Preparation

As the leader, there are a few things you should do to prepare for each meeting:

❖ *Read through the lesson.* This will help you to become familiar with the content and know how to structure the discussion times.

❖ *Decide which questions you want to discuss.* Each lesson contains forty Bible study questions (eight per day), so you will not be able to cover every question. Instead, select two to three questions in each day's reading that especially stood out to you.

❖ *Be familiar with the questions you want to discuss.* When the group meets you'll be watching the clock, so you want to make sure you are familiar with the Bible study questions you have selected. You can then spend time in the passage again when the group meets. In this way, you'll ensure you have the passage more deeply in your mind than your group members.

❖ *Pray for your group.* Pray for your group members throughout the week and ask God to lead them as they study his Word.

❖ *Bring extra supplies to your meeting.* The members should bring their own pens for writing notes, but it's a good idea to have extras available for those who forget. You may also want to bring paper and additional Bibles.

Note that in many cases there will no one "right" answer to the question. Answers will vary, especially when the group members are being asked to share their personal experiences.

*S*tructuring the Discussion Time

You will need to determine with your group how long you want to meet each week so you can plan your time accordingly. Generally, most groups like to meet for either sixty minutes or ninety minutes, so you could use one of the following schedules:

SECTION	60 MINUTES	90 MINUTES
WELCOME (members arrive and get settled)	5 minutes	10 minutes
ICEBREAKER (discuss the two opening questions for the lesson)	10 minutes	15 minutes
DISCUSSION (discuss the Bible study questions you selected ahead of time)	35 minutes	50 minutes
PRAYER/CLOSING (pray together as a group and dismiss)	10 minutes	15 minutes

As the group leader, it is up to you to keep track of the time and keep things moving along according to your schedule. You might want to set a timer for each segment so both you and the group members know when your time is up. (Note that there are some good phone apps for timers that play a gentle chime or other pleasant sound instead of a disruptive noise.) Don't feel pressured to cover every question you have selected if the group has a good discussion going. Again, it's not necessary to go around the circle and make everyone share.

Don't be concerned if the group members are quiet or slow to share. People are often quiet when they are pulling together their ideas, and this might be a new experience for them. Just ask a question and let it hang in the air until someone shares. You can then say, "Thank you. What about others? What came to you when you sat with the passage?"

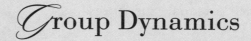

Group Dynamics

Leading a group through *Ten Women of the Bible* will prove to be highly rewarding both to you and your group members. However, that doesn't mean that you will not encounter any challenges along the way! Discussions can get off track. Group members may not be sensitive to the needs and ideas of others. Some might worry they will be expected to talk about matters that make them feel awkward. Others may express comments that result in disagreements. To help ease this strain on you and the group, consider the following ground rules:

❖ When someone raises a question or comment that is off the main topic, suggest you deal with it another time, or, if you feel led to go in that direction, let the group know you will be spending some time discussing it.

❖ If someone asks a question you don't know how to answer, admit it and move on. At your discretion, feel free to invite group members to comment on questions that call for personal experience.

❖ If you find one or two people are dominating the discussion time, direct a few questions to others in the group. Outside the main group time, ask the more dominating members to help you draw out the quieter ones. Work to make them a part of the solution instead of the problem.

❖ When a disagreement occurs, encourage the group members to process the matter in love. Encourage those on opposite sides to restate what they heard the other side say about the matter, and then invite each side to evaluate if that perception is accurate. Lead the group in examining other Scriptures related to the topic and look for common ground.

When any of these issues arise, encourage your group members to follow the words from the Bible: "Love one another" (John 13:34), "If it is possible, as far as it depends on you, live at peace with everyone" (Romans 12:18), and "Be quick to listen, slow to speak and slow to become angry" (James 1:19).

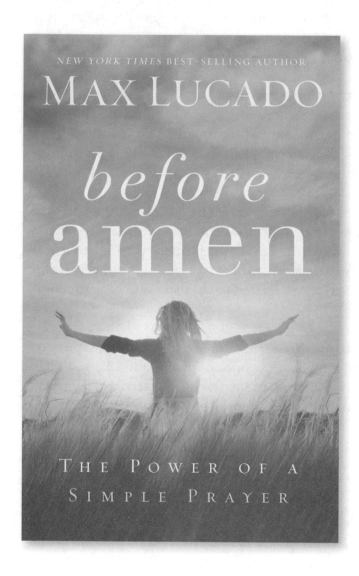